handbook
of photography

handbook of photography
of

James A. Folts
Ronald P. Lovell
Fred C. Zwahlen, Jr.

Oregon State University
Corvallis, Oregon

5TH EDITION

DELMAR
™
THOMSON LEARNING

Australia • Canada • Mexico • Singapore • Spain • United Kingdom • United States

DELMAR

™

THOMSON LEARNING

Handbook of Photography
Fifth Edition
by James A. Folts, Ronald P. Lovell, Fred C. Zwahlen, Jr.

Business Unit Director:
Alar Elken

Executive Editor:
Sandy Clark

Acquisitions Editor:
James Gish

Editorial Assistant:
Jaimie Wetzel

Executive Marketing Manager:
Maura Theriault

Channel Manager:
Mona Caron

Executive Production Manager:
Mary Ellen Black

Production Manager:
Larry Main

Production Editor:
Tom Stover

Copy Editor:
Alicia Saposnik

Cover Design:
Nicole Reamer

Cover Images:
Jim Folts

Full Production Services:
Liz Kingslien,
Lizart Digital Design

Library of Congress
Cataloging-in-Publication Data

Folts, James A.
Handbook of photography / by
James A. Folts, Ronald P. Lovell,
Fred C. Zwahlen, Jr.—5th ed.
p. cm.
ISBN 0-7668-2073-4 (alk. paper)
1. Photography—Handbooks,
manuals, etc.   I. Lovell, Ronald P.
II. Zwahlen, Fred C., 1924-   . III. Title.
TR146 .H19 2001
770—dc21
2001028303

ABOUT THE COVER

Although many of us think of photography as a single process, it is actually a collection of processes. The cover illustrates several types of photographic images. From left to right and top to bottom: a conventional silver-based black-and-white negative, a color positive, a Polaroid color emulsion transfer, a digital color image, a conventional black-and-white positive print, a color halftone screen, two examples of digital special effects, and a color negative.

NOTICE TO THE READER

Publisher does not warrant or guarantee any of the products described herein or perform any independent analysis in connection with any of the product information contained herein. Publisher does not assume, and expressly disclaims, any obligation to obtain and include information other than that provided to it by the manufacturer.

The reader is expressly warned to consider and adopt all safety precautions that might be indicated by the activities herein and to avoid all potential hazards. By following the instructions contained herein, the reader willingly assumes all risks in connection with such instructions.

The Publisher makes no representation or warranties of any kind, including but not limited to, the warranties of fitness for particular purpose or merchantability, nor are any such representations implied with respect to the material set forth herein, and the publisher takes no responsibility with respect to such material. The publisher shall not be liable for any special, consequential, or exemplary damages resulting, in whole or part, from the readers' use of, or reliance upon, this material.

contents

PART 1: CAMERAS AND PICTURE TAKING

Chapter 2

Chapter 3

PART 2: DEVELOPING AND PRINTING

Chapter 4

Chapter 5

Chapter 6

PART 3: HANDLING LIGHT AND COLOR

Chapter 7

Chapter 8

Chapter 9

PART 4: DIGITAL PHOTOGRAPHY

Chapter 10

Chapter 11

Chapter 12

PART 5: PROFESSIONAL ISSUES IN PHOTOGRAPHY

PART 6: PHOTO HISTORY

Chapter 15

preface

From its beginnings in the first edition, this book has been intended as an introduction to the possibilities of photography. This latest edition continues to aspire to open doors for those who want to discover more about photographic processes and the photographic image. This book will serve equally well as a beginning text in a one- or two-semester photography course or as a guide to someone learning photography independently.

Technical material throughout the book has been updated in the fifth edition. Captions have been extended to make them more explanatory. The chapters on lighting and on color photography have been reorganized and expanded. The discussion of lenses, once part of the first chapter, has been moved to the chapter on filters and accessories. The chapter on the history of photography has been expanded considerably to include many more contemporary photographers. Photography assignments, which used to be in a separate section at the end of the book, have been put at the end of appropriate chapters in sections titled "Try It Yourself."

Indeed, true understanding in photography comes only when you do try it yourself and this book encourages you to start taking pictures almost immediately. To that end, we begin in Chapter 1 with the camera and how it works to record images. In Chapters 2 through 6, the technique chapters, the book tries to get the would-be photographer into the darkroom as quickly as possible. We have chapters on operating the camera, taking the picture, developing film, printmaking, and advanced printmaking. Many of these chapters are unique in that they contain a detailed, how-to-do-it photo essay. Each essay is a simple, but complete, step-by-step guide that is intended to help beginners achieve success right from the start.

In Chapters 7, 8, and 9, the book turns to more specialized subjects: lighting, lenses and filters, and color photography. The goal of these chapters is to provide a basic understanding of more advanced equipment and techniques. We urge readers to experiment, evaluate, and experiment some more in order to progress to new levels of expertise.

Chapters 10 through 12 provide information on digital photography, from capturing digital images, to digital color photography, to the digital darkroom.

Chapter 13 discusses the legal rights of photo subjects and photographers. It also covers the moral issues and dilemmas faced by many photographers, especially those issues involving digital processes. Chapter 14 outlines the many kinds of careers available in photography. The final chapter briefly covers the rich and colorful history of photography. The final section of the book contains a glossary of terms.

The fifth edition retains a format that makes it portable, so it will fit into a backpack or camera bag easily for reference in the field. The thumb-indexed reference system will quickly lead the user to the needed information. Like all previous editions of this book, we have opened each chapter with photographs by well-known photographers to inspire readers (by their quality) and instruct them (by brief reviews of how and why the photographs were taken).

Many people helped in the preparation of all five editions of this book. We thank them now for their continued assistance and support. Perhaps we owe our greatest debt to our students, past and present, from whom we have learned so much. Their comments and questions have guided nearly every detail of the book. In many cases, photographs illustrating photographic issues have been taken by former students. In particular, we thank Elizabeth Miller, who assisted with numerous details in the preparation of the fifth edition. Her ideas, energy, and expertise were invaluable.

Reviews of the fourth edition that provided the beginning point for revisions were provided by Victor Lisnyczyj, Onondaga Community College; Edward Ross, II, Loyola College; Jerry L. Shaw, Texas State Technical College- Waco; Deborah A. Woodley, Eastern Illinois University; and John B. Zibluk, Ph.D, Arkansas State University. We appreciate their constructive advice and instructional insights.

We very much appreciate staff members at Delmar who helped see this fifth edition into print: James Gish, Acquisitions Editor; Tom Stover, Project Editor/Production Coordinator; Larry Main, Production Manager; and Jaimie Wetzel, Editorial Assistant. And we thank Nicole Reamer for the cover design and Liz Kingslien for the text design.

We are grateful to the photo teachers and their students who used this book in its earlier editions. We always appreciate hearing ideas and advice about how to make this book more effective. You can reach us via e-mail at jfolts@orst.edu.

Our families have supported us through the long hours and many months it took to create and revise this book. This edition would not have been possible without the help of Jeanene Louden, who suffered through early drafts of revisions, cooked when it was Jim's turn, and created the space in which it all happened.

Photography is many things to many people. It is a narrative form used by photojournalists. It is an artistic form used by creative photographers. It creates personal records in the hands of a portrait photographer. It provides fantasy and allure in the hands of fashion and advertising photographers. It can provide a medium of growth and inner discovery in personal photography. We wish you the best as you set out to discover what photography is for you and how photography can provide expression to your ideas and vision.

cameras
and picture
taking

"*As far as I am concerned, taking photographs is a means of understanding which cannot be separated from other means of visual expression. It is a way of shouting, of freeing oneself, not of proving or asserting one's own originality. It is a way of life.*"

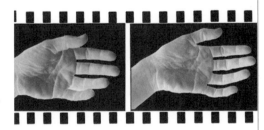

Henri Cartier-Bresson

CHAPTER 1

The camera

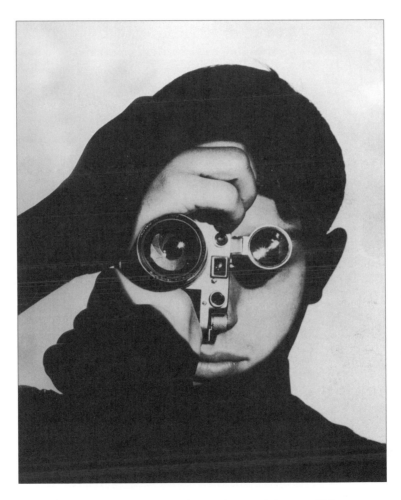

The Photojournalist, by Andreas Feininger, 1955

The camera

The Photojournalist, by Andreas Feininger, 1955

(Andreas Feininger/TimePix)

The subject of Feininger's photograph is Dennis Stock, who had just won *Life* magazine's Young Photographers Contest. The image shows the camera and photographer seemingly merged into a single being as though the photographer's entire identity is bound with the camera. Most photographers find that the camera does change how they see the world and most photographers find that they begin to see photographs even when they don't have a camera at hand.

Stock is holding a 35 mm rangefinder Leica, a descendant of the first 35 mm camera. Stock himself went on to become a leading photojournalist with Magnum Photos. Feininger, originally trained as an architect at the Bauhaus in Weimar, was known for his urban and architectural photography. He worked for *Life* magazine for a time and published several books on the techniques of photography.

The camera existed for centuries before a practical photographic process was discovered. The earliest cameras were small rooms with a tiny hole in an exterior wall that acted as a pinhole lens and focused light on the opposite wall. Such a device was known as a camera obscura, Latin for "dark room." Inventors searched for centuries for a way to fix the clear, precise image of the camera obscura on paper and capture what the sun had "written" on the wall. The word photography, in fact, means *light writing*.

By comparison with the early camera obscura, today's cameras are portable, versatile, and sophisticated. Modern cameras are available in a number of configurations and sizes, but nearly all have some basic features in common.

PARTS OF A CAMERA

An adjustable camera has seven basic parts: a viewfinder, a focusing mechanism, a shutter, an adjustable aperture, a lens, a body, and devices for holding and advancing film. Figures 1.1, 1.2, and 1.3 show a typical 35 mm camera and its various parts.

▸▸ A **viewfinder** allows the photographer to frame the subject to be photographed before the picture is taken. The viewfinder offers a preview in miniature of the

FIGURE 1.1. Front view of 35 mm camera

1. Built-in flash—a flash unit attached to the camera.
2. Mode select buttons—permit setting aperture priority, shutter priority, camera computer program or manual operation.

3. Camera back release—by sliding the release, the camera back can be opened.
4. Lens release button—when depressed, it permits the lens to be removed from the camera body.

5. Focus mode selector—allows the camera to be set on either manual, auto or continuous auto focus.
6. Lens—focuses rays of light to expose the film in the camera.

7. Shutter release button—used to activate shutter so a frame of film can be exposed.
8. Shutter speed dial—permits setting shutter speed either manually, during shutter priority, or by mode selection.

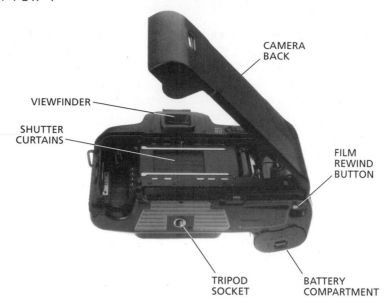

FIGURE 1.2. Back/bottom view of 35 mm camera

1. Camera back—keeps light from reaching the film and keeps the film flat during exposures.
2. Film rewind button—after pressing it, the film can be rewound from the take-up spool to its original cassette in the film-holding device.
3. Battery compart-ment—houses the battery or batteries necessary to operate the camera.
4. Tripod socket—permits the camera to be placed on a tripod when using a slow shutter speed or when necessary to be exacting when sighting in the area of the viewfinder.
5. Shutter curtains—control the amount of light reaching the film through the camera lens.
6. Viewfinder—shows the area that will be captured on film.

FIGURE 1.3. Top view of 35 mm camera

1. Focusing ring—makes it possible to view the anticipated photograph in and out of focus.
2. Aperture ring—permits setting the size of the lens opening.
3. Panel display—gives a computer-ized reading of the camera settings.
4. Accessory shoe—a place where a flash unit can be attached to the camera.
5. Self timer—permits taking a delayed action photograph.

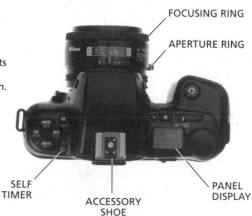

final image to be produced. Some viewfinders are separate optical devices, often attached to the top of the camera. This position causes a problem in some simple cameras; because the viewfinder and the lens are located on different planes, they don't see the subject in quite the same way. Accordingly, there is a discrepancy, called the **parallax effect,** between what the lens records on the film and what the eye sees in the viewfinder. This discrepancy is particularly apparent when the camera is close to the subject (Figure 1.4).

In some cameras, the problem is solved by building a parallax correction into the viewfinder system. The viewing system actually tilts as the camera's focusing mechanism is adjusted to compensate for differences in point of view. Other cameras avoid the problem altogether by making the viewfinder and the lens part of the same system. The viewfinder thus looks at the subject from exactly the same point of view as the lens that takes the picture, and parallax is not a factor.

▸▸ A **focusing mechanism** moves the lens closer to or further from the film where the image will be recorded. The focusing ring in Figure 1.3 is used to adjust the focusing mechanism. Proper focusing makes the image sharp and distinct; improper focusing makes it blurry and fuzzy.

There are two types of focusing systems: rangefinder and ground-glass viewing screen. In the **rangefinder system,** the photographer sees two images—a direct image through the viewfinder and a reflected image from a mirror-prism

FIGURE 1.4. The parallax effect. In a camera with separate viewing and taking lenses, the two lenses see the subject from slightly different positions. When close to the subject this difference can be significant.

As seen by viewing lens

As photographed by taking lens

arrangement. When the focusing ring is turned to focus the lens, the prism also turns, bringing the reflected image together with the direct image when the camera is in focus.

In the **ground-glass system,** light from the lens is projected onto a viewing screen. When the focusing ring is turned to focus the lens, the photographer sees the image formed by the lens on the ground glass and can judge when the camera is in focus. Various screens that are available to make focusing more precise are discussed in Chapter 2.

▸▸ A **shutter** controls exposure of the film to light by opening and closing at various speeds. The shutter thus determines the length of time light exposes the film. Shutters are of two basic types: the focal plane shutter and the leaf shutter.

The **focal plane shutter** is built into the camera body at a point directly in front of the film (Figure 1.5). It receives its name from the fact that it resides just forward of the **plane of focus,** the area where the image projected from the lens should be sharpest. The focal plane shutter usually consists of two overlapping curtains forming an adjustable window. The spring-powered window moves across

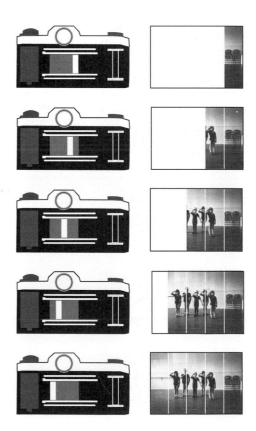

FIGURE 1.5. Focal plane shutter.
Located just in front of the film, the focal plane shutter consists of two curtains. One curtain opens to allow light to reach the film and the second follows along behind to block the light. The shutter speed is thus controlled by the delay between the release of the first curtain and the release of the second. At faster shutter speeds, as shown here, only a portion of the image is exposed at any one instant and the overall image accumulates as the two curtains move across the film frame. At slow shutter speeds, the first curtain travels all the way across the film frame before the second curtain is released.

the film and exposes it as it moves. The **leaf shutter** is located within the lens and consists of several small overlapping spring-powered metal blades (Figure 1.6). As the blades open, they form a circular opening through which light passes until the end of the exposure, when the blades close again. The time interval between opening and closing is adjustable for both types of shutters. The shutter control mechanism—the shutter speed dial—on the camera is shown in Figure 1.7 and discussed further in Chapter 2.

Both types of shutters have advantages and disadvantages. A camera with a focal plane shutter can use lenses that are less expensive because each lens does not need its own shutter. A focal plane shutter is also generally capable of faster shutter speeds because its design does not require the curtains to reverse direction during the exposure, as is the case with the blades of a leaf shutter. Leaf shutters, on the other hand, are quieter than focal plane shutters, which produce a distinct snap when released. Leaf shutters can also be used with electronic flash at higher speeds. A focal plane shutter is generally limited to maximum speeds of 1/60, 1/125, or 1/250 of a second (in some newer cameras) with flash because the window does not uncover the film completely at any one time at higher speeds.

FIGURE 1.6. Leaf shutter.
Usually built into the lens, leaf shutters consist of a series of blades that open and close in circular fashion. The shutter speed is controlled by how long the blades stay open. The entire frame is exposed simultaneously. The fact that the blades must open, then reverse and close, limits leaf shutters to speeds of about 1/500 second or slower.

**FIGURE 1.7.
Shutter speed dial.**
The shutter controls the length of time that the film will be exposed to light. It is calibrated in fractions of a second, so 125 means 1/125 second.

**FIGURE 1.8.
Aperture ring.**
The aperture controls the intensity of the light exposing the film. It is calibrated in f-stops.

Beginners should remember that the focal plane shutter is fragile and easily damaged and they should not touch it.

▸▸ An **aperture** also controls the exposure of film to light, this time by fixing the size of the lens opening. The aperture consists of overlapping metal blades that form a circular opening. The size of the opening is controlled by the aperture ring (Figure 1.8). When the ring is turned in one direction, it rotates the metal blades toward the outside of the circle and increases the size of the aperture. Turning the aperture ring in the other direction moves the metal blades toward the center and reduces the size of the aperture. Larger aperture sizes allow more light through the lens; smaller sizes allow less. The net result is that the aperture controls the brightness or dimness of the light that exposes the film. Aperture sizes are measured in f-stops and are discussed in Chapter 2.

▸▸ A **lens** projects a reversed image of the subject onto the film. In its simplest form, a lens is a single element, a solid piece of curved glass. Other optical elements of varying shapes are usually added to a lens to enable the lens to project a sharp image without distortion under all light conditions. The lens, sitting as it does between the subject and the film, sorts out various light rays, focuses them, and directs them to reproduce the subject accurately on film.

▸▸ The **body** of the camera houses all the parts and protects the film from light. Some camera bodies have a permanently attached lens. Others are designed to hold interchangeable lenses.

▸▸ A **film-holding mechanism** secures the film while it is being exposed and most cameras also have a **film-advance mechanism** that moves the film across the face of the shutter between exposures in order to expose the entire strip of film. The type of device for holding the film depends on the type of film used by the camera.

FILM FORMATS

Until recently, nearly all photographic film came in one of three formats: 35 mm film, medium format roll film, and sheets of film 4 x 5 inches and larger. Recently, a fourth format was added—the Advanced Photo System (APS) (Figure 1.9). The primary difference from one format to another is the size of the negative that results from the exposed film. In general the larger the negative, the sharper and more detailed will be the final print, but with the limitation of working with a larger, less flexible camera.

All 35 mm cameras use strips of film 35 mm wide and 2 to 3 feet in length. The film is packaged inside a cassette, which is held inside the camera, nearly always on the left side. The free end of the film attaches to a take-up spool on the right side. A pressure plate holds the film flat against the back of the camera. Medium format cameras use 120 roll film, similar to 35 mm film, but wider and lacking edge perforations. Roll film is 60 mm wide and comes wrapped around a spool with a paper backing to protect it from light. It is held in the camera much the same way as 35 mm film. View cameras use sheets rather than rolls of film. Sheet film must be first loaded into special film holders, which can then be

FIGURE 1.9. Film formats. At far left is 120 roll film, used in medium format cameras. In the center is a 35 mm film cassette. At the right is an APS (Advanced Photo System) film cassette.

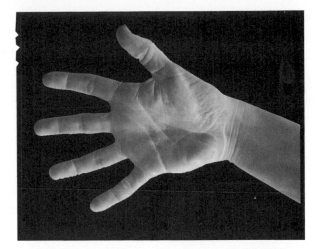

4 x 5 film is sold in sheets and must be exposed in a large view camera. Each negative contains 20 square inches of image area.

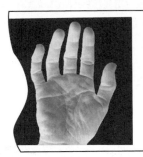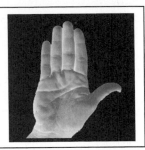

2 1/4 square format is 6 x 6 centimeters and is shot on 120 roll film using a medium format camera. Each frame contains about 5 square inches of image area.

35 mm film frames are 24 x 36 mm. Each frame contains about 1.3 square inches of image area.

APS film frames are about 17 x 30 mm. Each frame contains about 3/4 square inch of image area.

FIGURE 1.10. Film negative sizes. Shown here are the relative sizes of several common film formats. In general, the larger the frame of film, the less it will need to be magnified to make a print, making the final print that much sharper and less grainy. On the other hand, larger film sizes usually require larger cameras, take more trouble to shoot, and allow for less experimentation.

inserted into the back of the camera to take one picture at a time. The smallest sheet film in common use is 4 inches by 5 inches, but sheet film is also available in 8 x 10, 11 x 14, and even larger sizes. The smallest film format is the new APS film cassette. The APS format is aimed at consumers who want to simplify film handling. In the APS system, the film always remains in the cassette. APS cameras load the film automatically. The film is stored inside the cassette after processing. In many APS cameras, you can take a partially exposed roll out of the camera, put it back later, and the camera will keep track of where you left off. APS film has magnetic strips which can store exposure and processing information.

In comparing different film formats, it is wise to note the trade-offs. Larger negatives require larger cameras and are usually more difficult to expose. On the other hand, larger negatives can produce more detailed prints because they require less magnification when making an enlargement (Figure 1.10).

TYPES OF CAMERAS

Hundreds of camera designs exist: cameras designed to work underwater and cameras designed to make aerial photographs from space, cameras small enough

FIGURE 1.11. View camera. The view camera is one of the most versatile camera designs, but one of the most painstaking to use. It is usually used with sheet film.

A. In a monorail style view camera both the front and back camera standards can be moved in virtually any direction, allowing for maximum control and flexibility.

B. In a field camera design, the front and back standards are anchored to a flat base, limiting flexibility, but allowing the camera to be folded up into a compact package for portability.

to fit inside a watch and cameras large enough that you could park your car inside them, disposable cameras made of cardboard and plastic and expensive collectors cameras made of gold and precision ground glass. But most general purose photography makes use of four major camera types: view cameras, viewfinder cameras, twin-lens reflex cameras, and single-lens reflex cameras. Categorized by the kind of viewing system it has, each type has distinct advantages and disadvantages.

▸▸ **View cameras** (Figure 1.11) resemble accordions. The lens is in the front, a viewing screen is in the back, and a flexible bellows connects them. The design dates back to the earliest days of photography. Although simple, the view camera is very flexible and has capabilities possessed by no other type of camera. The lens produces an inverted image on a ground-glass plate at the rear of the camera. The image is composed and focused on the ground glass. To take the picture, a piece of film is inserted in front of the ground glass.

A view camera generally uses sheet film of 4 x 5 inches or larger. The large negative is capable of great sharpness and detail. But perhaps the greatest advantage of the view camera is the power it gives the photographer in composing the picture, in adjusting the field of focus, and in controlling perspective. The greatest disadvantage of the camera is its bulk. A view camera must be used on a tripod and is relatively slow to operate. And because the image projected on the viewing screen is dim, photographers using the camera have to put a dark cloth over their heads and the back of the camera, something that has characterized this camera since its appearance in the nineteenth century.

▸▸ **Viewfinder cameras** (Figure 1.12) see their subjects through a small hole containing a simple lens that provides an image of how the final picture will look.

FIGURE 1.12. Viewfinder camera.

A. The Leica is a descendant of the first 35 mm camera ever made. New Leicas are extremely expensive, but older models like the one shown here are often very reliable and much less costly.

B. This point-and-shoot viewfinder camera is aimed at the hobbyist photographer. It is intended to be easy to use, automatic in most respects, but still offer good quality negatives.

FIGURE 1.13. Twin-lens reflex camera. This camera design is defined by its two lenses, one for viewing the scene and a second for exposing the film.

A. The Rolliflex TLR (left) is a classic, used by serious photographers for decades, but relatively expensive.

B. The Lubitel (right) is a very inexpensive Russian-made twin lens reflex camera, but with fully adjustable apertures and shutter speeds.

The light from the subject travels separately through the lens to the film and through the viewfinder to the eye. Thus, the viewfinder and the taking lens see the subject from two levels and parallax error results. What you see in the viewfinder is slightly different from what will be recorded on film. Sophisticated viewfinder cameras compensate for the parallax problem at all but very close distances.

The greatest weakness of the viewfinder camera is that it generally cannot be used with telephoto lenses and is difficult to use with close-up lenses. The biggest advantages of viewfinder cameras are their compact construction, light weight, quietness, and fast handling. They are also easy to focus in low-light areas.

Better viewfinder cameras include a rangefinder focusing mechanism and thus the term **rangefinder** camera is used almost interchangeably with **viewfinder** camera. The first 35 mm camera, the Leica, was a rangefinder design. Rangefinder Leicas, although very expensive, are still used by many professionals.

▸▸ **Twin-lens reflex cameras** (Figure 1.13), as their name suggests, have two lenses. One is used for viewing and focusing while the other exposes the film. The two matched lenses are located one above the other on the front of the camera. The picture is composed and focused on a ground-glass viewing screen on the top of the camera. The camera is called a reflex because the light that forms the image on the ground glass is reflected off a mirror to turn the image right-side up. Twin-lens reflexes generally use medium format roll film.

FIGURE 1.14. Single-lens reflex camera. Because they allow the photographer to see exactly what will be recorded on film, the SLR is ideal for close-up and telephoto photography.

A. The 35 mm SLR is the most widely used camera design for serious photographers. It is portable and very flexible.

B. Medium format SLRs bring flexibility to a larger film format. They are very common in commercial and portrait photography.

The chief advantages of twin-lens reflex cameras are their simplicity, durability, and quietness. The larger negative tends to give a sharper and more detailed enlargement. Also, because the photographer uses the camera by looking down into it from above, he or she can use it at waist level or even ground level easily. It can also be held upside-down directly overhead to gain a high angle of view. The two disadvantages of the camera are its parallax error, which makes close-up work next to impossible, and its inflexibility. Few twin-lens reflexes can accept different types of lenses, a fact that considerably limits their versatility.

▶▶ **Single-lens reflex cameras** (Figure 1.14) allow the photographer to see directly through the lens that takes the picture (Figure 1.15). Light from the lens is reflected by a mirror inside the camera upward into the viewing system. When the picture is taken, the mirror swings up out of the way, allowing light to pass through the camera body and shutter, to the film at the back of the camera. The viewing system contains a prism that inverts the reversed image coming from the lens and projects it onto a ground-glass viewing screen. The photographer thus views the scene as it appears before the camera. Most single-lens reflex cameras take 35 mm film. Medium format models take roll film, which gives larger negatives, usually 6 x 4.5 cm, 6 x 6 cm, or 6 x 7 cm.

The major advantage of single-lens reflex cameras is the flexibility the viewing system gives. Because the photographer sees exactly what the film will record, there is no parallax error and nearly any type of lens may be attached. The camera is ideal for extreme close-up work and is equally adept when used with long telephoto lenses. Its extreme adaptability has made the 35 mm single-lens reflex by far the most popular of all camera types. But it is not without disadvantages. The addition of the mirror and viewing system tends to make the camera heavier and more bulky than 35 mm viewfinder cameras. And the movement of the mirror makes the camera rather noisy and causes camera shake.

DIGITAL CAMERAS

Digital cameras, once an expensive oddity, have become both affordable and very practical for a number of applications. Digital cameras create their images on computer chips rather than conventional film. Still expensive as cameras go, the digital camera nonetheless offers advantages to those who need them: no need for darkroom processing and thus images that are almost instantly available. If the need was for a digitized image anyway—for use on the World Wide Web or in a modest quality publication—there is no need for additional scanning. Digital cameras that cost less than $1,000 tend to offer the same features as 35 mm

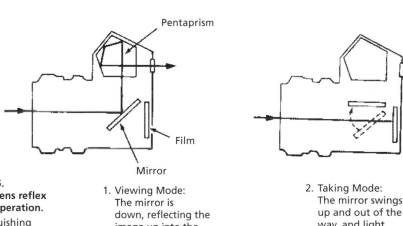

FIGURE 1.15.
The single-lens reflex camera in operation.

The distinguishing feature of an SLR design is the reflex mirror, which allows one lens to act as both the viewing and taking lens. The movement of the mirror also makes SLR somewhat noisy compared with other camera designs.

1. Viewing Mode: The mirror is down, reflecting the image up into the pentaprism where it can be viewed through the eyepiece.

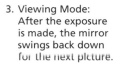

2. Taking Mode: The mirror swings up and out of the way, and light passes through the shutter to expose the film.

3. Viewing Mode: After the exposure is made, the mirror swings back down for the next picture.

FIGURE 1.16. Digital camera. These cameras do not use conventional film, but instead create an electronic image that can be transferred directly to a computer. They are relatively expensive and inflexible compared with 35 mm cameras, but offer the advantages of instantly available digitized images which can be used on the World Wide Web or in publications that do not require high quality.

point and shoot cameras. They are about the same size as a 35 mm camera, although the design may look somewhat more futuristic (Figure 1.16). They usually have autofocus lenses and automatic exposure. They do not take interchangeable lenses, but often sport zoom lenses. The differentiating features to consider in comparing digital cameras are their resolution, storage capacity, and ease of downloading images to your computer. Chapters 10, 11, and 12 contain a more detailed discussion of digital photography.

CHOICE OF A CAMERA

The selection of a camera depends entirely on the way you intend to use it. But it is probably safe to say that the serious student of photography should begin with a 35 mm single-lens reflex unless special considerations dictate some other type. The camera's flexibility allows you to explore many avenues of photography and to do so relatively inexpensively because 35 mm film allows many pictures per roll. As your skills develop and your photographic interests become more specialized, you may wish to obtain a different type of camera. But until then, the single-lens reflex offers you unparalleled opportunities to experiment and learn.

But even after narrowing your choice to a 35 mm single-lens reflex, you still have a wide variety of camera brands and models to choose from. They are available with such an overwhelming assortment of features that you almost expect one of the major camera manufacturers to introduce a model one day that will wash and dry the dishes when you're not busy photographing.

In the meantime, you still have to select between models with automatic versus manual exposure, with interchangeable versus fixed lenses, with greater or lesser flexibility in the attachments they will accept, and so on. Let's look at some of the major features available.

▸▸ **Built-in light meters.** Nearly all single-lens reflex cameras today have a built-in light meter located behind the reflex mirror, where the meter monitors the light coming through the lens. Depending on the model of the camera you have, you may interact with the meter in any one of three possible exposure modes: manual exposure, automatic exposure, or programmed exposure.

Some cameras with built-in light meters have **manual exposure**—that is, you manipulate both the aperture and the shutter speed to set the exposure indicated by the meter. Other cameras have **automatic exposure,** where you set either the shutter speed or aperture and the camera selects the other setting to produce correct exposure. Still other cameras have a **programmed exposure** mode, where the camera makes all exposure settings with no intervention from you. Many modern cameras combine two or more of these metering modes and allow you to choose between them. Most of these cameras are heavily electronic and use a panel display (Figure 1.17) to indicate the metering mode as well as other important camera information.

Since all three exposure modes are capable of accurate exposures, the choice is largely a matter of personal preference. Some photographers find automatic exposure or programmed exposure a convenience and say it lets them concentrate more on the picture itself. Others say setting the exposure manually is hardly difficult and want the extra sense of control over the exposure.

You should not get a camera with a built-in light meter that does not allow you to override the automatic or programmed feature. This limitation can be disastrous in certain lighting situations. Fortunately, it is a limitation found on

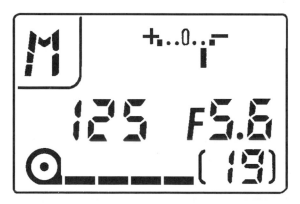

FIGURE 1.17. Electronic camera panel display. This panel shows the shutter speed (1/125), aperture (f/5.6), exposures taken (19), exposure mode (M for manual), and light reading (slightly underexposed).

FIGURE 1.18. Hand-held light meters.

 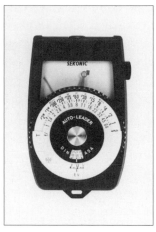 

A. An incident light meter measures the light falling on the subject.

B. A reflected light meter measures the light reflected from the subject.

C. A spot meter reads reflected light from a very tiny portion of the subject.

few cameras. If you choose a camera without a built-in light meter, hand-held light meters (Figure 1.18) are available to help determine exposures.

▶ **Interchangeable lenses.** If you plan to develop your interest in photography further, you should buy a camera that will take interchangeable lenses.

Eventually you are certain to feel limited by a choice of but one lens. The ability to use wide angle, telephoto, or macro (close-up) lenses greatly extends the versatility of your camera. Chapter 8 discusses lenses in greater detail.

▶ **Assorted power features.** Now, what about all those other features: shutter speed ranges, interchangeable viewfinders, electronic meter readouts, ability to take motor drives or winders, and so forth? Your pocketbook will probably have a great deal to say about these decisions. If you can afford it, it makes some sense to buy a little more camera than you need at the moment. That way, you can grow into it as your abilities develop. On the other hand, if you can't afford a camera body that has all the features you'd like, pick a camera brand you trust and buy a basic camera body that will accept the same lenses used by the more sophisticated bodies for that brand. As you accumulate lenses and eventually that more advanced camera body, you'll end up with a coherent system and your original camera will become a very handy second body.

▶ **How the camera feels.** In choosing a camera, there is one consideration that is more important than simply accumulating bells and whistles: How does the camera feel? Are you comfortable with it? When faced by camera brochures with multicolored charts extolling all the features of this or that model, how the camera feels may seem a rather trivial consideration. If it makes you feel any better, design engineers have a sophisticated word for it—ergonomics.

The feel of the camera is an important consideration if you and your camera are to become one functional unit. To photograph comfortably, your camera must feel as though it is a part of you. Does it fit your hand? Is the viewfinder easy to look through? (That is especially important if you wear glasses.) Are the camera controls easily accessible without taking your eye from the viewfinder? Is the camera the right weight? Will the camera be easy to carry with you?

Before you buy a camera, try it out under your normal shooting conditions. If you plan to use it in low-light conditions, try it there. Its viewfinder may be too dim to allow easy focusing. If you plan to take candid pictures of people, try that. It may be too noisy to allow you to work unobtrusively. Talk to other people who own that camera. Find out what problems they might have had and what they like about it. Talk to your instructor or advanced photographers about the suitability of the camera for your needs.

▶▶ **Used cameras.** Often you can find good value in a used camera. But first make sure it is in good working order. Check especially to make sure all shutter speeds are working properly, that the meter gives accurate readings, that the back closes securely, that film advances smoothly, that the lens mount isn't worn, that both the aperture and focusing rings operate smoothly, and that the lens itself is free of nicks and scratches. Shoot a test roll and process it to check overall operation. If you still aren't sure, have someone who knows cameras check it over for you.

FIGURE 1.19. Novelty cameras.

A. The Action Sampler is a little plastic camera with four lenses. It uses a rotating shutter to capture four tiny images, each one exposed a short time after the one before, on one frame of 35 mm film.

B. The Polaroid I-Zone takes miniature instant photographs on film that has an adhesive back so you can stick them to something besides your refrigerator.

And now for something completely different

Gimmicks have been part of photography since its beginnings. At one time, it was spy cameras that could be concealed in your hat, your lunchbox, or your walking cane. Then there was the miniature camera that could be strapped to a carrier pigeon for aerial photography. Here are a couple of recent entries, not to replace your regular camera, but to have some fun with and expand your creative vision (Figure 1.19).

REVIEW questions ?

1. What are the four common film formats? *APS 17 & 30 mm*

2. What is a view camera?

3. What is a viewfinder camera?

4. What is a twin-lens reflex camera?

5. What is a single-lens reflex camera?

6. Why is the parallax effect not a problem in single-lens reflex cameras?

7. What are the three common modes for built-in exposure meters?

8. What is the difference between a focal plane shutter and a leaf shutter? *—P.8*

9. What is the function of the camera's aperture? *P.9*

10. What factors are important in choosing what camera to buy?

— manual
— automatic
— programmed

CHAPTER 2

operating
the camera

Self-Portrait With Grandchildren in the Fun House, 1955, by Imogen Cunningham

operating the camera

Kossbeer

Self-Portrait With Grandchildren in the Fun House, 1955, by Imogen Cunningham
(Photograph by Imogen Cunningham © 1970 The Imogen Cunningham Trust)

In a charming family snapshot, Imogen Cunningham's twin lens reflex camera captures herself and her two granddaughters in the distortion of a fun-house mirror. Cunningham was one of the photographers who made the transition from the fuzzy, romantic photographs of Pictorialism to the ultra-sharp, geometric compositions of the modernist era. She learned photography from Pictorialist Gertrude Käsebier and worked for a time in the Seattle studio of Edward Curtis, known for his 20-volume set of photographs of Native Americans. Cunningham was a founding member of the f/64 Group, along with Ansel Adams and Edward Weston. The f/64 Group helped redefine photographic art as something grounded in the precision of the medium and not requiring the embellishment and handwork previously believed necessary to legitimize photography as an art form.

With experience, the process of operating a camera becomes almost automatic, like driving a car or riding a bicycle. At first, however, you have to learn how to use your camera—and in a way that is easiest for you.

Part of the process is selecting the film and loading it into the camera properly. Operating a camera also requires that you master the seemingly complex steps of adjusting the exposure, setting the shutter speed, and focusing the camera.

SELECTING 35 MM FILM

Most types of 35 mm film are available in rolls of 24 or 36 exposures. The 36-exposure rolls are more economical per frame. But you may want to begin by using 24-exposure rolls until you master film processing, because shorter rolls are easier to handle in the darkroom. The important issue, however, in selecting a film is its speed.

Film speed

Film is differentiated by its **speed**—that is, its sensitivity to light. Film speeds are noted by their **ISO Index,** a number designation assigned by the International Standards Organization.

The ISO number replaced the ASA (American Standards Association) number as the standard for identifying film speed a number of years ago. But only the name changed; the rating system and numbers are the same. Thus, even if your camera and light meter are marked for ASA numbers, they will work just as well with the newer ISO index. Films, cameras, and light meters may also be marked with another sensitivity scale called the DIN rating. DIN stands for *Deutsche Industrie Norm* (German Industry Standard) and is widely used in Europe.

FIGURE 2.1. Medium, fast, and super-fast films. A 100-speed film is a good choice when shooting outdoors where there is plenty of light. The 3200-speed film is used in very low-level light situations, like indoor sports photography. The 400-speed film is a good choice for general shooting. It is sensitive enough for indoor lighting but not too sensitive for daylight.

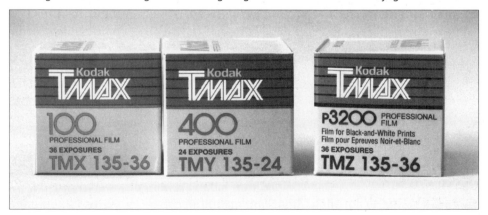

In the ISO rating system, high numbers mean films that are very sensitive to light. In the jargon of photography, they are called **fast** films because you can often use a faster shutter speed than with a **slower** film—that is, one that has a lower rating and is less sensitive to light.

Film sensitivity, or speed, combines with lighting conditions to determine the camera aperture and shutter speed settings needed for a properly exposed negative. A film with an ISO index twice that of another film is exactly twice as sensitive to light—that is, it will require half as much light to expose it properly. For example, a film with an ISO of 400 requires half as much exposure as an ISO 200 film. Therefore, you need to use an aperture one stop smaller or a shutter speed one notch faster than with an ISO 200 film. On the other hand, a film with an ISO index of 100 requires twice as much light (one stop greater) as an ISO 200 film.

Film ratings are divided into several categories:

Slow speed (ISO 25 to ISO 50),
Medium speed (ISO 100 to ISO 200),
Fast speed (ISO 400 to ISO 500),
Super-fast (ISO 1,000 and above).

In general, faster films are needed when shooting in low-level light and slower films can be used only when light levels are relatively high. Commonly used medium, fast, and super-fast films are shown in Figure 2.1.

If you are just getting started in photography, it is a good idea to begin with one of the "fast" black-and white films. These films allow you to shoot both indoors and outdoors under most light conditions. And, as a bonus, they tend to be more forgiving of exposure errors than slower speed films. After you've mastered the use of any of these films, then you'll be ready to tackle the somewhat more challenging slower films.

Whatever film speed you choose, you'll need to set your meter accordingly after you load the film. Most cameras have an ISO (or ASA) dial which can be

FIGURE 2.2. DX coding. The pattern of silver rectangles on the exterior of the film cassette allows electrical contacts in a camera's film chamber to detect and set the film speed automatically. Not all cameras can read DX coding, so you may still need to set film speed manually.

FIGURE 2.3. Manufacturer's instructions. To conserve paper, most film manufacturers print instructions for their films on the inside of the box. You can often find more extensive information on the manufacturer's Web site.

turned to the correct film speed. Some newer cameras set the film speed automatically for **DX coded film.** DX coded film cassettes are imprinted with a pattern of black and silver squares which represent the film's ISO index (Figure 2.2). A series of small electrical contacts inside the camera body translates this pattern into the appropriate film speed for the meter. Automatic DX coding can save you from the error of forgetting to set the ISO index when you change films. However, if you can't override the DX coding, it will make it difficult to push process film and to use bulk loaded film. Push processing and bulk loading will be discussed later, but suffice it to say that you should think twice before buying a camera that does not allow you to set the film speed manually when needed.

You should read and save the manufacturer's instructions packaged with the film (Figure 2.3). These instructions include information on exposure settings for all types of lighting and often give suggestions about developing the film.

BULK LOADING FILM

You can usually cut your film costs nearly in half by buying film in bulk rolls and loading it into cassettes yourself. Most common 35 mm films are available in 100-foot rolls, which yield the equivalent of 20 36-exposure rolls once loaded into cassettes. You use a bulk loader to transfer the film from the long roll to shorter lengths inside reusable film cassettes that will fit your camera (see How-to series). The bulk loader has a large chamber to accommodate the bulk roll and a smaller chamber to hold the cassette. Once the bulk roll is inside the bulk loader, the job of transferring the film to the cassettes can be done in room light. Bulk loading is a relatively simple process that will probably be well worth your while if you shoot much film.

How to

Bulk Load Film

Step 1: In a darkroom with all lights off (not even a safelight), unpackage the roll of film. The roll is usually wrapped inside a plastic bag which is inside a can and the can is taped shut.

Step 2: Insert the roll of film into the bulk loader so the film unspools counterclockwise and threads through the opening to the film loading chamber on the side of the bulk loader.

Step 3: Replace the lid on the bulk loader and fasten it shut. Replace or shut the trap door which gives access to the film loading compartment. The rest of the process can be done in room light.

Step 4: Take one end off a reusable film cassette to free the film spool. Open the door to the film loading compartment and tape the end of the film to the film spool. Note that one end of the film spool is longer than the other. The longer end should be oriented as shown here or the emulsion side of the film will be backwards in the camera. The tape should go completely around the spool and fasten to both sides of the film.

How to

Bulk Load Film

Step 5: Slip the film cassette over the film and spool and replace the end of the film cassette. Position the cassette inside the bulk loader and close or replace the door.

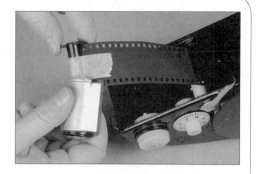

Step 6: Turn the loader crank to pull film from the bulk roll to the cassette. You can load different lengths of film up to a maximum of about 36 exposures. Some loaders have a frame counter. Others require you to count revolutions of the crank.

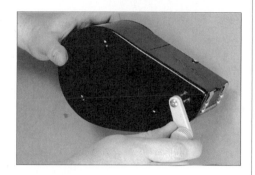

Step 7: When you have loaded as many frames of film as you want, open the bulk loader door and snip the film.

Step 8: Cut a tongue on the free end of the film so it will fit the take-up spool in your camera.

LOADING A 35 MM CAMERA

When loading film into the camera, it is important to stand in subdued light or to turn your back to the sun so that the camera is shaded. You begin by checking to see that the camera has no film in it. If you can turn the rewind knob in the direction of the arrow marked on it with no resistance, the camera is empty. When you open the back of the camera, you should always be careful not to touch the pressure plate or the shutter curtain.

In most cameras, you insert the film cassette in a cassette chamber on the left side of the camera and draw the film across the back of the camera to the take-up reel. You put slight tension on the film with the film-advance lever and make sure you engage the sprocket wheel in the film sprocket holes along the edge of the film. After closing the camera, the last step is to turn the rewind knob gently in the direction of the arrow to take the slack out of the film (Figure 2.4).

You will need to shoot off two or three waste exposures to move exposed film out of the way and position unexposed film behind the shutter. At the same time, you can watch the rewind knob to make sure it turns backwards. If it does, the film is advancing properly. If it doesn't, you should open the camera to see what went wrong.

ADJUSTING THE EXPOSURE

Correct exposure involves getting the right amount of light to the film. Too much light will **overexpose** the film. Too little light will **underexpose** the film. Neither will result in a satisfactory negative, and without a good negative, you won't be able to make a good print. The camera exposure is set with two controls: the aperture ring and the shutter speed dial. Exposure is determined by using a light meter. In some cameras, meters are built in. With others, you must use a

FIGURE 2.4. Rewind knob. The rewind knob on a 35 mm camera is a useful way of checking to be sure you have loaded the film correctly. After you have loaded a roll of film, turn the knob gently as if to rewind the film until you feel slight resistance. That will take the slack out of the film. Then as you advance the film, the knob should turn backwards. If it doesn't, the film is not advancing correctly.

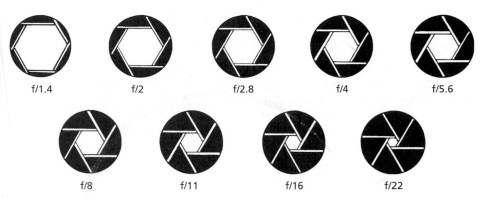

FIGURE 2.5. Aperture openings and f-stops. Larger f-stop numbers represent smaller lens openings because the number is actually the bottom part of a fraction. Thus, larger f-stop numbers represent apertures that let less light through to expose the film.

separate (hand-held) meter. In either case, the film speed rating—the ISO index— must be set properly on the meter or the entire roll will be incorrectly exposed.

Aperture: controlling light intensity

The aperture controls the intensity of the light passing through the lens. As can be seen in Figure 2.5, a large aperture lets through a lot of light, while a small aperture allows little light to pass through. The size of the aperture, also called the lens opening, is designated by the f-stop.

F-stops on the camera are noted—usually on the lens barrel—in a rather odd series of numbers like this:

1.4, 2, 2.8, 4, 5.6, 8, 11, 16, 22.

Such numbers are a shorthand way of expressing fractions. They give the ratio of the focal length of the lens (50 mm or 55 mm for a normal lens) to the physical diameter of the aperture opening. The ratios are used so that an f-stop on one lens gives the same exposure as the same f-stop on another lens. Thus, f/2 on a telephoto lens admits as much light as f/2 on a wide angle lens.

The larger f-stop numbers (like f/16) indicate smaller lens openings; the smaller numbers (like f/4) represent larger openings. When you change the lens opening from one f-stop to the next, you are adjusting the aperture "one stop." The f-stop series has been arranged so that each such change either doubles the intensity of light or cuts it in half. When you go down to the next smaller aperture (from f/4 to f/5.6, for instance), you are "stopping down" one stop and letting in half as much light. When you move a stop up to a larger aperture (say from f/8 to f/5.6), you are "opening up" the lens and allowing twice as much light in.

Shutter speed: controlling exposure length

The shutter speed controls the length of the exposure. A closed shutter means that no light may enter the camera body and strike the film. Opening the shutter allows light to strike the film until the shutter closes again. Shutter speed, then, is the length of time the shutter remains open. Simple cameras often have a single, fixed shutter speed. Adjustable cameras have a wide range of shutter speeds.

Shutter speeds appear on a camera in a series like this:

B, 1, 2, 4, 8, 15, 30, 60, 125, 250, 500.

These numbers are a quick way of noting fractions of a second. A shutter speed of 30 means 1/30 of a second, for instance. The larger numbers thus represent smaller fractions, or shorter exposure times.

Camera shutter settings are organized so that each one is either half or double the length of time of the one next to it. For example, moving from a setting of 30 to one of 60 lets in half as much light because the shutter stays open only half as long. Going from 500 to 250, on the other hand, allows in twice as much light because the shutter is open twice as long. Most cameras include shutter speeds larger than 1/2 second. Speeds like 4s or 2s denote speeds of 4 seconds and 2 seconds. In addition, most cameras include a "B" shutter speed, which allows you to hold the shutter open for as long as you want. When the shutter is set to "B," the shutter opens when you depress the shutter release button and stays open for as long as you hold it down. The "B" stands for "bulb" and is sometimes used for special effects in flash photography.

As you have probably noticed, the shutter speed series and aperture series parallel one another. In both, each time you move a notch up or down the scale, you halve or double the amount of light reaching the film during exposure. This is no coincidence, of course. The exposure controls were designed so that you can trade off shutter speeds and apertures.

The law of reciprocity

The basic principle of exposure is called the **law of reciprocity.** It simply means that you can reciprocate (or compensate) for a change in one exposure control with a change in the other. That is, you can trade off shutter speeds for apertures and vice versa.

You can trade off a shutter speed for an aperture setting because both shutter speed and aperture affect things besides exposure. Various settings will give the same exposure, but not the same picture. For instance, there will be differences in the ability of the camera to record moving subjects without blur. The way a camera records action is controlled by the shutter speed. And there will be differences in the overall sharpness of the picture from foreground to background. This overall sharpness of the image is called "depth of field" by photographers, and it is controlled by the aperture.

TABLE 2.1. Equivalent exposure settings. All of these shutter speed-aperture combinations will give equivalent exposure, but those at the top of the table will have greater depth of field while those at the bottom of the table will arrest subject movement more effectively.

Appearance of moving subjects	Shutter speed	Aperture setting	Overall sharpness (depth of field)
blurred, fuzzy	1/8	f/22	large
	1/15	f/16	
	1/30	f/11	
	1/60	f/8	
	1/125	f/5.6	
	1/250	f/4	
	1/500	f/2.8	
	1/1000	f/2	
sharp, clear	1/2000	f/1.4	shallow

Here is how the law of reciprocity works. Say your meter says you will obtain a correct exposure using a shutter speed of 1/60 of a second and an aperture of f/8. If you change your shutter speed from 1/60 to 1/125, you will allow half as much light to reach the film because the exposure time will be cut in half. But you can compensate for the decrease by doubling the intensity of the light striking the film—that is, by opening the aperture from f/8 to f/5.6. Thus, 1/125 at f/5.6 will give the same exposure as 1/60 at f/8.

You can continue making alterations: Speed the shutter up to 1/250 and compensate by doubling the light intensity again by changing the aperture to f/4. Or, you can go in the other direction from the original settings of 1/60 at f/8. Slowing the shutter down to 1/30 will let in twice as much light. But you can compensate for the increase by changing the aperture from f/8 to f/11 to decrease the light intensity. By continuing the trade off process, you can create an entire series of equivalent exposure settings, as shown in Table 2.1.

If you are using a hand-held light meter, the series of equivalent exposure settings is usually obvious because the meter's dial gives them all to you at once. A built-in meter, on the other hand, gives them to you one at a time. But even the built-in meter will yield the same series if you change the shutter speed and aperture settings. If you have a built-in meter, you can try this experiment: Point your camera at something and make a meter reading. Note the shutter speed and aperture settings. Now change the shutter speed to the next fastest speed. Then change the aperture to compensate. You should find that you had to move to the next larger aperture opening. By continuing the process, you will find an exposure setting series similar to the one in the example above. That series will give you the various shutter speed and aperture combinations for the subject you were metering and the speed of the film you were using.

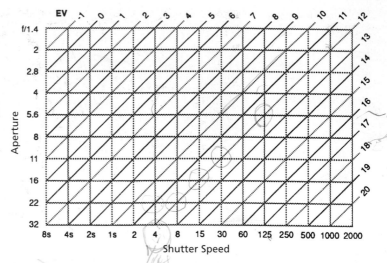

FIGURE 2.6. Chart of exposure values. Each diagonal line represents a series of equivalent shutter speed-aperture combinations. For example, EV 12 is 1/2000 second at f/1.4, and 1/1000 second at f/2, and so on down to 1/4 second at f/32.

Photographers have devised a shorthand—called the **exposure value**—that can be used to refer to the group of all the shutter speed-aperture combinations that give correct exposure with a certain brightness level. For instance, an aperture of f/2.8 and a shutter speed of 1/60 is equivalent to EV 9. All equivalent shutter speed-aperture combinations—from f/1.4 at 1/250 to f/32 at 2 seconds—are also EV 9. An exposure value of 10 refers to the set of shutter speed-aperture combinations that would be used when the brightness level is one stop greater—that is, combinations like f/2.8 at 1/125, or f/1.4 at 1/500, or f/22 at 1/2.

Figure 2.6 shows the common range of exposure values in chart form. The diagonal lines intersect all the aperture and shutter speed settings for a particular exposure value. For example, the diagonal line for EV 12 intersects the upper right corner, which represents an aperture of f/1.4 and a shutter speed of 1/2000. If you track that same diagonal line leftward and downward, it next intersects a point that represents an aperture of f/2 and a shutter speed of 1/1000 (which the law of reciprocity tells us is equivalent to the first combination). As you continue tracking the diagonal line downward and leftward, you'll find more equivalent combinations of shutter speed and aperture until you finally reach f/32 at 1/4 second.

Although you won't often find exposure values inscribed on modern photographic equipment, you will find charts similar to Figure 2.6 used to depict the exposure characteristics of programmed exposure mode systems. We'll see more about that when we look at exposure meters later in this chapter.

Shutter speeds control how objects appear when they are moving

FIGURE 2.7. Effects of shutter speed

A. The camera is held steady and a slow shutter speed allows the moving subject to blur; the background stays sharp.

B. A fast shutter speed freezes the action of both the subject and the background.

C. Moving the camera with the subject, called panning, stops subject motion and blurs the background, creating the impression of movement.

FIGURE 2.8. Focusing aids. These are two of the most common focusing screens found on 35 mm cameras. In both cases, you need to be careful to keep your eye centered in the viewfinder, especially when using lenses with apertures that do not open up to more than about f/4.

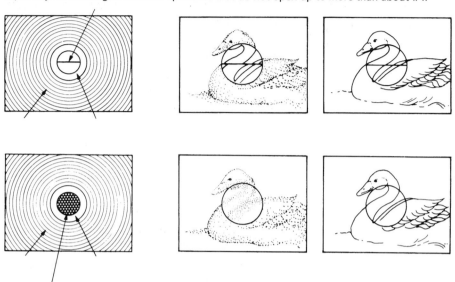

RECORDING MOTION

The shutter speed affects the way cameras record action. If you use a very slow shutter speed to record a moving subject, there is time during the exposure for the subject to trace its image on the film. In other words, you create a blur (Figure 2.7A). A faster shutter speed, on the other hand, tends to "freeze" a moving subject, recording it sharply (Figure 2.7B). By selecting the shutter speed, you can control how much or how little blur a moving subject creates. Other factors affect how moving subjects are recorded: how fast they are moving, how close they are to the camera, and whether they are moving toward the camera or across the viewfinder.

The shutter speed determines how camera movement affects the final image. If the camera is moved during a long exposure, the entire scene in front of the camera will streak across its field of view and produce a blur. Faster shutter speeds decrease the effects of camera movement. A common rule of thumb says that if you hand-hold the camera and want sharp results, you should not use a shutter speed any slower than the focal length of the lens you are using. For a normal (50 mm) lens, then, you should stick to shutter speeds of 1/50 (or 1/60) or faster. For a moderate **telephoto** (say, 135 mm), the minimum speed would be 1/125. For a wide angle like a 35 mm, you can use a speed as slow as 1/30.

The shutter speed can create special effects. Faster shutter speeds arrest motion and prevent blur, but blur is not always a bad thing. It depends on the picture you want. Many times, blur is an excellent way to produce an image of motion. You can control the degree of blur by controlling the shutter speed (probably 1/30 or slower).

You can also use a technique called **panning,** which involves moving the camera with the subject so the subject maintains the same position in the viewfinder during a long exposure. Because the subject doesn't move relative to the film frame, it is not blurred, but the background is (Figure 2.7C). The result is often an excellent impression of movement from the perspective of the moving subject. Panning takes some practice to do well: You begin the pan before you release the shutter, and continue panning after it has closed. As in any other sport, follow-through is the key to success.

ACHIEVING SHARPNESS

The camera is in focus when the subject is sharp in the viewfinder. To help you determine focus critically, the ground-glass viewing screens on most 35 mm cameras incorporate various focusing aids (Figure 2.8). A **fresnel screen,** with concentric line patterns, is used to brighten the outer edges of the screen. The central focusing spot may be either a **split-image rangefinder prism assembly** or a **microprism grid,** or some combination of the two.

The rangefinder focusing spot consists of two small prisms that cause an out-of-focus image to appear split in half in the viewfinder. Focusing brings the two halves of the split image together to form a whole image. Some types of rangefinders are designed to project two superimposed images, rather than a single split image. The superimposed images appear slightly offset from each other when out of focus and are perfectly aligned when in focus. The microprism grid focusing spot consists of many tiny prisms that break up, or exaggerate the blur of, an out-of-focus image. When focused, the image is clear and intact.

A camera can only focus sharply at one distance at a time. If your camera is focused on a subject 6 feet away, only objects 6 feet from the camera will be recorded truly sharp. Other objects, in front of or behind the subject, will be less than sharp. The further the objects are from the plane of focus, the less truly sharp they will be. Some may be so unsharp as to be unidentifiable blurs. Others, those close to the plane of focus, may be so nearly sharp as to be in focus for all practical considerations. They are said to lie within the camera's depth of field.

The aperture affects the depth of field. Depth of field means "zone of apparent image sharpness"—that is, the area in front of and behind the point of focus where, although objects won't be exactly sharp, they will be so nearly sharp you won't know the difference. Small apertures (like f/22 or f/32) give a large depth

FIGURE 2.9. Depth of field and aperture setting. The camera is focused on the eight ball in both images. With the wider aperture (f/4) the depth of field is shallower and the balls in the foreground and background are blurred. With the smaller aperture (f/32) nearly all the balls are relatively sharp.

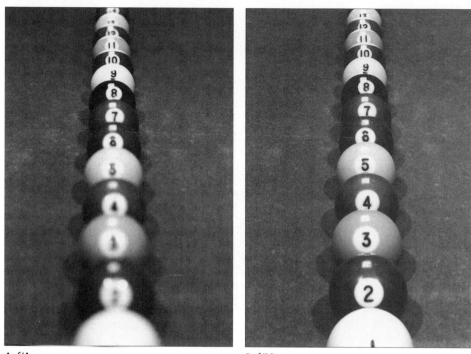

A. f/4   B. f/32

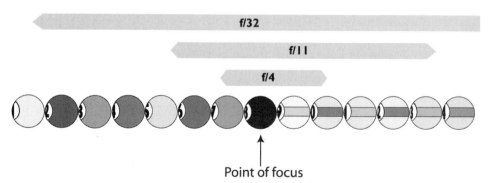

Point of focus

FIGURE 2.10. Relationship of various aperture settings and depth of field. As you stop down the lens aperture, the depth of field increases, encompassing more of both the foreground and background. At f/4 the depth of field is shallow and only three or four balls are sharp. At f/32 the depth of field is extended considerably and all the balls are relatively sharp.

FIGURE 2.11. Using depth of field to isolate subject. When the lens is stopped down to f/32, the resulting large depth of field renders the background sharply and provides a distinct pattern that distracts from the subject. By opening the aperture to f/4, the depth of field is made more shallow, the background softens, and the subject stands out more clearly.

A. f/32   B. f/4

TWO

of field, while large apertures (like f/2 or f/4) give a shallow depth of field. Figure 2.9 shows the differences in depth of field in photos taken from the same vantage point with the camera focused in the same spot (the eight ball), but with different aperture settings. In practice, you can control the zone of apparent sharpness by changing the aperture (Figure 2.10).

You can use this technique to isolate a subject against a distracting background (Figure 2.11). For example, you may be focused on a subject 6 feet away. With a small aperture like f/32, anything from 4 feet in front of the subject to about 20 feet behind the subject will also be acceptably sharp. By opening the aperture to f/4, you can reduce the depth of field. Now, still focused at 6 feet, only objects from 5 feet away (1 foot in front of the subject) to 7 feet away (1 foot behind the subject) will be sharp. By reducing depth of field, you can "pop" the subject loose from a distracting background.

The distance from camera to subject affects depth of field. If you keep the aperture the same and focus on a subject closer to the camera, the depth of field becomes shallower. On the other hand, if you focus on a subject farther away from the camera, the depth of field is increased. This point is made primarily for the sake of completeness. How far you are from the subject is usually dictated by your

A Note on

Sharpness

Both depth of field and shutter speed affect the sharpness of a negative, although in different ways. Depth of field controls the foreground to background sharpness—that is, which objects will be sharp and which won't. The shutter speed controls the effect of movement—that is, whether or not it will produce a blur.

The law of reciprocity implies that as you gain one type of sharpness, you lose the other (Figure 2.12). As you close down the aperture to gain depth of field, you must slow the shutter, thus losing the ability to freeze action. Conversely, if you speed up the shutter to decrease blur due to motion, you must open the aperture, thus collapsing the depth of field. The only ways to gain both depth of field and also faster shutter speeds are to increase the amount of light available or to use a faster film.

Some photographers, in an effort to increase sharpness, attempt to use slower, sharper film. It may work, but you shouldn't throw out your rolls of fast film too soon. While it is true that slower films generally are capable of producing finer detail, there must be enough light to expose them. Ironically, if light levels are low, the increased sharpness of the slower film may be lost on a blurred image or one with inadequate depth of field. On the other hand, although you can use faster shutter speeds and smaller apertures with faster films, the film itself may not be capable of adequately recording the extra sharpness. In the end, you can produce overall increased sharpness on all fronts only by increasing the amount of light available to expose the negative (Figure 7.1).

picture's composition, or the frame you want to put around the subject. Rarely would you move forward or backward merely to establish a certain depth of field.

The focal length of the lens affects depth of field. If you have a variety of lenses to shoot with, you will notice that they have different depths of field for given aperture settings. Wide angle lenses have a relatively large depth of field. Telephoto lenses have a correspondingly shallow depth of field. Occasionally, the depth of field you wish to establish will determine your choice of lens.

There are two ways of determining the amount of depth of field. Nearly all lenses are inscribed with a depth of field scale. They will tell you, for the aperture you are using, how far forward of and behind the subject will be sharp. The scale gives you distance, but you will have to imagine how the finished picture will look. As an aid to overcoming this problem, many single-lens reflex cameras also have a depth of field preview button. If you use that, you can get a

FIGURE 2.12. Trading off depth of field for shutter speed. Exchanging shutter speeds for apertures inevitably involves trading sharpness due to depth of field with sharpness due to arresting motion. In the image on the left, the depth of field is greater but the moving ball is blurred. In the image on the right, the faster shutter speed arrests the movement of the ball, but the depth of field is now very shallow.

A. f/32 at 1/4 of a second

B. f/4 at 1/250 of a second

close approximation of the finished image by simply looking through the viewfinder. The button works by actually stopping the lens down to the aperture you have selected. Because the viewfinder goes dim when the lens is stopped down, using the preview feature takes some getting used to.

Depth of field is one of the creative controls of an adjustable camera. There will be times when you want considerable depth of field. If you want to establish a visual relationship between something in the foreground and something in the background, you will need enough depth of field so they are both sharp. There will be other times when you want to limit depth of field. If you are taking a portrait and the subject is standing in front of a busy, distracting background, you will want a shallow depth of field to throw the background out of focus. That way attention will be centered on the subject.

UNLOADING THE FILM

When you have completed a roll of film, the exposure counter on your camera should indicate 24 or 36, depending on the length of the roll of film you shot. In

FIGURE 2.13. Incorrect use of a light meter. If the meter reading includes the bright sky, you are very likely to underexpose the subject and create a near silhouette.

A. Meter pointed skyward

B. Underexposed negative and dark photo

addition, the camera's film-advance lever will no longer operate easily. The advance lever should never be forced because the film may be pulled out of its cassette inside the camera. If this happens, you will have to take the camera into a darkroom before opening it to unload the film.

Normally, you simply rewind the film into the light-tight cassette, unload the film in subdued light, and load another roll if you wish to continue shooting. To rewind the film, nearly every camera has a film rewind button or lever, which, when pressed, disengages the sprocket wheel so it can turn backwards. You then

FIGURE 2.14. Correct use of a light meter. By aiming the meter carefully or by getting close enough to the subject to exclude extraneous light sources and bright sky areas, your meter will give you more accurate reflected light readings.

A. Meter pointed at subject

B. Properly exposed negative and usable photo

rewind the film by turning the rewind knob in the direction of the arrow marked on it. You should turn the knob until you feel a slight resistance and then wind past the resistance to pull the beginning of the film off the take-up reel and into the cassette. Unless you plan to process the film immediately, it is a good idea to return the cassette to the canister it came in and store it in a cool, dry place.

Sometimes, you may want to leave a bit of film extending from the cassette. In this case, you stop rewinding immediately after you feel the film come loose from the take-up reel. This trick can be handy if you do not finish a roll of film and want to be able to reload it later. You should mark the number of frames already shot on the leader extending from the cassette with a grease pencil for reference. If you plan on using this trick, it is a good idea to get in the habit of rewinding completed film all the way inside the cassette. That makes it easy to tell which rolls of film have been fully shot and which haven't. (It's very embarrassing to shoot the same roll twice and not nearly as economical as it sounds.)

USING A LIGHT METER

Some light meters are built into cameras; others must be held separately. Whatever their physical appearance, light meters have one purpose: They determine the exposure settings (aperture and shutter speed) needed to record a usable image on film.

Light meters are of two types: reflected and incident. A **reflected light meter** is pointed at the subject to measure the amount of light reflected from the subject back toward the camera. An **incident light meter** is held in front of the subject, but facing the camera, to measure the light falling on the subject.

Nearly all meters built into cameras are of the reflected type. In order to use a reflected light meter effectively, you should be aware of its personality. A reflected light meter expects to look at a subject that is an "average gray." Although that sounds informal and approximate, **average gray** is a precisely defined photographic term; it represents 18 percent reflectance of the light that falls on a subject. You can even buy a photographic **gray card**—one that reflects 18 percent gray—to use as a meter target if you need to make exact exposure measurements. However, most subjects are very close to average and do reflect something like 18 percent of the light that hits them.

If the meter gets fooled, it's usually because not all the light coming toward it is reflected light. That is, it's because the meter is looking directly at a light source of some kind, rather than at the indirect light reflected off the subject. Figure 2.13 shows the wrong way and Figure 2.14 the right way to use a light meter.

The problem of backlighting

A backlit subject is one where the light coming from behind the subject is as strong or stronger than the light falling on the front of the subject. It could be someone standing against a bright window, or a subject with the sun setting behind it. The meter expects only reflected light, but primarily picks up the light from behind the subject. In effect, the meter "thinks" there is more light reflected from the subject than there really is. As a result, the meter indicates settings that are less than needed for proper exposure. The subject comes out too dark, perhaps even as a silhouette. The picture is underexposed.

Backlighting can be dealt with in several ways. In general, you want to avoid pointing the meter at anything except subject matter that reflects light. If the backlight is due to an expanse of bright sky behind the subject, you may be able to point the meter downward. In other cases, you may be able to move in very close to the subject so the meter avoids reading the backlight. If you can't get close to the subject, you may be able to use a technique called "substitute metering"—that is, pointing your meter at a substitute subject that receives the same front light as the subject, but one that allows you to avoid metering the backlight.

A convenient substitute subject is a gray card, or you can even use your hand. But because skin doesn't reflect the same as a gray card, you will need to make a correction. For dark skin, you meter the back of the hand and then close down one stop. You can remember to close down by noting that your thumb will point down when you hold the back of your hand toward you. For light skin, you meter the palm of the hand and open up one stop; your thumb will point upward as you hold the palm of your hand toward you. In any case, once the meter reading is made from a substitute subject and the exposure controls are set, you can reframe the picture the way you want and shoot.

Some types of reflected light meters deal better with backlighting than others. Built-in meters differ in what part of the scene they take exposure information from: **Averaging meters** consider the entire viewfinder frame; **spot meters** read only a small area in the center of the viewfinder; and **center-weighted meters**

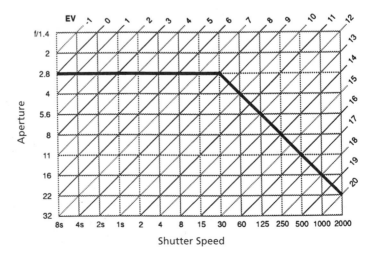

FIGURE 2.15. Example exposure program for an f/2.8 lens used with ISO 100 film. As exposures increase, the program keeps the aperture wide open at f/2.8 and gradually increases the shutter speed to minimize blur. At 1/30 second, it begins both to stop down the aperture and increase shutter speed to enhance sharpness.

give most attention to the center area, although they don't entirely ignore the edges of the frame.

Spot and center-weighted meters are more likely to give correct exposures in backlight than averaging meters because both tend to ignore the backlight itself. You should know which type of meter your camera has so you can use it effectively. But keep in mind that no meter is foolproof. It has to be used with intelligence and with its limitations in mind.

EXPOSURE METER MODES

Three metering modes are in common use today in cameras with built-in meters: manual, automatic, and programmed.

In a manual exposure camera, you set both the shutter speed and aperture. Your camera's meter will usually have some sort of indicator inside the viewfinder that tells you whether the shutter speed-aperture combination you've selected will yield a correct exposure. If it shows under- or over-exposure, you adjust either the aperture or shutter speed until the indicator shows the exposure will be correct. The manual approach gives you complete control over exposure, but it also makes it easy to make exposure errors by setting the shutter or aperture incorrectly.

When using the automatic exposure mode, you select either the shutter speed or the aperture, and the camera automatically selects the other to produce a correct exposure. In an **aperture priority** system, you select the aperture and the camera automatically sets whatever shutter speed is needed to yield a correct exposure. In a **shutter priority** system, you set the shutter speed and the camera sets the aperture accordingly. In theory, a shutter priority system would be of most value when photographing action because you would be able to select a fast shutter speed to freeze the action, while the metering system would select whatever aperture was needed for accurate exposure. On the other hand, an aperture priority system would theoretically be of most value when depth-of-field considerations outweigh the need to stop action. In practice, both systems are flexible enough to accommodate nearly all shooting situations because, while you have direct control over only one of the two exposure controls, you also have indirect control over the other. For instance, if you had an aperture priority camera and wanted to force a fast shutter speed, you would only need to select a wide open aperture setting (like f/1.4). The exposure system would then be forced to select the fastest shutter speed possible for the film and lighting conditions.

A programmed exposure camera selects both the aperture and shutter speed based on a table of exposure settings stored electronically within the camera. Once you've selected a certain speed film to use, the programmed system measures the light available for exposure and automatically selects a certain aperture and shutter speed combination. Figure 2.15 shows a typical program for an f/2.8 lens used with an ISO 100 film. When light levels are very low (EV-1 through

FIGURE 2.16. Bracketing exposures. Bracketing is no substitute for accurate exposure, but it can be very helpful in lighting that is tricky to meter and can be instructive in seeing how film reacts to varying degrees of exposure.

A. Negative strip showing (left to right) correct exposure, one stop overexposed, and one stop underexposed

B. Proof print of bracketed negatives

EV8), the exposure system keeps the lens aperture wide open so as to use the fastest possible shutter speed. At higher light levels (EV9 through EV20), the exposure system gradually speeds up the shutter and closes the aperture to improve overall sharpness. Many programmed exposure cameras contain more than one program, each tailor-made to suit a given shooting situation. One program might maximize depth of field for shooting still-life subjects, while another would use the fastest possible shutter speed when shooting action.

Many cameras will give you a choice among several metering modes. You'll learn more about exposure if you work in the manual mode until you become familiar with the basics of metering and exposure. After that, you'll know when it's safe to let your camera make some or all of your exposure decisions for you.

Bracketing exposures

There will be times, despite your equipment and your intelligence, when you just cannot be certain of exposure. That's when you guess. But photographers have a special name for it: **bracketing,** which means taking the same shot at several exposure settings as insurance against incorrect exposure.

When you bracket an exposure, you guess systematically (Figure 2.16). You take the first shot at the exposure you think is correct. Then you take a second picture, but overexpose it. Finally you take a third shot that is underexposed. If you are using black-and-white film, you will probably want to bracket in intervals of at least a full stop. That is, if your first exposure is f/5.6 at 1/125, then your second might be f/4 at 1/125 (overexposed a stop), and the third might be f/8 at 1/125 (underexposed a stop).

When you bracket, the hope, of course, is that one of the exposures will be correct. But don't let bracketing become a substitute for careful exposure measurement. It can help when the lighting is tricky, but it costs a lot of film and obviously won't work if you are shooting something fleeting. Imagine trying to bracket as you are taking pictures of a football game.

The f/16 exposure guide

At some point your meter will fail. It will never be the right time, but fortunately there is an exposure guide you can fall back on. The **f/16 rule** says that correct exposure in direct sun (no clouds covering the sun) is always f/16 at a shutter speed equal to 1/ISO. For T-Max 400, for example, sunlight exposure would be f/16 at 1/400 second (or 1/500 second, the closest shutter speed on most cameras). For T-Max 100, the exposure would be f/16 at 1/100 (or 1/125). Of course, equivalent exposures would also work: if f/16 at 1/125 is correct, so would f/11 at 1/250, or f/22 at 1/60. If you are photographing under a hazy sun (clouds with soft-edged shadows), then you need to open one stop from the basic full sunlight rule: f/11 at 1/ISO. Table 2.2 summarizes a series of exposure guides that are surprisingly accurate. You can even use them to check your light meter if it doesn't seem to be working properly.

TABLE 2.2. The f/16 exposure guide. In direct sun, correct exposure is always f/16 at a shutter speed equivalent to 1/ISO. For Tri-X, for example, correct exposure would be f/16 at 1/400 (or 1/500). Other weather and lighting conditions require you to adjust the aperture as shown in the table.

Lighting conditions	Shutter speed at an aperture of f/16
Bright sun (well-defined shadows)	Shutter equal to ISO index film speed
Hazy sun (weak, soft-edged shadows)	Open one stop
Cloudy bright (no shadows)	Open two stops
Dark overcast (light rain, gray sky)	Open three stops
Open shade on a sunny day	Open three stops
Heavy overcast (heavy rain, dark sky)	Open four stops
Sand or snow in bright sun	Close one stop

How to

Operate a Camera

Step 1: Check to make sure there is no film in the camera by turning the rewind knob in the direction of the arrow marked on it. If the knob turns freely several times, the camera is empty and safe to open.

Step 2: In subdued light or shade, open the back of the camera and pull out the rewind knob. Remove the roll of film from its canister and insert the cassette in the left side of the camera.

Step 3: Push down the film rewind knob to lock the cassette in place, and draw the film across to the take-up reel by pulling the narrow end of the film. Insert the end of the film into the slit of the take-up reel.

Step 4: Make sure the holes along the edges of the film engage the sprocket wheel next to the take-up reel.

How to

Operate a Camera

Step 5: Close the camera back and turn the rewind knob in the direction of the arrow to take the slack out of the film.

Step 6: Shoot off two or three waste exposures to see whether the film is advancing properly. The rewind knob should turn backwards.

Step 7: Make certain your light meter is set for the correct ISO index for the film you are using.

Step 8: Take a meter reading and set the aperture accordingly.

How to

Operate a Camera

Step 9: Set the shutter speed. Both aperture and shutter speed should be set according to the reflected light reading made with your camera's meter.

Step 10: Focus your camera on the subject.

Step 11: Release the shutter smoothly.

Step 12: Advance the film.

TWO

How to

Operate a Camera

Step 13: At the end of the roll, be careful not to pull the film out of the cassette. The film advance will be difficult to move, and the film counter should indicate that 24 or 36 exposures have been shot.

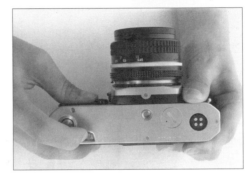

Step 14: Press the rewind button (usually on the bottom of the camera) to disengage the sprocket wheel.

Step 15: Rewind the film into its cassette using the rewind knob. When the film is nearly rewound, you will feel a slight resistance; wind past that point to pull the film completely inside the cassette.

Step 16: In subdued light or shade, open the back of the camera and remove the cassette.

What Can Go Wrong

Even experienced photographers occasionally have problems operating their cameras. Sometimes it is the fault of the camera; more often, it is the fault of the photographer.

Problem 1: Image out of focus

An out-of-focus shot can usually be distinguished from other blurred shots because often some area just in front or just behind the subject will be sharp.

P.36

Probable Cause:

You probably have not concentrated on focusing your camera carefully enough.

Solution:

Be more careful in focusing your camera for each shot. If the problem persists, it may be due to an out-of-adjustment viewfinder.

Problem 2: Film with light streaks

Light streaks or fogged areas on film.

Probable Cause:

You may have opened the camera back before the film was rewound into the cassette (in which case, the fogged areas will form stripes across the width of the film), or you might have a faulty shutter, a damaged film cassette, or a camera back that doesn't close properly.

Solution:

Make sure the camera back is closed properly or, in the case of the other problems noted above, proper repairs are made.

What Can Go Wrong

Problem 3: Blank film

Probable Cause:

Film not exposed in camera, probably because it was misloaded and did not advance between exposures. Note that this is not a processing error. The visible film edge numbers indicate that the film was developed properly.

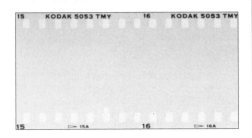

Solution:

Be sure to check the rewind knob as you advance the film to make sure it is turning backwards.

Problem 4: Blurred picture

Probable Cause:

The subject or camera moved during the exposure, and the shutter speed was too slow.

Solution:

Make sure you have the proper setting to freeze the image on film.

Problem 5: Double exposure

Two images appearing on the negative, one on top of the other.

Probable Cause:

You have not advanced the film between each shot.

Solution:

Be sure to advance the film between each shot if you do not have a camera with built-in protection against unintentional double exposure.

REVIEW questions ?

1. Why is speed important in selecting a film?

2. What is the primary advantage of bulk-loaded film?

3. What does the aperture do and why is shutter speed important?

4. What is the law of reciprocity?

5. What are the points to remember in recording motion by a still camera?

6. What is depth of field and what affects it?

7. What are the three kinds of light meters and what are the advantages of each?

8. What is backlighting and why is it sometimes a problem?

9. What is the difference between aperture priority and shutter priority metering modes?

10. What is the f/16 exposure rule?

[handwritten note: SUNNY DAY — f 16 @ equivalent to film speed]

try it YOURSELF

1. Shoot a roll of film in which you make some tests to see how your film, camera, and meter react in different exposure situations.

   a. See how great an exposure error your film will tolerate. Make an exposure at the metered setting. Then make eight more exposures: four underexposed in steps from one to four stops, and four overexposed in the same manner. After the film has been developed, estimate which of the negatives are usable.

   b. Make a series of equivalent exposures—that is, in which you trade shutter speeds and apertures to maintain identical exposure. Try to use as many apertures and shutter speeds as possible. After you've processed the negatives, check them to make sure all frames are exposed alike. Note differences in depth of field. (If any frame differs significantly from the others in exposure, it may indicate that your shutter is not operating correctly at that speed.)

    c. Make a series of pictures using backlight. In one, make no special compensation for the backlight. In another, meter the background and underexpose by two stops to produce a silhouette. In a third, meter the subject very closely, so as to ignore the backlight. Make prints from the three negatives to see how metering affects exposure in backlight.

2. Most of us, interested in maximum sharpness, use the fastest shutter speed possible under given lighting conditions. But sharpest isn't necessarily best. Try your slow shutter speeds. Take pictures of moving subjects at speeds like 1/4, 1/8, or 1/15. Try panning your camera with the moving subject so the subject itself is sharp, but the background is blurred. Often, pictures like these will be much more evocative of movement than shots in which subject and background are frozen in time. While you're at it, see how much you can slow the shutter speed and still safely hand-hold the camera. Most photographers, if they are careful, can achieve reasonably sharp pictures at speeds as slow as 1/15.

3. Make a deliberate study of depth of field. Remember that three factors influence depth of field: the lens aperture, distance from the subject, and the focal length of the lens you are using. Depth of field effects are usually clearer if you use a subject that repeats from background to foreground, like a series of railroad ties or a picket fence. Keep notes as you shoot the pictures so you can judge the final results.

    a. Make a series of exposures of the same subject (like bicyclers, joggers, cars) from the same distance. Trade off shutter speeds and apertures so you maintain the same exposure. Be sure to include the extremes of the possible apertures for your lens, both wide open and closed down as much as possible.

    b. Now keep the aperture and shutter speed constant, but vary the distance from the subject to the camera. Begin by getting as close as your lens will allow to the subject. Then move back a foot or two, refocus, and take another picture. Keep moving back a few feet at a time and shooting pictures until you are about 25 feet from the subject.

    c. If you have a zoom lens or different focal length lenses available, shoot a series of pictures in which you keep lens aperture and distance from the subject constant, but change lenses. After you've processed your film, make prints of some of the frames to see how depth of field increased or decreased.

CHAPTER **3**

shooting for composition

Place de l'Europe, by Henri Cartier-Bresson, 1932.

shooting for composition

Place de l'Europe, by Henri Cartier-Bresson, 1932.
(© Henri Cartier-Bresson/Magnum Photos)

    Henri Cartier-Bresson is often described as a documentary photographer because he finds his subjects in everyday life. He describes himself as a surrealist, however, because what he looks for in everyday subjects are "decisive moments" that seem to transcend the ordinary, when the arrangement of elements in the frame creates a strong visual composition and offers insight into the subject. In looking at _Place de l'Europe_ it is easy to misunderstand the decisive moment as the moment of peak action, but Cartier-Bresson refers to something much more significant. In his book _The Decisive Moment_, he describes it as "the simultaneous recognition, in a fraction of a second, of the significance of an event as well as a precise organization of forms which gave that event its proper expression." Note, for instance, the visual echoes of the scene in the poster in the background: the leaping figure and the semicircular shapes.

A good photographer must know more than what dials to set and what knobs to turn. A good photographer has to visualize a scene and realize that it contains a photograph long before pressing the shutter. Some people are born with an "eye" for photography, but most of us have to develop it—by taking pictures, by analyzing them, and by taking more pictures.

There are no simple absolutes to guide the search for effective photographs. The process begins simply with knowing how to hold the camera properly. From there, it goes to effectively "working the subject"—that is, visually exploring a subject with a camera. And, finally, it involves putting the guidelines for good composition into practice.

USING THE CAMERA

From a mechanical point of view, taking a picture requires that you know how to hold a camera and how to press the shutter. Taking a good picture is a bit more complicated, but these two basics provide a good place to begin.

Hold the camera properly. Holding a camera involves more than simply supporting the camera body in your hand. You should hold it in such a way that you can operate all essential controls without taking your eye from the viewfinder.

The proper way to hold a 35 mm camera is to cradle the lens and base of the camera body in the palm of your left hand. You should be able to operate both the aperture and focusing rings with your left hand. Your right hand grips the right side of the camera body in such a way that you can press the shutter release with your forefinger and work the film advance lever with your thumb. When necessary, you should also be able to operate the shutter speed dial with the thumb and forefinger of your right hand. This camera position is used to take horizontal photographs.

To take vertical pictures, most people simply turn the camera 90 degrees counterclockwise. Your right hand still grips the side of the camera, but it's positioned above. Your left hand cradles the lens and left side of the camera, now positioned below. You should still be able to work the camera controls without taking your eye from the viewfinder.

Steady the camera while you shoot. Steadying the camera while you shoot can eliminate blurred pictures. For most shots, you can brace the camera by tucking your left arm in against your body and gently pressing the camera back against your cheek and forehead. You can also use the neck strap of the camera to help you steady it by getting your hands inside of the strap or by wrapping the strap around one wrist several times. By turning that wrist, you can place tension on the strap around the back of your neck.

If you are using particularly slow shutter speeds, you should try to find a support to help you keep the camera from moving. You can lean up against a wall, for example, or support your elbows on a table. If you are sitting on the ground, you can place your elbows on your knees. At slow shutter speeds, the steadier you can hold the camera, the sharper your pictures will be.

For all types of shots, it's a good idea to practice holding the camera until you arrive at a posture that is both steady and comfortable for you. You can even look at yourself in a mirror to see whether your arms, hands, and fingers are positioned properly.

Snap the shutter properly. "Snapping" the shutter is not as mundane as it sounds. Actually, it is better to think more in terms of pressing or squeezing the shutter, rather than snapping it. Those words suggest more of a deliberate gentleness, but whoever heard of "press-shots" or "squeeze-shots"? Still, you shouldn't punch down on the shutter release. When you're ready to take a picture, you should be relaxed: Take careful aim, take a breath and release it, hold very still, and press down on the shutter release smoothly and firmly. Jabbing or jerking the release button may cause you to move the camera and blur the photo.

If you are using slow shutter speeds, you should place your right thumb under the camera, then squeeze thumb and shutter-finger together. Your thumb will counterbalance the movement of your forefinger and help prevent camera movement.

WORKING THE SUBJECT

You should never worry about making every frame a masterpiece. One of the advantages of the 35 mm camera is that you can take many photographs on one roll of film. Your camera should be used as something of an exploratory device—as a scratch pad, as some photographers call it. If you take but one frame of each subject you encounter, chances are you will wind up with nothing worth printing. When you use a 35 mm camera, you need to be able to recognize that a scene or situation has the potential for a successful photograph. Once you decide that, you can begin "working" the subject—exploring it with your camera (Figure 3.1).

Change your proximity to the subject. You can think of yourself as a film director developing a scene. A movie scene frequently begins with a long, overall shot to establish the general location, for example, the New York skyline or a panorama of cactus and sagebrush. After that, the camera often moves in for a medium shot, concentrating on the subject of interest. Then, it usually comes in for a tight close-up, perhaps the expression on someone's face. You can do much the same thing by circling around your subject from a distance, watching for effective lighting and visually interesting backgrounds. When you make your long shots, you will want to be careful to avoid backgrounds that are cluttered and that distract from the subject. As you move in closer, still circling, you continue shooting photographs each time you see something that looks like it may work. Eventually, you get in tight on the subject, so it fills the frame completely if possible.

Closing in on the subject is important. If there is a single common error by

FIGURE 3.1. "Working" the subject. In 35 mm photography it is common to take a series of photographs of a single subject, varying how close you are to the subject, changing the angle of view, and mixing horizontal and vertical views. This allows the photographer to explore the visual possibilities in the subject and work toward the strongest possible image.

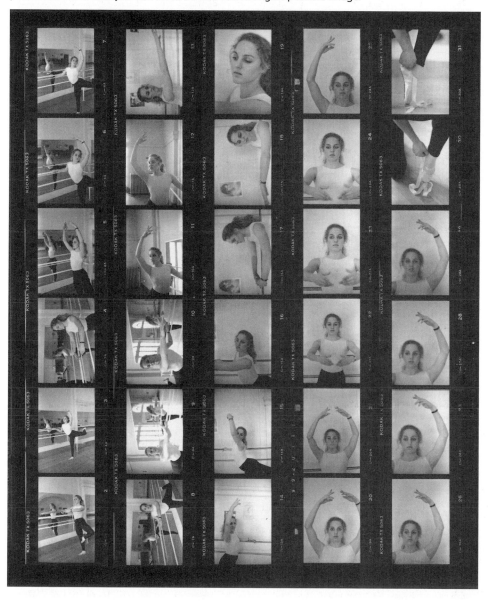

beginning photographers, it is that they take their photographs from too far away. As a result, the viewer can't see the subject well because it's too small. At the same time, many distracting details creep in to compete with the subject for attention. You can almost always improve your photographs by getting closer.

Go high/Go low

Vary your vantage point. While you are moving in on the subject, vary your vantage point. Shoot from high and low angles, always looking for the interesting angle. The vast majority of photographs are taken from eye-level. But that's the way we all look at the world anyway. Your pictures will be more interesting if you try to find something fresher: Try bird's eye views and worm's eye views. You can climb up on things and get down on the ground. It's good exercise—and often leads to good photographs.

Prop

Keep your subjects occupied. When you are taking pictures of people, you will get stronger photographs if you can get them to relax and be themselves. Many times, it will help to give them something to do or a prop to work with. A prop can be anything that fits the person and the picture: a flower, a hat, a book.

eliminate extraneous background junk

Frame your subject tightly. You will also get stronger pictures if you eliminate unessential backgrounds by framing tightly—that is, by isolating the subject alone in the frame of the viewfinder. If you do include backgrounds, they should complement the subject and help tell the story. For instance, a portrait of a painter beside one of her paintings tells a story on two levels. We see what she looks like. At the same time, we are allowed a glimpse at her thought processes by studying the painting.

Avoid taking all pictures as horizontals. For some reason, that seems to be the most natural way to hold the camera when you're first getting started. But it's not the most effective frame for many subjects, including most portraits. If you're in doubt, you can shoot the picture both as a horizontal and a vertical.

Don't be afraid to experiment. You should always be willing to risk an occasional failure to see whether something will work. Later, when going through your shots after the film is processed, you can decide what worked well and what didn't.

Taking good photographs is a deliberate process of discovery. As you gain experience, you'll know better which angles won't work and which are more likely to yield results. You will be able to narrow down the field of experimentation and concentrate on strong possibilities. Eventually, you may arrive at the point where you are able to "previsualize" your photographs—that is, see the image in your mind's eye and then set about creating it in your camera.

Read

It may comfort you to know that most professional photographers are satisfied if they get two or three successful photographs from a roll of film. If you find that you are getting many more than that, perhaps your standards are too low.

If you expect to grow as a photographer you will always need to experiment and try things you're not sure of. But you must be careful of sloppiness. No amount of experimentation is a justification of sloppy or haphazard shooting.

PRINCIPLES OF COMPOSITION

The title of this section is misleading—in fact, a lie. It is not going to list any principles of composition.

Photographic composition has been aptly defined as the strongest way of seeing. You usually hear about composition in the form of a set of principles. But you really learn about composition by taking photographs, by studying them, and by taking more photographs. Eventually composition becomes second nature; it is simply incorporated into the way you see photographs. Edward Weston said it well: "To consult the rules of composition before taking a photograph is like consulting the laws of gravitation before taking a walk."

All of this isn't to say that composition is unimportant, but rather that it is not usually in the forefront of your mind as you photograph. Composition, the design of the photograph, is crucial. It lies at the center of photography as a visual form. While there is a fairly well-recognized set of principles for analyzing composition—concerning things like balance, contrast, proportion—they tend to be useful primarily in analyzing photographs after they are made. What we have here is a set of guidelines and shooting strategies that should assist you in strengthening your own compositions as you shoot. To make them a little more interesting, we've overstated them as absolutes. As rules, all of them ache to be broken at one time or another. As guidelines, you can take them as a challenge to strengthen your photographic eye and personal style.

The key to a strong image lies in its simplicity. Ideally, there should be nothing in the photograph that doesn't contribute to its overall quality (Figure 3.2). This isn't to say that a photograph must be simplistic, but rather that all its

FIGURE 3.2. **Simplifying the shot.** Staying too far back from your subject allows competing elements to distract. Getting closer and deliberately selecting simple backgrounds puts more emphasis on the subject.

A. Loosely framed.

B. Tighter framing.

elements must add up to something coherent. You must always be on guard against backgrounds that distract, elements that compete, and inclusion of the extraneous and unessential.

Every photograph must have a central subject or a focal point. Even when you have more than one person or object, you can achieve a good photo by developing a "center of interest" around which to organize the picture. When you have a group of three or more, you should avoid

FIGURE 3.3. The rule of thirds. Divide the rectangular film frame into thirds both vertically and horizontally. Compositions can often be strengthened by placing your subject at one of the four intersection points.

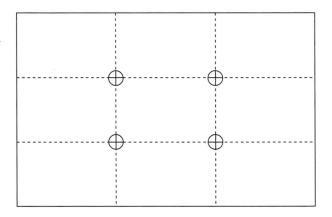

FIGURE 3.4. Composing by the rule of thirds. In most cases, centering your subject will not yield the strongest composition. Here, following the rule of thirds, the subject's face is located at the **upper right intersection point.** *(Photo by Chris Johns; published with permission)*

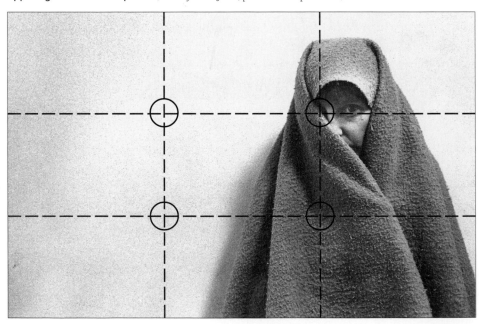

FIGURE 3.5. Using the corner. Some subjects lend themselves to placement in the corner of the frame. This is an unusual enough composition that it may offer a bit of a surprise to viewers.

(Photo by Randy Wood; published with permission)

Rule of 3rds

arrangements that waste space and look trite or static. Instead, you can keep your subjects close together and stagger the arrangement, overlapping them and varying the height. Giving the subjects something to do can also help to develop a strong focal point. Manipulating depth of field is another way to create a central focal point. By controlling it, you can contrast a sharply defined subject against a more diffuse foreground and background.

The center of interest rarely belongs in the center of the photograph. The center of a rectangle is graphically its weakest point. Stronger points of placement are suggested by the **rule of thirds.** The rule of thirds refers to a rectangular frame divided into thirds both horizontally and vertically with four points located where the lines intersect (Figure 3.3). Placing your center of interest at one of the

FIGURE 3.6. Symmetrical subjects. A symmetrical subject, in which one half of the subject is essentially the mirror image of the other half, is often most strongly composed by centering it. Centering gives the subject a formality and directness it would not otherwise have.

four points will generally result in much stronger composition than centering it (Figure 3.4). As an alternative and for a bit of surprise in your compositions, you can also try placing the center of interest in one of the corners (Figure 3.5).

Centering your subject is an easy trap to fall into because the focusing aid in your viewfinder is dead center in the frame. That makes it tempting to put the focusing aid over your subject, then focus and shoot. You can avoid the temptation by making focusing and framing two distinct steps in picture taking.

Center symmetrical subjects. The rule of thirds is extremely useful for images that are asymmetrical, that is, images where shapes and patterns are not balanced around a central axis. And while you'll find that most images are indeed asymmetrical, you'll occasionally discover others that will yield the strongest images when treated as symmetrical patterns. In those cases, the photograph will usually work best if the subject is centered, thus enhancing its symmetrical appearance. Symmetrical composition often gives the photograph a formal tone. Compare the two renditions of the same subject in Figure 3.6.

Dominant lines help organize a photograph. A dominant line might be the edge of an object. It might be the horizon. It might be a stream winding its way through some rural landscape. Dominant lines are useful because they can help establish points of interest or can give the photograph direction (Figure 3.7). They can provide a kind of visual backbone that helps structure the rest of the photograph. But a dominant line should not divide the picture in half: Halves and fourths are boring. Thirds are more interesting, but the ancient Greeks said the best proportion was the "golden section": roughly 3/5.

Be aware of subject-background relationships. When you've got a number of technical details on your mind—aperture, shutter speed, focus, etc.—and you're concentrating on getting what you want from your subject, it's easy to overlook the background. But in the final print, the background will be as much a part of the image as the subject. You need to train yourself to look past your subject in the viewfinder to study the background. You need to look into the far corners of the viewfinder as well as the center.

In general, you'll probably want the background to be as simple as it can be, but that doesn't mean the background should always be stark and bare. It depends on whether the background contributes or distracts from the meaning and graphic qualities of the photograph. If the background carries information that is essential to your image or helps create a striking visual image, then you'll want to keep it sharp and give it presence. But if the background just happens to be there or even distracts, then you'll want to make it as simple and unobtrusive as you can. You can resort to a number of strategies to simplify backgrounds. Probably the most effective is to get closer so your subject fills the frame and the background becomes a less significant part of the image. You can also make the depth of field shallower either by using a larger aperture, or by moving in closer, or by using a longer focal length if you're using a zoom lens or have more than one lens. You can often find simpler backgrounds merely by changing camera angles so you're shooting against the sky (north sky works well) or shooting against a grassy area or a plain wall.

You should also be aware of tonal relationships between subject and background. By putting a light subject against a dark background (Figure 3.8) you can emphasize the subject. You can, of course, accomplish the same thing by

FIGURE 3.7. Dominant lines. In this image, the curve of the fence provides a kind of structural "backbone" and leads the eye into the scene. The fact that the overall line of the fence is countered by the diverging lines of the pickets creates an interesting tension.

(Photo by Elizabeth Miller; published with permission)

FIGURE 3.8. Emphasis by contrast. The dark background in this image contrasts with the lighter subject and seems to push it forward in the frame.

(Photo by Stuart Wong; published with permission)

FIGURE 3.9. Negative space. The considerable empty space surrounding the subject isolates and emphasizes it. In photographs for publication, this negative space may also be useful for typography.

putting a dark subject against a light background. At the same time, there are images that work better when the subject and background are similar in tone.

You can also use the background as a frame for the subject. The background in a photograph is often called negative space. Large amounts of negative space can create dramatic compositions (Figure 3.9).

You'll generally want to keep subject and background distinct by avoiding what photographers call mergers. A **merger** is a confusing association of subject with background.

There's really no right or wrong in any of this. Sometimes mergers create fascinating images. Sometimes intricate backgrounds are successful. Sometimes large amounts of negative space weaken the composition. One thing is reasonably certain, however—your photographs will be stronger if you are aware of and manage subject-background relationships when you shoot.

In fact, there's nothing sacred about any of these guidelines for creating stronger composition. As you photograph, you'll almost certainly find ways to break the rules and create yet stronger compositions. The important thing is to develop an eye for organizing spatial relationships within the frame of the photograph. It is rare, however, that spatial relationships are the only thing you need to consider— a photograph is taken in time as well as space. (See *A Note on Timing,* Page 70.)

Beyond Saying "Cheese"

There is more to taking good photographs than the mechanics of camera operation and an eye for composition, although both are obviously essential. You should also pay attention to the content of your images. One way to do this is to ask yourself why you take photographs of the subjects you select and what you are trying to capture about those subjects in your pictures.

If you are taking pictures of people, what interests you about that particular person? If it is his or her face alone, bring the camera in close enough to make the face the main emphasis in the final picture. If it is something he or she does, show your subject in action or try to incorporate visual elements that help tell this person's story. You might include a pet cat, a shawl your subject knitted, or the watercolor brush this person paints with. These props will add interesting information to the picture and will usually help put your subject at ease. Most people are defensive about having their picture taken. They frequently put up a front, put on an artificial smile, or do whatever it takes to get it over with. (Photographers are usually worse than anyone else.) It is worth taking some time to establish a rapport with your subject to help put him or her at ease.

You can also put people at ease by giving them roles to play. This is usually as simple as getting them to do something they normally do. For example, if you are taking a photograph of a potter, get him or her to make a pot. Philippe Halsman, who shot more than one hundred covers for *Life* magazine, often asked subjects to jump in place while he photographed them. He felt that having them do something a bit silly helped subjects relax and avoid self-conscious poses.

If you are shooting photographs of inanimate objects, you should still ask yourself what you find visually interesting about those particular objects. Are you drawn to their formal qualities: their shape, their surface, how they reflect light? Are you drawn to the way in which they contrast with their environment in texture, or size, or color? Are you interested primarily in documenting their use as a tool or ornament? Are you interested in establishing some sort of relationship among a number of separate objects? As you examine what you want to show in your pictures, you very likely will find yourself refining how you shoot to make that aspect of the subject clearer.

Some photographers work very intuitively and might be inhibited by questions about why they shoot as they do. But most of us find that one of the rewards of photography is that it gives us a way to examine the world and our relationship to it. By asking ourselves what we find compelling in certain subject matter, we can discover something about the subject and something about ourselves. Our photographs allow us to make those insights concrete and share them with others.

A Note on

Timing

A photograph represents the scene in front of the camera—at the instant the shutter is released. For most subjects, some moments are more interesting than others. A strong photograph is the result of timing as well as an eye for composition. The French photographer Henri Cartier-Bresson called it the "decisive moment"—that single instant when objects within the frame organize themselves into a strong composition and also reveal something about themselves that is worth capturing on film (see Cartier-Bresson's image at the beginning of this chapter).

A good photographer, catlike, stalks that moment. Sometimes, when things move quickly before the camera, it's a matter of reflex and instinct. You take pictures rapidly and deliberately, ready to pounce when that single revealing instant comes. Sometimes it's a matter of patience, of waiting in one spot long enough for the moment to arrive. You might be taking portraits, working your subjects and waiting for the moment when they finally begin to relax, let down their guard, and reveal themselves as they really are.

Sometimes you have absolute control and create the moment yourself. You might, for instance, be working in a studio creating a still-life, arranging and rearranging things, when suddenly you know you've got it. You may take lots of pictures in search of that moment, but when you finally get it, it will be The Picture on the roll. The ability to find moment photographs consistently is what distinguishes strong from weak photographers. The quest is what makes photography so fascinating.

How to

Take Pictures

Step 1: Cradle the camera in your left hand so that you can operate both the focusing and aperture rings. Grip the right side of the camera with your right hand. You should be able to operate the shutter speed dial, the shutter release, and the film advance lever without taking your eye from the viewfinder.

Step 2: For horizontals, gently press the top of the camera against your forehead. Brace your left elbow against your body and use the camera strap for additional rigidity.

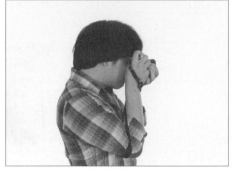

Step 3: For verticals, cradle the left side of the camera in your left hand. The right side of the camera, positioned upward, is pressed gently into your forehead. Sometimes, the strap can be used for additional support.

Step 4A: Seek additional support to keep the camera steady if you are using slow shutter speeds. Brace yourself against a wall

How to

Take Pictures

Step 4B:
or, place your elbows on a table

Step 4C:
or, sit on the ground and place your elbows on your knees.

Step 5: Make a meter reading, being careful to avoid stray light sources or backlight. If needed, make a meter reading off your hand. For light skin, read off the palm and open up one stop. For dark skin, read off the back of the hand and close one stop.

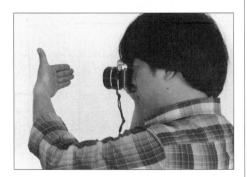

Step 6: Set the aperture and shutter speed according to the meter reading.

How to

Take Pictures

Step 7: Focus carefully on the subject. Then frame the photograph, perhaps according to the "rule of thirds."

Step 8: Release the shutter to take the picture, making sure to squeeze and not jerk the camera.

Step 9: Work the subject. Start back with long shots . . .

Step 10: . . . and then move in for close-ups.

How to

Take Pictures

Step 11: Try different vantage points. Try some shots from high angles . . .

Step 12: . . . and some from low angles.

What Can Go Wrong

Experience will eliminate most of the common mistakes you might make early in your photographic career. This guide should help you eliminate them quickly.

Problem 1: Tilted horizontal line

Probable Cause:

You probably tilted the camera when you took the picture.

Solution:

Make sure the back of the camera is parallel to the ground or to the horizontal plane of objects.

THREE

- A little it distracting

- A lot can be interesting

Problem 2 (A): Subject too small in picture

Probable Cause:

You were not close enough to your subject.

Solution (B):

Get closer; use a telephoto lens if necessary.

A. Problem print

B. Solution print

What Can Go Wrong

Problem 3 (A): Subject lost in photograph

Probable Cause:

You were not careful in selecting the background.

Solution (B):

Frame the subject tightly, and throw the surrounding area out of focus by limiting the depth of field.

A. Problem print

B. Solution print

Problem 4: Subject distorted: Wrong lens used

Probable Cause:

You shot the picture too close with a normal or wide angle lens.

Solution:

Move back or use a telephoto lens.

What Can Go Wrong

Problem 5 (A): Trite group shots

Probable Cause:

The subjects are arranged awkwardly or statically, and space is wasted.

Solution (B):

Move your subjects closer together, stagger the arrangement, and, if possible, give them something to do.

THREE

A. Problem print

B. Solution print

REVIEW **questions** ?

1. How should you hold a 35 mm camera when shooting horizontal photographs? vertical photographs?

2. What is meant by "working the subject"?

3. When is it best to get close to your subject? far away?

4. How should you "frame" your subject?

5. Should all your photos be horizontals? Why or why not?

6. Is experimentation in 35 mm photography important? Why?

7. What are the main factors in photographic composition?

8. What is the rule of thirds and how can it improve the composition of a photograph? When is it not helpful?

9. What should you look for in assessing subject-background relationships?

10. What did Cartier-Bresson mean by "the decisive moment"?

try it YOURSELF

1. Take some shots where you isolate your subject from a busy background using a shallow depth of field (lens aperture wide open). For example, you could take a portrait against a brick wall or some shrubbery. This will be easiest with a telephoto lens (if you have one) and working relatively close to the subject. Make a habit of using your depth of field preview button frequently and then adjusting your aperture to give the depth of field you want.

2. Take a series of pictures of a single subject in which you deliberately "map" the subject. You will probably get best results shooting pictures of a person, but the technique will work with other subjects too. Begin by taking a series of pictures from about 20 feet away, circling the subject to get shots against different backgrounds. Then move in to about 10 feet, and take another series of pictures. Repeat at about 5 feet. Take some photos from bird's eye views and worm's eye views. Finally, take a series of close-up shots of various parts of the subject. If you are shooting pictures of a person, don't confine your close-ups to the face.

Get close-ups of hands and feet as well. Study the contact sheet for the roll to see which shots are strongest. You may not always work a subject as mechanically as this, but this assignment should give you some feel for the variety of possibilities contained in a single subject.

3. Take a series of pictures of the same subject or visual situation, never shooting a frame from eye-level. Try to shoot from unusual angles, both high and low: from tops of buildings, cliffs, ladders, whatever will safely hold you; then get down on the ground, crawl under things, shoot up where it will make the picture more interesting. Review your contact sheet to select the best "down" shot and the best "up" shot.

4. Make a series of photographs of a subject in which you never include the entire subject, only a small portion of it. Let that part stand for the whole. Portrait photographers use the approach all the time, when a head-and-shoulders portrait of the face alone becomes the visual representation of the whole person. Try it another way: Take pictures of people's hands or feet, and let them represent the person.

5. Make a series of photographs in which you leave the camera in the same spot, but take your exposures over a period of time. One way to do this is to find a window where you can point your camera outside. Set the camera on a tripod if possible, and take a series of shots at half-hour or hour intervals from early in the morning until late at night. Or take them over a period of several days if time permits. If you are really patient, take them over a year's time and watch the seasons change.

THREE

developing
and printing

"*The contemplation of things as they are, without error, without substitution or imposture, is in itself, a nobler thing than a whole harvest of invention.*"

Francis Bacon

—Quotation from Francis Bacon pinned to
Dorothea Lange's darkroom door, circa 1930s

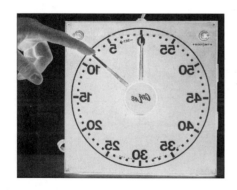

developing
the film

Normandy Invasion, by Robert Capa, 1944

developing the film

Normandy Invasion, **by Robert Capa, 1944**
(© *Robert Capa/Magnum Photos*)

Robert Capa covered the wars in China and Spain from 1935 to 1940 for various European magazines and the North African and Italian campaigns for *Life,* before being selected as one of four photographers to accompany the first troops going ashore in the invasion of France in June 1944. As Capa ran down the ramp, bullets tore holes in the waist-deep, cold water around him. "It was still very early and very gray for good pictures," he later wrote, "but the gray water and the gray sky made the little men dodging the surrealistic designs for Hitler's anti-invasion brain trust, very effective."

He shot film for an hour and a half, then returned to Portsmouth by ship. There he gave the film to an Army public relations officer for transport to London. In a rush to process the film quickly, a technician put the negative in the dryer with the heat on high and closed the door. With no air circulating, the film emulsion melted. Of the 72 images on the two rolls of 35 mm film Capa had shot during the landing, only 11 pictures were printable. These were slightly blurred, however, like the one reproduced in this chapter. In its caption, *Life* noted that Capa had moved his camera in the "excitement of the moment." He did not learn the truth until he returned to London in July.

Always dismissive of his own personal safety, Capa once said, "If your pictures aren't good enough, you're not close enough." He was killed by a land mine in Indochina in 1954.

When you take a photograph, your film is exposed to light and forms a **latent image**—an image that is not visible to the eye, but that can be developed to make it visible. During development, that latent image is made both visible and permanent by converting it into a negative that can be used to make positive prints.

In some ways, developing negatives is the most crucial step in the photographic process. Developing errors are difficult or impossible to correct later on. A bad negative will probably have to be reshot (if that is possible) or discarded altogether. There is no substitute for a good negative, one that is properly exposed and developed.

LIGHT-SENSITIVE PROPERTIES OF FILM

Photographic film is designed to be a precise light-sensitive recording medium. Film is constructed of several layers and contains chemicals to record the image. These chemicals determine basic characteristics of the film including its speed and grain structure, its color sensitivity, and its contrast.

Structure of film

Black-and-white film is a sandwich of four primary layers (Figure 4.1). The photographically active layer is the **emulsion,** which consists of light-sensitive silver salts, or silver halide crystals, suspended in transparent gelatin. The emulsion is coated with a **scratch-resistant substance** to prevent abrasion in handling. The emulsion is fixed onto a transparent plastic film base, usually cellulose-acetate in modern film. The backside of the **film base,** opposite the emulsion, is coated with an **anti-halation layer,** designed to keep light rays from being reflected back up through the film base and exposing the emulsion a second time.

Film reaction to light

The most important ingredient in photographic film is the light-sensitive silver salts in the emulsion. The silver salts are actually silver halide crystals, which include silver chloride, silver iodide, and silver bromide. During exposure of the film, a few of the silver ions in the crystals that are exposed to light are selectively

FIGURE 4.1. Cross section of black-and-white film. Of the several layers that make up modern film, the most important is the light-sensitive emulsion layer which records the image. The emulsion layer contains light-sensitive silver salts suspended in transparent gelatin.

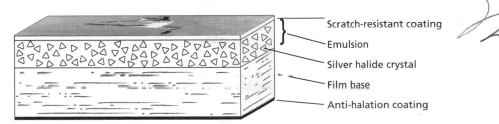

Scratch-resistant coating
Emulsion
Silver halide crystal
Film base
Anti-halation coating

converted into metallic silver atoms. However, no silver ions in the crystals that aren't exposed to light are converted to metallic silver. The degree of exposure—the brightness of the light that reaches the emulsion—determines the number of silver crystals converted to metallic silver.

When a silver halide crystal is exposed to light, only a few of the silver ions in the crystal are converted to metallic silver atoms. At this stage, the image on the film is invisible—that is, it is a **latent image** (Figure 4.2). Not enough silver ions have been converted to make a **visible image.** But the few metallic silver atoms make it possible for the developer to "recognize" exposed crystals during processing and convert the remaining silver ions in them to metallic silver. Developing, then, greatly magnifies the effect of exposure and makes the latent image visible. Unexposed silver crystals, which contain no metallic silver atoms, are left unchanged by the developer because they contain only ions and no metallic silver for the developer to convert. During fixing, the unexposed crystals are removed from the emulsion. At this stage, the image is not only visible from the action of the developer, but it is also permanent because the fixer removes the unexposed and still light-sensitive crystals from the emulsion.

FIGURE 4.2. Film development. Only the emulsion layer is shown in this diagram. Exposure creates a latent image, exposing silver salts in proportion to the amount of exposure they receive. Development creates a visible image, but remaining silver salts could be subsequently exposed and ruin the image. The fixing step removes those remaining silver salts and leaves the visible image light-safe.

1. Before exposure: The emulsion layer contains silver salts suspended in gelatin.

Deep shadows: Film unexposed	Midtones: Film partially exposed	Highlights: Film completely exposed

2. Exposure to subject: Areas of the subject that are dark will cause little or no exposure. Bright areas will completely expose the film.

3. After exposure: Sensitivity centers are formed in the exposed silver salt crystals, creating a latent image.

4. After development: Exposed silver salts with sensitivity centers are converted to metallic silver, creating a visible image.

5. After fixing: The undeveloped silver salts are removed by the fixer, leaving an image that is light-safe.

Key: △ Unexposed silver salt
      ◭ Exposed silver salt
      ▲ Metallic silver

FIGURE 4.3. Slow and fast films. Fast films contain larger silver salt crystals, which make larger targets for light. Slower films contain smaller silver salt crystals. The smaller crystals in slower films give these films greater resolution and sharpness.

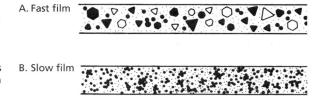

A. Fast film

B. Slow film

FOUR

Characteristics of film

▸▸ **Speed.** Black-and-white films differ principally in the size of the silver halide crystals in their emulsions (Figure 4.3). Generally, the larger the size of the crystals, the more light-sensitive (or faster) the film is. The higher the film's speed rating, the larger the silver halide crystals in the film's emulsion.

But the increase in speed is not without trade-offs. Because the image-recording substance—the silver halide crystal—is coarser, the film cannot record as much detail as a slower film with finer crystals. Fast films are not as sharp as slow films. Also, when fast films are enlarged, they tend to have a speckled, or grainy, appearance. The prominence of the grain pattern depends on the degree of enlargement as well as the size of the silver halide crystals. The important point is that you gain in light sensitivity as you move from a slower to a faster film, but you lose in ability to record extremely fine detail.

▸▸ **Color sensitivity.** Most common black-and-white films are **panchromatic**—that is, sensitive to about the same colors of light as those seen by the human eye. Silver halide crystals themselves are sensitive only to blue light. Film manufacturers add sensitizers to panchromatic films to extend the sensitivity to include green and red light also. Some films contain additional sensitizers to make them sensitive to infrared light, which is not visible to the human eye. These emulsions, aptly named **infrared films,** are useful for haze penetration (haze does not scatter infrared as much as visible light) and for special effects (Figure 4.4A). They also have scientific applications.

▸▸ **Gradation of tone.** Most films are designed to render a series of tones, or shades of gray, from black to white. When you don't want such gradations of tones but prefer blacks and whites only, you can select a film that gives high contrast. A **high-contrast film,** usually used with special developing chemicals, records only blacks and whites with few shades of gray in between (Figure 4.4B). This type of film is useful in photographing line work, like the type on this page, where tonal shading is undesirable. High-contrast films can also be used to create interesting special effects. When used to record a normal scene, they drop out gray tones and render the scene as patterns of black and white.

FIGURE 4.4. Special films. Infrared film extends the sensitivity of normal film into the infrared, beyond the perception of human vision. Green vegetation, an excellent reflector of infrared light, photographs as white. In the example below, what appears as snow-covered ground is actually a green lawn. High contrast films minimize variations in gray values, rendering the image in blacks and whites. The result is usually an emphasis on shadow and shape.

A. Infrared film

B. High contrast film

CHEMICALS AND BASIC EQUIPMENT FOR DEVELOPING FILM

Chemicals

You need to use a number of chemicals to develop film. These chemicals are developer, stop bath, fixer, hypo clearing agent, and a wetting agent (Figure 4.5). These chemicals come in either powder or liquid form and must be mixed for use. To lengthen the life of the developer, it should be stored in dark brown glass bottles or other containers that keep out light. To safeguard the environment and yourself, never pour any of these chemicals down the drain.

FIGURE 4.5. Film developing chemicals. You will need film developer, stop bath, fixer, hypo clearing agent, and a wetting agent. Once mixed, you should keep processing chemicals in airtight containers.

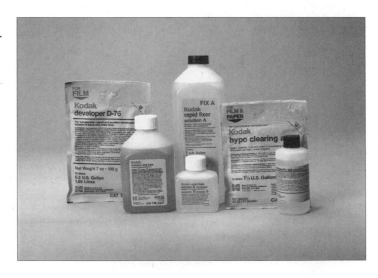

➤ Developer. A variety of developers in liquid and powder form are available (Figure 4.6). Typically, developers consist of a **developing agent** and several other chemicals that make the developer practical. The developing agent reduces the silver ions in the exposed silver halide crystals to metallic silver to make the latent image on the film visible. Since the developing agent acts slowly, practical developers also contain an **activator** that accelerates development by making the developer alkaline. This is why the developer feels "soapy"—soap, too, is an alkaline substance. Practical developers also contain a **preservative**, which slows down oxidation, or spoilage, of the developing agent by air, and a **restrainer**, which helps keep the developing agent from converting unexposed silver ions into metallic silver atoms.

FOUR

The two key ingredients in the developer are the developing agent and the activator, however. The developing agent does the actual work—it provides the "brains" by making the distinction between exposed and unexposed silver halide crystals. But the developer works too slowly to be practical and requires an activator—the "brawn" that reduces developing times from hours or even days to minutes.

The strength of the developing solution is important. Some types can be mixed to recommended strength and used as "one-shot" developers. That is, the

FIGURE 4.6. Film developers. A wide variety of film developers are available, many intended for special purposes. It is best to stick with one general purpose developer at first until you learn its characteristics.

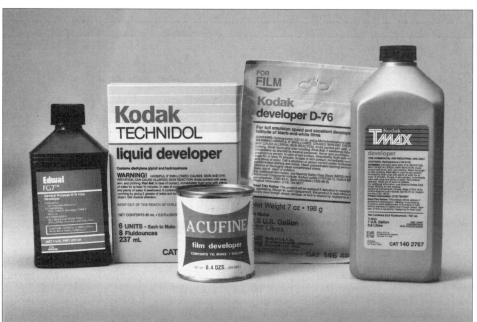

FIGURE 4.7. Developing tanks and reels. Plastic tanks and reels, on the left, are usually easier for beginners to get used to, but stainless steel tanks and reels, on the right, are faster to load once you get used to them. Most professional processing equipment is designed for stainless steel reels.

developer is used once and discarded. Other types can be used in a replenishing system in which fresh solution is added to a stock solution in proportion to the number of rolls that have been developed. Different developers also have different storage periods, so you should read the manufacturer's instructions carefully.

▶▶ **Stop bath.** Two types of stop bath are in common use. In one, fresh water is poured into the tank to dilute the developer and halt its action. In the other, a weak acid solution is used to chemically neutralize the developer. The water stop is the most common with film processing. Your film instructions will indicate if an acid stop bath is required. You should throw it away after one period of use.

▶▶ **Fixer.** This solution stabilizes, or fixes, the photographic image by removing unexposed silver halide crystals from the film emulsion. The formal chemical name for fixer is sodium thiosulfate, once known as sodium hyposulfate. Fixer is still often called by its historic nickname, "hypo." It can be reused until it becomes exhausted. A testing solution is available to check whether the fixer is worn out or still working.

▶▶ **Hypo clearing agent.** This solution cuts down the time needed for washing the negatives by making the fixer, or hypo, more soluble in water. The storage life varies from type to type. Generally, the liquid types are mixed, used once, and discarded.

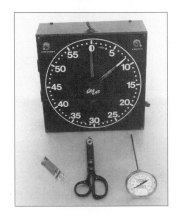

FIGURE 4.8. Other film developing equipment. You will need a thermometer and a reliable timer for accurate processing. A can opener and scissors are useful for opening film cassettes and snipping the film loose from the spool.

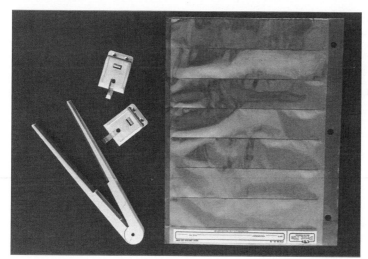

FIGURE 4.9. Equipment for drying and storage. Use squeegee tongs or a sponge to strip excess liquid from your film after it is processed. You can use film clips to hang the film to dry if you don't have a film dryer. Once the film is dry, negative sleeves will keep your negatives organized and protected during storage.

FOUR

▶▶ **Wetting agent.** This solution helps the negatives to dry evenly and helps to eliminate water spotting. One such wetting agent is Kodak's Photo-Flo. Although it can be reused several times if you mix a large amount, it is best to discard it after each developing session.

Basic equipment

Any well-equipped darkroom must have a number of essential pieces of equipment. It is a good idea to buy high-quality, rustproof items that are made of plastic, stainless steel, or glass.

▶▶ **Developing tanks and reels** (Figure 4.7). The film goes on a reel and into the tank so it can be developed. Plastic reels and tanks are less expensive than stainless steel reels and tanks, and they are easier to learn to use. Stainless steel tanks and reels, however, are more durable and once mastered, more efficient. Both plastic and stainless steel tanks can be purchased to hold a single reel or several reels. Unless you frequently plan to develop several rolls of film at one time, a single-reel tank is adequate.

▶▶ **Can opener and scissors** (Figure 4.8). The can opener is used not only to open the chemical containers, but to pry open the film cassette. The scissors are needed to cut the leader off the film before winding it onto the developing reel. They are also needed to cut the negatives into strips after they have dried.

▶▶ **Thermometer and timer** (Figure 4.8). The thermometer enables you to test the temperature of chemicals and water. The timer gives you the correct time for all the various steps you must follow. A special photographic timer is best, but you can use your wristwatch if it has a sweep second hand.

▸ **Squeegee tongs and film clips** (Figure 4.9). The squeegee tongs or a sponge help you remove excess water from both sides of the film before drying it. The film clips hold the film for drying. A film dryer is a piece of equipment designed to dry film in heated conditions. If you don't have a dryer, however, you can hang the film by the clips in any dust-free location for about one hour.

▸ **Negative sleeves** (Figure 4.9). These cellophane or plastic holders protect your negatives from damage. By using fingernail clippers, you can put curved edges on the four corners of a negative strip, allowing for easier insertion of the negatives into the sleeve.

PROCESSING THE FILM

Despite its critical importance, negative development is one of the simplest and most mechanical steps in photography. The secret to successful film developing is consistency and care. After you carefully establish a technique that yields good negatives for you, you will want to follow that technique consistently roll after roll.

▸ **Preparing the chemicals.** The first step in developing film is preparing the chemicals you need. The manufacturer's instructions should be followed when mixing the chemicals. Only appropriate containers, usually glass or plastic jugs, should be used. You should avoid using metal containers. After the chemicals are mixed, the containers for each of the solutions should be labeled and dated. You should be sure not to contaminate the chemicals by interchanging the containers.

▸ **Organizing the equipment.** It is important to lay out your equipment so that you can locate it easily in the dark. Most darkrooms are organized into a wet side and a dry side. The film and the equipment you need are located on the dry side, an area where no chemicals are allowed, to prevent accidental contamination of the film with spots of chemicals. On the dry side, you should have the opener, cassette of exposed film, scissors, reel, and developing tank. On the wet side, you should place the thermometer, developer, and mixed chemicals.

▸ **Loading the film.** With all lights in the darkroom turned off, take the film out of its light-tight cassette, roll the film onto a developing reel, put the loaded reel into a developing tank, and put the cover firmly on the tank. You should be sure your hands, the tank, and the reel are dry before you start loading the film. You should try to handle the film by its edges as much as possible to avoid getting fingerprints on it. The film must be fed into the reel accurately; if it jumps out of the groove and touches itself during processing, the emulsion will be damaged and some frames will be lost. Once the loaded reel is inside the covered tank, you can turn on the room lights and complete the rest of the processing steps in the light. The film will be protected inside the light-tight tank.

▶▶ **Developing and fixing the image.** The developing process consists of giving the film several chemical "baths" and water rinses while it is in the developing tank. The first is the developing solution, followed by other chemical solutions that stop the developer's action and then "fix" the image for permanency.

You must be sure the film is developed for the exact length of time and at the particular temperature recommended by the manufacturer. If time/temperature instructions are not followed, overdeveloped or underdeveloped negatives result. Incorrectly developed negatives will be more difficult to print.

When development is complete, pour the developer out of the tank through the small opening in the cover of the tank and pour in water or stop bath. When stop bath time is up, pour out the water stop or stop bath and pour in the fixer. The cover must remain on the tank through the fixing step. When the fixing time is up, you can remove the cover of the tank for the remaining chemical and water rinses. The film is no longer light sensitive.

To be sure development occurs evenly, you must agitate the film and developer in the tank. For stainless steel tanks, you cap the small opening in the tank cover and turn the tank upside down and back at the rate of three inversions in 5 or 6 seconds. Plastic tanks come with an agitator rod or a thermometer that you turn at the rate of three revolutions in 5 or 6 seconds. In either case, you should agitate for 30 seconds after you first pour in developer. After that, you should agitate for 5 seconds every 30 seconds.

Agitation during the development step affects the final results, so it is important to establish a consistent development technique. Agitation during the subsequent steps is not as critical, but you must agitate periodically to ensure even processing.

When the film is fully rinsed and processing is complete, remove the reel from the tank and carefully unwind the film from the reel. Remove excess water from both sides of the film with a sponge or squeegee before hanging it up to dry.

▶▶ **Storing negatives.** When the developed film is dry, it's a good idea to cut it into strips of 5 or 6 frames and store the strips in a negative holder. Negatives must be stored carefully; damaged negatives are essentially useless. They must be protected from scratches that produce dark lines on the final print. They should also be stored flat to ensure sharp prints. And, they should be stored in a relatively cool and dry location to prevent stains or chemical contamination.

A Note on

Controlling Contrast

You can control negative contrast—the range of tones in the negative—by altering development time. After developing a few rolls of film, you might find that your negative contrast is unsatisfactory. If your negatives are consistently overdeveloped and too contrasty, you can try reducing the recommended development time by 25 percent. On the other hand, if they are consistently underdeveloped and too flat, you can try increasing time by 25 or 50 percent. You should consider the manufacturer's developing time as only a starting point. It may take two or three adjustments of the developing time to achieve consistently satisfactory negatives.

It's important that you keep the temperature of the developer consistent from roll to roll as you work toward an optimum development time. Developer that is too warm will develop the image faster, while cooler developer will develop more slowly. Manufacturers' directions will usually contain a time/temperature compensation chart, but the best option is to adjust the temperature of the developer to a consistent temperature.

You manipulate development time in order to control the contrast of your negatives, which, in turn, allows you ultimately to control the contrast of the prints that you make from your negatives. You should be able to achieve consistently good negatives—and thus good prints—by fine-tuning your film development procedures to suit your equipment, shooting techniques, and materials.

How to

Develop Film

Step 1: On the wet side of the darkroom, with the lights on, prepare the chemicals you need (developer, stop bath, fixer, hypo clear, and wetting agent) by mixing them as directed by manufacturers' instructions.

Step 2: Be sure that the temperature of the chemicals reaches 68°F by putting the bottles of mixed chemicals in a pan containing water that partially covers the bottles. Test the temperature of the developer with a thermometer, and simply add hot or cold water to the pan until you get the desired 68°F.

Step 3: Organize the equipment you need so you can find it in the dark on the dry side of the darkroom. (From lower left clockwise: a can opener for the film cassette, a developing reel, a single-reel developing tank and its cover and cap, and scissors.)

Step 3A: If you will be developing several rolls at once in a multi-reel tank, fill the developing tank with developer almost to the top. Put the tank in the pan of water on the wet side of the darkroom. The cover should not be on the tank, but should be placed in a spot where you can locate it in the dark.

FOUR

How to

Develop Film

💡 **Step 4:** Set the timer to the time indicated on the manufacturer's instruction sheet or at the time you have determined from previous development trials. At this point, however, do not start the timer.

💡 **Step 5:** Turn off the darkroom lights, and use the can opener to pry the end off the film cassette. (Note: For simplicity, these instructions deal with 35 mm film; other film sizes are covered in manufacturers' directions.) Remove the film from the cassette, and cut off a short section of the end to make it square.

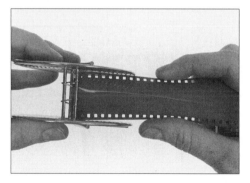

💡 **Step 6:** Pick up the reel, and hold it in one hand. With the thumb and forefinger of your other hand, insert the end of the film into the clip that holds it in place in the center of the reel.

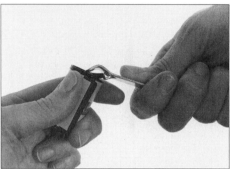

💡 **Step 7:** Pinch the film slightly between thumb and forefinger to bow it as you turn the reel with the other hand. The film should clear the outside edges of the reel and seat itself in the groove that begins at the center and spirals outward to the outside edge. You must be sure to thread the film onto the groove evenly so it does not touch itself at any point.

How to

Develop Film

Step 8: If you are developing only one roll, drop the loaded reel into the developing tank and put the cover firmly on the tank.

Step 8A: If you are developing several rolls of film, place the loaded reels on the loading hook and put them in the tank filled with developer all at once. Start the timer.

Step 8B: If you are using a plastic tank and reel, drop the loaded plastic reel into the plastic developing tank place the lid on the tank, and then twist it to lock in place.

Step 9: Pour the developer in the tank through the small opening in the cover, and then cap the opening tightly. Start the timer, and turn on the darkroom lights.

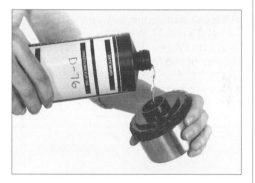

Step 10: Rap the tank gently on the edge of the sink to dislodge air bubbles.

How to

Develop Film

💡 **Step 11:** Pick up the tank and agitate it gently—that is, turn it upside down and back—to make sure the developer flows freely and continuously over the entire film surface. You should agitate for 30 seconds initially, then 5 seconds every 30 seconds throughout the developing time.

💡 **Step 11A :** If you are developing several rolls of film, push the reels up and down to remove air bubbles. Then place the cover, with the small cap firmly in place, on the tank, and turn on the darkroom lights.

💡 **Step 11B:** If you are using a plastic tank, agitate the developer by inserting the thermometer that comes with the tank and twisting it in a clockwise direction. Note that if you twist the thermometer counterclockwise, you will unwind the film.

💡 **Step 12:** When the timer shows that the end of the development step is near, remove the small cap from the cover, and pour the developer out of the tank. Do not remove the tank cover. Begin pouring about 10 seconds or so prior to the end of development so all developer will be out of the tank at the end of the timing period.

💡 **Step 13:** Pour stop bath or water stop into the tank through the small opening in the cover. Agitate the tank. If you are using water, change the water every 15 to 20 seconds. The cover should remain on the tank.

How to

Develop Film

Step 14: At the end of the stop step, pour the stop bath back into its container, or pour out the water. Do not remove the tank cover.

Step 15: Fill the tank with fixer, again through the opening in the tank cover. Set the timer for 2 to 4 minutes and start it.

Step 16: Agitate the tank, again 30 seconds initially; then 5 seconds every 30 seconds.

Step 17: At the end of the fixing step, remove the cover, and then pour the fixer back into its container. It is now safe to take the cover off the tank since the film is no longer light sensitive.

How to

Develop Film

Step 18: Rinse off the film with running water at 68°F for approximately 30 seconds to remove excess fixer.

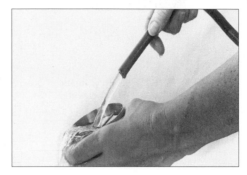

Step 19: Immerse the film in the hypo clearing agent for 1 to 2 minutes. To agitate the hypo solution, you can rock the tank gently or turn the reel in the tank periodically to swirl the solution.

Step 20: Wash the film for 5 minutes in running water at 68°F. A specialized film washer is shown here, but you can also hold the tank under a faucet or run a hose with running water into the top of the film tank.

Step 21: Immerse the film for 30 seconds in the wetting agent. Agitation is not necessary at this step.

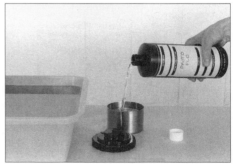

How to

Develop Film

💡 **Step 22:** Take the reel out of the tank and carefully unroll the film. Remove excess water from both sides of the film with squeegee tongs. (Make sure the tongs are clean so the film doesn't get scratched.)

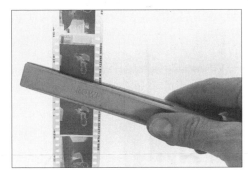

💡 **Step 23:** Hang the film to dry in a dust-free location, or place it in a film dryer if you have one. If you hang the film, weight the bottom end to take the curl out of the film.

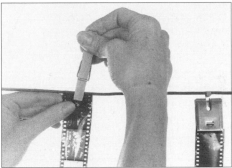

💡 **Step 24:** When the film is thoroughly dry, cut it into strips of five or six frames, depending on the negative carriers that you have acquired.

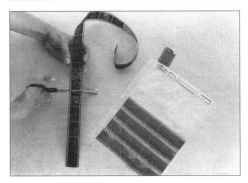

💡 **Step 25:** Store the negative strips safely in a negative sleeve.

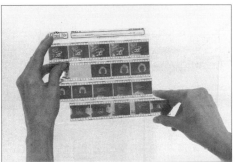

FOUR

PUSH PROCESSING FILM

Push processing is a widely used technique for "increasing" film speed. In fact, it does nothing of the sort, but it's a useful approximation. In simple terms, there are two steps in push processing. First, you pretend your film is more sensitive to light than it really is by inflating its speed rating when you are taking the pictures. That will consistently and precisely underexpose the film. Then, you attempt to compensate for the underexposure during development.

Push processing is most often used with films that are relatively fast to begin with—Kodak's Tri-X or Ilford's HP-5, for instance. These films tend to yield better results than slow or medium speed films, and if it's speed you are after, you're better off with an inherently fast film to begin with. Either of these films can be successfully pushed one or two stops.

You begin pushing film by setting your light meter with an inflated ISO exposure index (E.I.). To push one stop, you double the manufacturer's rating, from 400 to an E.I. of 800, for instance. To push two stops, you quadruple it, from 400 to 1,600. Meter readings will thus be based on a faster film than you are really using and the film will be precisely and consistently underexposed.

If you were to develop the underexposed roll normally, you would find two deficiencies in the negatives. The frames would lack detail in the shadow areas (the dark areas of the original scene) and they would lack contrast. A print made from such negatives would be flat (lack contrast) and would show little or no detail in the dark areas. There is little that can be done about the loss of shadow detail; if it's not recorded on the film, it is difficult to salvage it later. But it is possible by push processing to increase negative contrast to acceptable levels.

The push processing methods described here involve changes in the development step only. All other film processing steps—stop, fix, hypo clear, wash, and wetting agent—remain the same.

The most common method of push processing uses a special high-energy developer, quite often Acufine or Diafine. Either can be used for a two-stop push of T-Max 400, Tri-X, or HP-5 with relatively good results. There will be some loss in shadow detail, but the negatives are generally contrasty enough to be printable.

The ultimate combination for push processing, however, is T-Max developer coupled with one of the new super-fast films—Kodak's T-Max p3200 film or Fugi's Neopan 1600 Professional film. The ISO index of T-Max p3200 film is actually about 1000, but, as its name suggests, it is intended to be pushed to an E.I. of 3200 or higher. Fugi's Neopan 1600 is likewise intended to be pushed to an E.I. of 1600 or above. Very acceptable results can be found even when pushing these films as high as 6400 or 12,800. Best results will be obtained by using a push process developer especially suited to T-Max films, like Kodak's T-Max developer or one of the similar developers from other manufacturers.

Some photographers search as diligently for the perfect "hot soup"—the perfect push process developer—as the knights of old searched for the Holy Grail. But pushing is inherently a compromise. Push processing methods almost always entail some loss in quality—an increase in grain and a loss of shadow detail. In the case of push processing, this is the cost of getting the picture.

What Can Go Wrong

Even when you have the best of intentions, things can go wrong when you are developing film. When they do, try to determine what caused the problem so you can avoid it next time.

Problem 1 (A and B): Pinholes on negative

Pinholes (small clear spots) on the negative.

Probable Cause:

Air bubbles clung to the film during development.

Solution:

Agitate

Be sure to rap the tank at the beginning of development to dislodge air bubbles.

A. Negative

B. Positive proof

Problem 2 (A and B): Negatives with glitches

Glitches or undeveloped areas on the negative.

film touches itself

Probable Cause:

You may have improperly loaded film onto the reel so that it touched itself in places and the developer couldn't reach the emulsion.

a melt

A. Negative

Solution:

Be more careful next time. In the light, practice loading an already-developed film onto a reel until you are confident

B. Positive proof

What Can Go Wrong

Problem 3 (A): Overexposure

Overexposure that causes negative to be too dense (too black) and contain blocked-up highlight detail.

Probable Cause:

You may have set the ISO index too low on your light meter.

Solution (B):

Make sure that you set the ISO index correctly for the film you are using. If the problem persists, check your meter against another meter.

A. Problem negative   B. Correct negative

Problem 4 (A): Underexposure

Underexposure that results in lack of contrast and shadow detail.

Probable Cause:

You may have set the ISO index too high on your light meter.

Solution (B):

Make sure you set the ISO index correctly. If the problem persists, check your meter against another meter.

A. Problem negative   B. Correct negative

What Can Go Wrong

Problem 5 (A and B): Ragged-edged areas on negative

Probable Cause:

Your negatives may not have been fully dry when you inserted them into the envelopes or sleeves, and the sleeve stuck to the emulsion, pulling it off the film base; or, in drying, the film touched another negative.

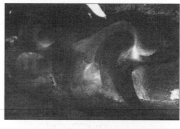

A. Negative

B. Positive proof

Solution:

Make certain your negatives are absolutely dry before you put them into the envelope.

Allow film today

FOUR

Problem 6 (A and B): Scratches on negative

Probable Cause:

Fingernails or abrasive material like dust or dirt have rubbed against the emulsion; sometimes abrasive material on the camera rollers can cause scratches when loading the film.

A. Negative   B. Positive proof

Solution:

Handle the film very carefully, particularly while it is wet and the emulsion is soft; keep your camera free of dust and dirt.

— *Scratched Negatives*

What Can Go Wrong

Problem 7 (A and B): Fibers imbedded in film

Fibers that become imbedded in the emulsion of the film.

Probable Cause:

You tried to dry your negatives with a paper towel, or you hung them in a location that was not free of dust.

Solution:

Be sure to dry your negatives in a dust-free location. Do not allow them to come in contact with anything except squeegee tongs until they are dry; let them dry on their own without the aid of a paper towel.

A. Negative   B. Positive proof

Problem 8 (A): Overdeveloped negative: too contrasty

Probable Cause:

Timer may be set improperly, or temperature of the developer is too high.

Solution (B):

Make sure that you set the timer correctly and that the temperature of the developer isn't too high.

A. Problem negative

B. Correct negative

What Can Go Wrong

Problem 9 (A and B): Light crescents on negative

Probable Cause:

You pinched the film, probably when you loaded the film onto the developing reel.

Solution:

Handle the film more gently.

A. Negative　　　　B. Positive proof

[handwritten: film BENT]

[handwritten: FOUR]

Problem 10 (A): Underdeveloped negative: no contrast

Underdeveloped negative that lacks contrast.

Probable Cause:

Timer may be set improperly, or developer temperature is too low.

Solution (B):

Check the timer and make sure the temperature of the developer isn't too low.

A. Problem negative

B. Correct negative

[handwritten: didn't develop long enough too cool a temp]

Problem 11 (A and B): Streaks on negative

Probable Cause:

The film was not consistently agitated during development.

Solution:

Be sure to follow proper agitation procedures.

A. Negative

B. Positive proof

[handwritten: ALSO may indicate a light leak in camera]

REVIEW questions ?

1. How does film record its images?

2. Describe the basic structure of black-and-white film.

3. How does film react to light?

4. What are the main characteristics of film?

5. What chemicals are needed to develop film?

6. How do developer, stop bath, and fixer work on film?

7. What is the role of hypo clearing agent and wetting agent?

8 What basic equipment for film developing should be in every well-equipped darkroom?

9. What is "negative contrast" and how can it be controlled?

10. What is push processing and how is it accomplished?

CHAPTER 5

printmaking

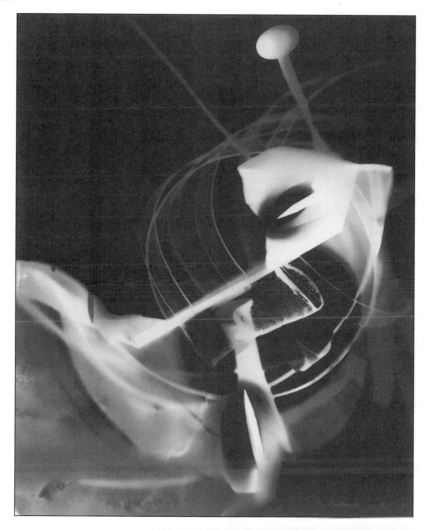

Untitled (abstraction), by László Moholy-Nagy, c. 1930

■printmaking

Untitled (abstraction), by László Moholy-Nagy, c. 1930
*(Gelatin Silver Print, n.d. 50 x 40 cm, Gift of George and Rita Barford, 1968.264. Courtesy of
The Art Institute of Chicago. Published with the permission of Hattula Moholy-Nagy)*

László Moholy-Nagy, once a member of the Bauhaus in Germany, came to the United States in 1937 to escape the Nazis and helped establish the Institute of Design, the American reincarnation of the Bauhaus. He experimented with images made without a camera by putting objects on photographic paper and exposing them directly to light—a kind of contact print he called "Photograms." This approach was also taken by Man Ray, who called his creations "Rayographs." Moholy-Nagy created his works using collages, montages, reflections, refractions—almost all camera-less images made by manipulating light through various devices. Portraiture, landscapes, nudes, architecture, machines, organic form, and urban street scenes were among his themes.

Most serious photographers are very selective about what they print. Professional photographers and serious students carefully select the frames that will be made into enlarged prints by first looking at a contact sheet containing an unenlarged positive print of each frame on the roll of film they have shot. Making a contact sheet is a good introduction to handling and processing photographic paper.

A GUIDE TO PHOTOGRAPHIC PAPER

To make a positive print from a negative, the first thing you need is photographic paper. There are two basic kinds of paper: fiber-base paper and resin-coated paper. Both types of paper are light-sensitive and, like film, have several layers (Figure 5.1). The most important layers are a gelatin supercoating, a light-sensitive emulsion containing silver halide crystals, and a paper base.

The **gelatin supercoating** protects the emulsion from scratches. Just as with film, when the **light-sensitive emulsion** is exposed to light, a few of the silver ions in the silver halide crystals are converted to metallic silver atoms to make a latent image. Processing makes the image visible and permanent. The **paper base** is the support for the other two layers.

In **resin-coated paper,** generally known as RC paper, the paper base is coated on top and bottom with water-resistant plastic. This coating prevents chemicals from seeping into the paper base during processing. Because the paper base does not absorb the chemicals, RC papers process and wash more quickly than

FIGURE 5.1. Cross section of black-and-white photographic paper. Fiber-base paper consists of a light-sensitive emulsion coated on a paper base. In resin-coated (RC) paper, the paper base is coated on top and bottom with water-resistant plastic.

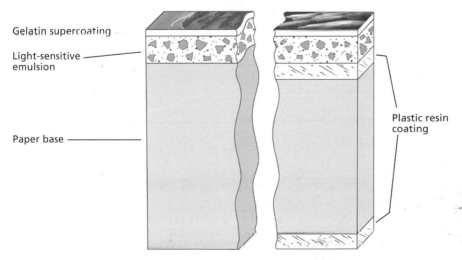

Gelatin supercoating

Light-sensitive emulsion

Plastic resin coating

Paper base

A. Fiber-base photographic paper   B. Resin-coated photographic paper

FIGURE 5.2.
Various types of photographic paper. Many manufacturers produce both fiber-base and RC papers in a variety of sizes, surfaces, contrasts, and weights.

fiber-base papers. They also require fewer chemicals. Nearly every major photographic paper manufacturer has both fiber-base and RC papers.

Fiber-base paper is preferred for some purposes since it tends to be more permanent than RC paper. If care is taken, fiber-base paper can also produce better looking prints. But fiber-base papers take more time and work to process. Because processing chemicals are absorbed into the paper, prints must be washed four or five times longer than those made on RC paper. Usually, a hypo clearing agent is used—as in film processing—to shorten the wash time. Fiber-base paper also takes longer than RC paper to dry, and special care must be taken if a glossy surface is desired.

Both RC and fiber-base photographic papers are manufactured by a number of companies and are boxed and packaged to be protected from light (Figure 5.2). Most papers come in various sizes, weights, contrasts, and surfaces. The paper you decide to use will depend on the kinds of photos you take and your own preferences gained by experience in the darkroom. Many people like the simplicity of RC papers and begin with them while others appreciate the feel and look of fiber-base papers and don't mind the extra trouble in getting used to them.

Characteristics of paper

▶▶ **Surface.** Paper surfaces vary from smooth to highly textured. A smooth surface is glossy and shiny, while the textured ones have a matte finish or dull appearance. Samples of common paper surfaces are available for inspection at nearly all photographic supply stores. Each manufacturer has its own system for classifying paper surfaces. Some use letter designations, such as "F" or "N," while others use descriptive words like "smooth" or "rough."

The choice of surface depends on the use of the photo. In photojournalism, for example, where photos are to be screened and reproduced by a printing press, they are usually printed on a glossy (F surface) paper. The glossy surface works well because it renders detail well and has a slightly longer tonal scale (range of tones from black to white) than other kinds of paper. Photographs to be used for other purposes are often printed on other surfaces. If a photograph is to be viewed directly, a glossy surface is usually undesirable because reflections from the shiny surface detract from the image itself. A matte (N surface) paper may be more suitable. Other surfaces (like E or "Pearl") offer a compromise: They produce nearly the same tonal scale as a glossy paper, but are slightly textured to reduce reflections.

▸ Weight. Weight corresponds to the thickness of the paper. Fiber-base paper usually comes in single weight and double weight. RC papers, however, are medium weight. Most prints made on fiber-base paper are single weight. Double weight paper resembles the stiffness of light cardboard and is more expensive than single weight.

▸ Contrast. Most papers are also available in several contrast grades to compensate for less-than-ideal negatives. As the paper grade increases, the contrast between the black tones and the white tones increases. By adjusting film developing time, you can control negative contrast and attempt to achieve an optimum negative. By selecting the proper contrast grade of paper, you can adjust for slight deviations from an optimum negative.

Most papers are available in contrast grades from 0 to 4 or 0 to 5 (Table 5.1). The lower the grade number, the less contrasty is the paper, and the less contrasty is the final print (Figure 5.3).

With some papers, it is necessary to purchase separate packages of paper to get different contrasts. That is, you need to have five boxes of paper on hand to obtain contrast grades of 1, 2, 3, 4, and 5.

▸ Variable-contrast papers. Variable-contrast papers allow contrast control on the same paper through use of filters. These papers are coated with two emulsions: One is equivalent to a grade 1 paper and the other equivalent to a grade 5. The

TABLE 5.1. Paper contrast grades

#0 Extra soft/very flat	#3 Hard/contrasty
#1 Soft/flat	#4 Extra hard/extra contrasty
#2 Normal/medium	#5 Extreme contrast

FIVE

FIGURE 5.3. Using paper grades or filters to control contrast.

A. Contrast grade #1 paper or #1 filter with variable contrast paper produces low contrast and would ordinarily be used to compensate for an overly contrasty negative.

B. Contrast grade #3 or #3 filter produces moderate contrast and would usually be used for a negative of normal contrast.

C. Contrast grade #5 or #5 filter produces high contrast and would usually be used for a low contrast negative.

grade 1 emulsion is sensitive to yellow light. The grade 5 is sensitive to purplish light (Figure 5.4). To obtain the various grades, you use special filters that color the light coming from the enlarger. If you use a yellow filter, for example, the top emulsion layer is exposed and a contrast grade of 1 is obtained. With a purplish filter, on the other hand, the bottom layer is exposed, resulting in a contrast grade of 5. Filters of intermediate colors are used to produce intermediate contrast grades. If you don't use any filter, you'll get the equivalent of a contrast grade 2.

Storing photographic paper

Whatever type of paper you use, it is vital that you store it carefully. Adverse storage conditions cause deterioration of both the physical and photographic properties of paper.

You should store the paper you use regularly in a cool, dry place. A temperature below 70°F is recommended, with the relative humidity between 40 and 50 percent. If you store your paper for long periods, you should put it in an area with temperatures between 40°F and 50°F and be sure to keep it away from steam pipes, radiators, or any source of heat. Many photographers refrigerate new packets or boxes of paper to keep it fresh. If you do, allow the paper to warm to room temperature for one to two hours before opening the packaging or water may condense on the paper and ruin it. Once the packaging moisture barrier is broken, the paper should not be put back into the refrigerator.

You should be certain that you securely close the package or storage container for your paper. If you will be storing it for any extended period or carrying it around with you, tape the box so it doesn't come open accidentally. You should also be careful to keep photographic paper out of reach of curious friends who might open the package to see what it contains and end up ruining it by exposure.

FIVE

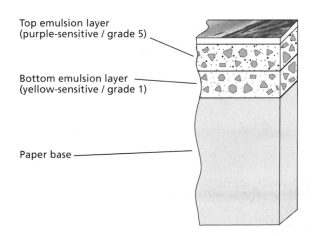

Top emulsion layer
(purple-sensitive / grade 5)

Bottom emulsion layer
(yellow-sensitive / grade 1)

Paper base

FIGURE 5.4. Variable-contrast photographic paper. Two emulsion layers allow one paper to produce a range of contrasts. One layer is purple-sensitive and high contrast. The other is yellow-sensitive and low contrast. By using special filters to control the color of the enlarger light, you can change the effective contrast of the paper.

FIGURE 5.5. Chemicals for making prints. You will need paper developer, stop bath, and fixer. For fiber-based paper, a washing agent like Kodak's Hypo-Clear is also advised. Most of these chemicals are available as both liquids and powders. Liquids are usually easier to mix.

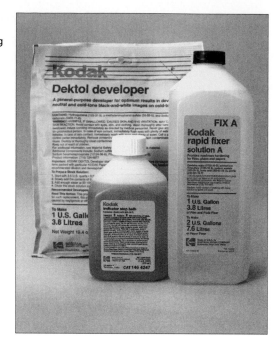

CHEMICALS AND EQUIPMENT

Whether you intend to make a contact sheet or enlarged prints from your negatives, you need chemicals to develop and fix the image on the photographic paper. You also need an enlarger and certain other basic pieces of equipment.

Chemicals

You process positive prints on photographic paper with chemicals similar to those used in developing film: developer, stop bath, and fixer (Figure 5.5). All three come in liquid and granular form. You should always follow manufacturers' instructions in mixing them.

▸▸ **Paper developer.** Developer brings out the image that has been exposed onto the paper by the enlarger. Paper developers are generally stronger than those used in film processing and development times are correspondingly shorter. A commonly used paper developer is Dektol, which is first dissolved in water to make a stock solution. Then you mix one part of the Dektol stock solution with two parts of water to make a working solution. You mix up enough working solution to fill the bottom of your tray to a depth of at least 1/2".

▸▸ **Stop bath.** This solution stops the action of the developer. An acid stop bath, usually dilute acetic acid, is used in print processing. Oftentimes an indicator stop bath is used. The indicator is a chemical additive that causes the stop bath to change color when it is exhausted and needs to be changed.

▸ **Fixer.** This chemical removes the unused silver salts from the print and makes the image permanent. If you leave a print in fixer for too long, it will begin to bleach out the image. The same fixer can be used for both film and print processing, although fixer for printing is usually mixed to half the strength as that for fixing film.

Basic equipment

▸ **Trays** (Figure 5.6). You need one each for developer, stop bath, fixer, and wash water. Trays come in various sizes; 5" x 7", 8" x 10", or 11" x 14" are the most common. You should use a tray that is larger than the print you plan to make in order to give yourself room to work. For example, you use an 11" x 14" tray when you are working with 8" x 10" prints.

Trays for chemicals come in stainless steel, enamel, and plastic. Plastic trays are most commonly used because they are the least expensive. Plastic trays have another advantage: They come in different colors (yellow, white, black, and red, for example), and you can use the color to distinguish the type of chemicals you put into the trays without labeling them.

One tray should be set up to wash the prints. Washing can be done in a variety of ways. The simplest involves running water into a tray or bucket and letting it overflow into the sink. You may also purchase specially built wash trays that are connected to the water supply by a hose. One of the most common and

FIGURE 5.6. Printmaking equipment. You will need three or four trays for chemicals, tongs, a thermometer, a wash tray, and a print squeegee.

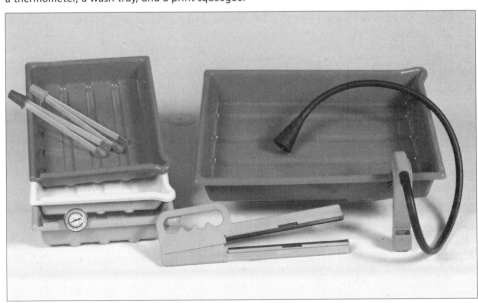

FIGURE 5.7.
Equipment for making contact sheets.
A hinged printing frame (left) or a plain sheet of glass can be used to hold negatives in place on photographic paper.

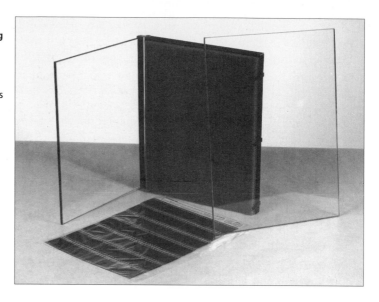

efficient washing devices is Kodak's tray siphon, which attaches to a tray and siphons off the fixer-laden water as it adds fresh water.

▶▶ **Tongs** (Figure 5.6). You use these wood, plastic, or metal devices to move prints along the line of trays in a darkroom and thus avoid putting your hands in the chemicals. Two pairs of tongs—one pair for developer and one pair for stop bath and fixer—are needed to prevent contamination of the developer with the other chemicals. Be careful not to carry any stop bath or fixer back to the developer because either one will quickly neutralize it. Different colored tongs will help keep you from mixing them up.

▶▶ **Thermometer** (Figure 5.6). The same thermometer you use to check the temperature of the chemicals for film developing is needed for the same purpose in making prints.

▶▶ **Print squeegee** (Figure 5.6). This tong-like implement has rubber on both edges. You use it to wipe excess water off your prints when you have finished rinsing them.

▶▶ **Contact printing frame** or **sheet of glass** (Figure 5.7). To hold the negatives in place on the photographic paper when you are making a contact sheet, you need a contact printing frame or a sheet of glass. If you use a sheet of glass, it must be large enough to cover an 8" x 10" sheet of paper. You can use window glass, but it breaks easily and has sharp edges. It is usually best to go to a glass shop and have a piece of plate glass cut to size and the edges beveled.

FIGURE 5.8. Photographic timers. Any timer or clock will work as long as it will read seconds.

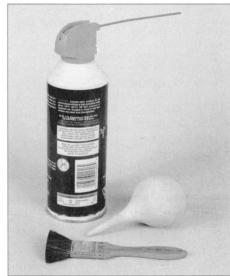

Figure 5.9. Dusting equipment. You can use pressurized canned air, an ear bulb, a soft brush, or a blower brush to remove dust from your lens and negatives.

FIGURE 5.10. Carrier to hold negative in enlarger. The carrier will be specifically designed to fit your enlarger.

A. Open carrier

B. Carrier loaded with negative strip

FIGURE 5.11. Grain magnifier. You can use this to check the sharpness of the image projected by the enlarger.

FIGURE 5.12. Contrast filters. These filters alter the color of the enlarger light and thus control the contrast of prints you make.

▶▶ **Timer** (Figure 5.8). It is best to use a timer with a large face that is easy to read under the dim illumination of a safelight. Specialized photographic timers are excellent, but your wristwatch or any wall clock will do. Whatever you use, though, must allow you to time seconds.

▶▶ **Dusting equipment** (Figure 5.9). You need a soft brush to remove dust and pieces of lint from your negatives and from the enlarger lens. Brushes are available

FIGURE 5.13. Safelights. These lights emit wavelengths of light which are visible to the human eye but will not expose photographic paper. In truth, however, safelights are only semi-safe and they will fog paper after an exposure of several minutes. You should not leave paper out under the safelight.

in various styles and sizes. Some are anti-static to help loosen the dust and some have built-in blowers. You can also purchase pressurized cans of air that you use to blow dust away. An inexpensive alternative is an ear bulb, available at most pharmacies and which never needs to be refilled.

▶ **Negative carrier** (Figure 5.10). This device is used with an enlarger to hold the negative flat while the image is being projected onto the paper. The size of the carrier opening corresponds to the size of the negative.

▶ **Grain magnifier** (Figure 5.11). This special magnifying device is used to examine the projected negative image when you are focusing the enlarger.

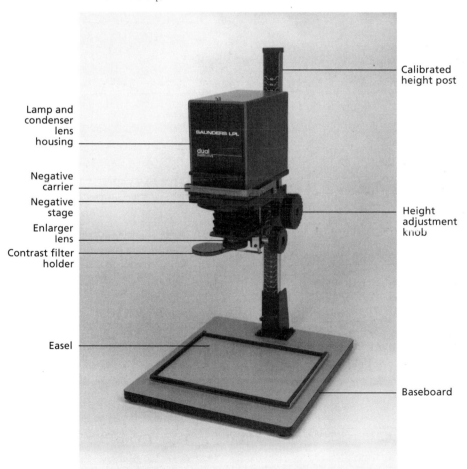

FIGURE 5.14. An enlarger
(Saunders/LPL 35 mm enlarger; published with permission, The Saunders Group)

Calibrated height post

Lamp and condenser lens housing

Negative carrier

Negative stage

Enlarger lens

Contrast filter holder

Height adjustment knob

Easel

Baseboard

FIGURE 5.15. Enlarging easels. Shown are adjustable and fixed easels which hold photographic paper on the enlarger baseboard. The fixed easel has three windows corresponding to commonly used print sizes and can be turned over to print a full 8 x 10 sheet.

▸▸ **Contrast filters** (Figure 5.12). These small sheets of colored plastic are used in the enlarger to control the contrast of the finished print, when using variable contrast paper.

▸▸ **Safelight** (Figure 5.13). This light is specially designed to illuminate the darkroom without exposing the light-sensitive photographic paper. A safelight works by emitting wavelengths of light visible to the human eye but to which photographic paper is insensitive. Your safelight must thus have the proper filter for the photographic paper you are using. Even so, safelights are not perfectly safe and will begin to fog paper after several minutes. Keep your paper in a light-safe box or package when you are not exposing or processing it.

▸▸ **Photographic paper.** You will need a supply of 8" x 10" light-sensitive paper. Most beginners find it easier to use RC paper to begin with.

The enlarger

An enlarger (Figure 5.14) projects light through a negative onto light-sensitive paper to make a positive print. By adjusting the enlarger, prints can be made in varying sizes. In most enlargers, the head contains a lamp with a condenser lens that concentrates light on the negative held below it in a metal carrier. The negative carrier slides onto the negative stage above the enlarging lens. The enlarger head as a whole moves up and down on a post. The movement alters the size of the image projected onto the baseboard of the enlarger. A fixed or adjustable easel (Figure 5.15) can be placed on the baseboard of the enlarger to hold the photographic paper in place and to mask the edges of the print to produce white borders.

Your enlarger must match the film size you use. Most enlargers can handle negatives made from 35 mm film and can enlarge each frame to about 11" x 14". Other enlargers can accommodate 2 1/4" x 2 1/4" roll film frames or even 4" x 5" sheet film, as well as smaller sizes.

The enlarger has exposure controls similar to those on your camera. The enlarging lens has an aperture like your camera lens. Instead of a shutter, however, it is plugged into a timer that controls the length of time the enlarger is turned on. Despite this difference, the principle is the same. You control the intensity of the exposing light with the enlarger's aperture and you control the length of exposure with the timer. Although you can turn the enlarger lamp on and off with the switch that is attached to it, it is far more accurate to use a timer. An enlarging timer can be set to a preselected time, usually between 0 and 60 seconds. Then, whenever the "expose" button is pressed, the timer will switch on the enlarger for precisely that amount of time. Since the enlarger lacks a light meter, you do have to experiment a bit—by making a test strip—to find the correct combination of lens aperture and exposure time.

CONTACT SHEETS: SEEING WHAT YOU'VE GOT

A **contact sheet** is a print of an entire roll of film on a single piece of photographic paper (Figure 5.16). The contact sheet allows you to see what you've

FIGURE 5.16. A contact sheet. This proof sheet shows positive images of all frames on your roll of film. Because the proof sheet is made with the negatives in direct contact with the photographic paper, the images are the same size as the negatives.

got on the roll of film and to make decisions about which frames you want to enlarge. You make a contact sheet in much the same way you develop film: in the darkroom, using similar chemicals, but different equipment and techniques. In fact, now the darkroom need not be literally dark since you can use a safelight with photographic paper.

Preparing to make a contact sheet

As with film developing, you begin by mixing the chemicals according to manufacturers' instructions and checking to be sure they are at the correct temperature. You next assemble all the equipment you need. Line up the trays from left to right in the order you will use them: developer tray, stop bath tray, fixer tray, and wash tray. You should keep photographic paper on the dry side of the darkroom and in the light-tight package or in a specially built paper safe. Pour the appropriate chemicals in their respective trays and check the temperature of the chemicals and the wash water.

Your next step is to adjust the enlarger head to a height where its light projects generously over an 8" x 10" area on the baseboard. You should also check the enlarging lens to make sure it is free of lint and fingerprints. If not, carefully clean both sides of the lens with a soft brush.

If you are going to make your contact sheet on variable contrast paper, you may or may not want to use a contrast filter. If you do not use a filter, you will get the equivalent of a grade 2 paper. Whichever way you decide, you should be consistent: If you use a filter, use the same one all the time. That way, you can make more accurate judgments about contrast when you refer to the contact sheet. (More about contrast filters appears in Chapter 8.) By the same token, if you are using graded paper, be consistent about which contrast grade you use.

With the white lights off and the safelight on, assemble the paper, negatives, and glass sheet into a sandwich by placing a single sheet of paper on the enlarger baseboard with its emulsion side up (that is usually the glossy side). Position the paper in the center of the enlarger baseboard so it will be completely covered by light when the enlarger is turned on.

Next, place the negatives on top of the paper, emulsion side (dull side) down. It is faster and requires less handling of the negatives if you leave the strips in their transparent sleeves to make contact prints, even though the contact sheet may not be quite as sharp. Alternatively, you can take the negative strips out of their sleeves and arrange them individually on the paper. Either way, when the negatives are in place on the paper, you put a sheet of glass over the negatives to hold them flat against the paper. At this point, before you turn on the enlarger to make your prints, it's a good idea to get in the habit of checking your package of paper to make sure you've closed it tightly.

Making a test print or a test strip

A **test print** is one that contains trial exposure times. A **test strip** is the same as a test print except only part of a piece of photo paper is used, to avoid wasting paper. You make a test print or test strip by setting the enlarger lens aperture at a reasonable f-stop and then making a series of exposures to find the time that works best with it. For contact sheets, you can begin by leaving the enlarging lens wide open (the brightest setting). Then begin the test print by making the first exposure, say, for 3 seconds, with all but a small section of the paper covered by cardboard. On the second exposure, you move the cardboard to uncover a second section of the paper and expose it, again, for 3 seconds. Meanwhile, the first section is still uncovered and receives and additional 3-second exposure for a total of 6 seconds. On the third 3-second exposure, the first section is exposed for a total of 9 seconds, the second section for a total of 6 seconds, and the newly uncovered third section for 3 seconds. If you make a series of six 3-second exposures in this fashion, you will end up with a series of exposure times from 3 seconds (on the last section) to 18 seconds (on the first section). Then, when you have developed the test print, you can select the exposure time that works best with the f-stop you selected and make your final print.

To develop the exposed paper, you immerse it quickly and evenly in the tray of developer by sliding it beneath the surface. Agitate the tray gently by rocking it. Agitation prevents streaking because fresh developer swirls over the paper during development. A few seconds before the developing time is up, pull the print from the tray to allow excess developer to drip back into the tray.

When you transfer your print from the developer to the stop bath, you should be careful not to let the tongs touch the stop bath solution in the tray. And when you remove it from the stop bath to put it into the fixer tray, you should use a second pair of tongs. You must be very careful not to contaminate the developer with either of the other two chemicals.

After the test print is totally submerged in the fixer for about 15 seconds, you can look at it under white light. It is not necessary to fully process the test print, only to fix it long enough so it is stable for a few minutes under white light. You look for the section of the paper (and thus the exposure time) that gave you the best results. This section of the paper will not be so dark that detail is blocked up in the dark areas or that the whites appear dingy. On the other hand, it will not be so light that light areas are washed out and blacks are only a light gray.

If your test print is too light or too dark overall, you'll need to make another. If it is too light, it did not receive enough exposure. To correct the problem, you can increase the time of each exposure interval or open the lens aperture to a brighter setting. If it is too dark, it is overexposed. In this case, decrease the time interval or close the lens aperture to a dimmer setting to correct the problem.

Making the contact sheet

Once you have determined an exposure time based on the test print, go back and repeat the process to make your contact sheet. This time, make a single exposure of the negative-paper-glass sandwich at the selected exposure time. This time, you should fully fix the print according to the paper manufacturer's instructions. If you are using fiber-base paper, you may want to use a washing agent. Lastly, wash the print according to the paper manufacturer's instructions.

Now you're ready to dry the print. If you haven't a dryer suitable for RC paper, you can simply remove excess water from the print surface with squeegee tongs or a paper towel and allow it to air dry by placing it in a rack or by hanging it on a line with film clips or clothespins. Air drying RC paper takes about 15 minutes. If you want to speed it up, you can use a hair dryer. If you have an RC paper dryer, drying takes about 2 to 3 minutes. Fiber-base paper is usually placed on racks to air dry overnight.

A contact sheet makes it easy to decide on the frames you want to enlarge and print. You can use a magnifying glass for this purpose and mark the frames you like with a grease pencil. You can also make tentative **crop marks** that indicate what portion of the frame you intend to use in the final print.

Save your contact sheets along with your negatives and identify them by date and subject. You may want to print other frames at a later date.

A Note on

Darkroom Safety

Many photographers used to get their hands wet in the developing chemicals when printing. Normally, such contact with the chemicals didn't cause problems. But professional photographers, many of whom have extended contact with processing solutions, have begun to be wary. Most now use tongs.

Some people are hypersensitive to processing chemicals, usually the developer. They can develop contact dermatitis, a flaming red rash, all over their hands. If that happens to you, you must get medical treatment and always wear rubber gloves when printing.

Because many of the chemicals used in processing give off fumes, it is also very important for your darkroom to have good ventilation.

How to

Make Contact Sheets

Step 1: Prepare the chemicals you need by mixing them according to the manufacturers' instructions. If your developer was mixed by using warm water, allow it to cool to about 70°F before you begin processing.

Step 2: Pour the chemicals into the appropriate trays that have been assembled close to each other in the order you will use them. Fill the trays to a depth of 1" with developer (left), stop bath (center), and fixer (right). If you plan to use a siphon wash tray, rather than the sink, for the running wash water, it should be set up next to the fixer tray.

Step 3: Check the temperature of the developer. Also check and adjust the temperature of the running wash water.

Step 4: Clean the glass you will use to hold the negatives in place on the paper.

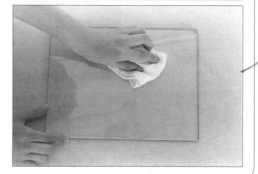

FIVE

(handwritten notes in margin:) I do this & this this — NOT TO WORRY — You may want to do this

How to

Make Contact Sheets

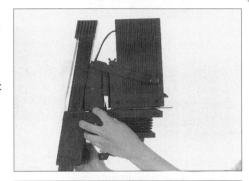

💡 **Step 5:** Turn off the white lights in the darkroom, and turn on the safelight and the enlarger light. Then, adjust the enlarger head so that the light projected onto the baseboard is sufficient to cover an 8" x 10" sheet of paper generously.

💡 **Step 6:** Set the enlarging lens aperture to its brightest setting.

💡 **Step 7:** Set the enlarger timer to 3 seconds, and turn off the enlarger light.

💡 **Step 8:** With only the safelight on, take out a sheet of RC paper, and lay it on the baseboard of the enlarger with the emulsion side up. Position the paper so that it will be completely covered by the light projected from the enlarger when you turn it on.

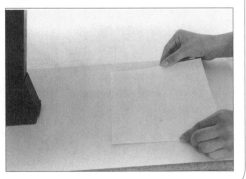

How to

Make Contact Sheets

Step 9: Place the sheet of negative sleeves on the paper. Or, if you prefer, arrange the individual negative strips on the paper, being careful not to touch the paper and to handle the strips only by the edges. In either case, be sure the negatives are positioned with the emulsion (dull) side down.

Step 10: Cover the negatives and paper with the sheet of glass.

Step 11: Begin to make a test print by using a sheet of cardboard and covering all but one row of frames on the negative strips.

Step 12: Press the timer button to turn on the enlarger light and expose that row of frames for 3 seconds.

FIVE

How to

Make Contact Sheets

Step 13: Move the sheet of cardboard to uncover another row of frames. Make another 3-second exposure. Continue moving the cardboard and making 3-second exposures until the entire set of negatives has been exposed.

Step 14: Handling it by the edge, remove the exposed paper from beneath the negatives.

Step 15: Set the timer or note the time on your wristwatch, and then, using tongs, slide the paper beneath the surface of the developer in the first tray.

Step 16: Agitate the developer by gently rocking the tray throughout development. Leave the print in the developer for approximately 1 minute or for the amount of time specified by the paper manufacturer.

How to

Make Contact Sheets

Step 17: About 10 seconds before the recommended time is to expire, remove the print and allow it to drip over the tray.

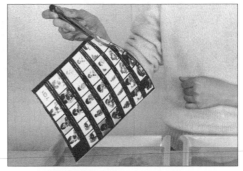

Step 18: Slide the print beneath the surface of the stop bath for 10 to 15 seconds. Then, using a second pair of tongs, remove it and let it drip over the tray.

Step 19: Slide the print into the fixer for about 15 seconds (since it is only a test print).

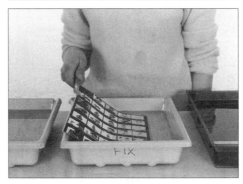

Step 20: Inspect the test print under white light to determine the correct exposure time to use, and set the enlarger's time accordingly.

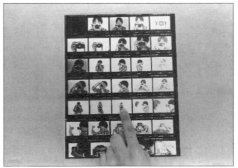

How to

Make Contact Sheets

Step 21: Repeat the process of assembling paper, negatives, and glass to make a contact sheet. Then, turn on the enlarger to expose all of the negatives at one time.

Step 22: Develop the contact sheet as you did the test print, but extend the fixing time to a full 2 to 4 minutes, as recommended by the paper manufacturer.

Step 23: Wash the print for 5 minutes in running water.

Step 24: Use the print squeegee to mop off excess water from the print and hang it up until dry, about 15 minutes. If you have a print dryer, drying will only take a couple of minutes.

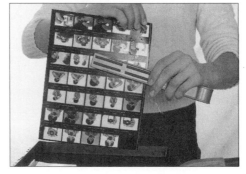

How to

Make Contact Sheets

Step 25: Inspect the dry contact sheet with a magnifying glass and mark frames you may want to enlarge later. Make any notes on the contact sheet you might need for later reference.

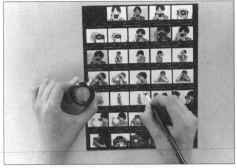

Step 26: Store the contact sheet and negatives so they will be accessible but protected.

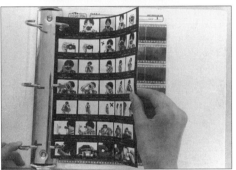

FIVE

ENLARGEMENTS: GETTING THE BIG PICTURE

Ansel Adams once said that as the negative is the score, the print is the performance. It is when you print that you bring the picture alive.

The enlarger allows you to do some of the things you couldn't do (or neglected to do) when shooting the picture. The composition can often be strengthened. Extraneous elements can be eliminated. Print tonalities can be adjusted. If you have an underexposed or thin negative, you can select a higher contrast paper and less exposure (smaller aperture and/or shorter time) to avoid a muddy print. If you have an overexposed or dense negative, you can increase exposure to compensate.

Making an enlargement

The enlarging process is quite similar to the one you followed in making your contact sheets. You will need the same equipment and chemicals.

▸▸ **Preparation.** You begin by carefully removing all dust from the negative with a soft brush. An easy way to make sure it is clean is to hold the negative at an angle under the enlarger light. The reflecting light will reveal the dust as little sparkles. Any dust specks that are not removed will be enlarged right along with your negative and appear on your print as white blobs.

When you insert the negative into the metal negative carrier of the enlarger, you should be careful not to touch anything but the edge of the film to avoid getting fingerprints on it. The emulsion side of the negative should face down, toward the emulsion side of the paper. (The general rule, whether making contacts or enlargements, is emulsion to emulsion.)

Note that if your enlarger can be adjusted to different film formats, you must be sure to put it on the 35 mm setting at this point. Slide the negative carrier into the enlarger and set the lens aperture wide open. By setting the lens wide open—the lowest numbered f-stop—you're provided with the brightest light to focus the projected image.

You must turn off the white lights in the darkroom and turn on the enlarger to see the negative image projected on the enlarger easel. Now you have several adjustments to make before starting to print. You can raise or lower the enlarger to change magnification. You can position the easel to capture only a portion of the negative frame and eliminate extraneous elements. With some easels, you can adjust the metal edges to the exact shape and size you want in the final print.

If you will be using a contrast filter, you should place it in the enlarger before you focus. Once you've arranged things as you want them, focus the enlarger carefully. Various types of focusing aids are available to assist you. A grain magnifier of some type is best; they are more difficult to learn to use but are very accurate. The enlarger should always be focused with the lens aperture wide open—that is, at the brightest setting. Once focused, however, you should close the aperture to f/8 or f/11—usually the optimum aperture for an enlarging lens—before you turn off the enlarger.

FIGURE 5.17. Test print. This test series was made at intervals of 2 seconds. Most photographers use a quarter sheet for test strips to conserve expensive photographic paper.

FIVE

▶▶ **Test print or test strip.** You make a test print or test strip for an enlargement (Figure 5.17) in much the same way as you make a test print or test strip for a contact sheet. To save paper, most photographers use one-fourth of a full sheet when making test prints. As with the contact sheet test strip, you want to determine the exposure time that gives the best detail in both shadows and highlights. Experience will eventually guide you in the selection of a trial exposure time for test prints. For now, you can try using an interval of 5 seconds. Begin by covering all but about 2" of the sheet of paper with cardboard and making a single 5-second exposure. Then you move the cardboard to expose another 2" and make a second 5-second exposure. You keep moving the cardboard and making exposures until the entire sheet of paper has been exposed.

Process the exposed paper for an enlargement just as you did the contact sheet: Develop for 1 minute (or time recommended by paper manufacturer), stop for 15 to 20 seconds, and fix for about 15 seconds. This fixing time isn't long enough for permanence, but it will allow you to inspect the print in white light. Select the exposure strip that gives the best detail in both shadow and highlight areas and set your timer for the exposure time used for that section.

▶▶ **Final print.** To make the final print, use a fresh sheet of paper, expose it for the selected time, and process it as you did the test print, extending the fixing time to a full 2 to 4 minutes for permanence and wash the print for 5 minutes before drying it.

You now have what photographers call a "straight" print—one that hasn't been manipulated at all. Usually, it's only the beginning. It is a rare print that can't be improved with some extra work. We will look at how to improve your prints in the next chapter.

How to

Make Enlargements

Step 1: Pour the prepared chemicals into assembled trays as you did to make contact sheets.

Step 2: Check the temperature of the developer and running wash water. They should both be close to 68°F.

Step 3: Use a soft, anti-static brush to clean the enlarger lens.

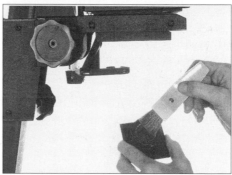

Step 4: Clean the negative you plan to print using a soft brush. Be sure all dust specks are removed.

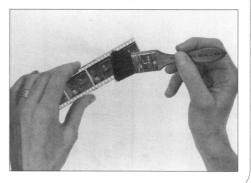

How to

Make Enlargements

Step 5: Insert the negative strip into the negative carrier, being careful not to touch anything but the edge. Position the strip so that the frame you want to enlarge is centered in the opening of the carrier.

Step 6: Place the carrier containing the negative strip in the enlarger head on the negative stage.

FIVE

Step 7: Set the enlarging lens aperture wide open (brightest setting). Then, turn off the white lights and turn on the safelight.

Step 8: Turn on the enlarger to project the negative image on the enlarger easel. Then, adjust the enlarger head, as well as the easel, so the negative will be enlarged and cropped as you want it.

How to

Make Enlargements

Step 9: If you intend to use a contrast filter, insert it in the filter holder of the enlarger.

Step 10: Focus the enlarger by turning the focusing knob. You can use a grain magnifier, if you have one, to check the sharpness of the image projected on the easel.

Step 11: Set the enlarger aperture to either f/8 or f/11.

Step 12: Set the enlarger's timer to a trial time interval: for example, 5 seconds. Experience will guide you in choosing a reasonable time for the degree of enlargement and density of the negative you are using.

How to

Make Enlargements

💡 **Step 13:** Turn off the enlarger, and put a sheet of RC photographic paper in the easel.

💡 **Step 14:** Using a sheet of cardboard as you did with the contact sheet, make a test print by giving several exposures to the paper.

💡 **Step 15:** Process the test print just as you did the test print for the contact sheet: Develop for 1 minute, stop for 10 to 15 seconds, and fix for about 15 seconds.

💡 **Step 16:** Inspect the test print to determine the best exposure time, and set the enlarger's timer to that time.

FIVE

How to

Make Enlargements

💡 **Step 17:** With only the safelight on in the darkroom, place a fresh sheet of paper in the easel, and turn on the enlarger to expose it.

💡 **Step 18:** Process the print in developer for 1 minute or so and in the stop bath for 10 to 15 seconds.

💡 **Step 19:** Fix the print for a full 2 to 4 minutes, and wash in running water for a full 5 minutes.

💡 **Step 20:** Remove excess water from the print with the print squeegee, and dry the print by hanging it up or by putting it in an RC paper dryer.

What Can Go Wrong

Gradually, your work in making prints will come naturally. You will be able to follow all of the procedures without difficulty. At first, however, you may run into some of these common problems.

Problem 1 (A): Overly contrasty print

Contrasty print with blacks where there should be shadow detail and whites where there should be highlight detail.

Probable Cause:

You selected the wrong filter or paper grade.

Solution (B):

Use a lower contrast filter in the enlarger or select a lower grade of paper.

A. Problem print   B. Solution print

*[handwritten:] * not generally a problem*
*[handwritten:] * film dev. time effects contrast*

Problem 2: Yellow stains on print

Yellow stains on print, frequently appearing several days or several weeks after the print was made.

Probable Cause:

You did not fix long enough or you used fixer that was weak and exhausted. This problem can also be caused by contaminated developer or insufficient washing.

Solution:

Do not use old chemicals, and be sure to wash and fix your prints sufficiently.

[handwritten:] — Generally not a problem with RC
[handwritten:] — But it may be you didn't fix long enough

What Can Go Wrong

Problem 3: Fuzzy print

Fuzzy, out-of-focus print.

Probable Cause:

You may not have properly focused the enlarger, or your negative may not be sharp.

Solution:

Use a grain magnifier to check the projected negative image for sharpness. When your enlarger is not in focus, the grain of the negative will not be sharp. If the grain is sharp but the image is fuzzy, the negative is not sharp and you cannot correct the problem in printing.

Problem 4: Dark print

Probable Cause:

Print is overexposed, either because the exposure time is too long or because the enlarger lens aperture is too large.

Solution:

Decrease your enlarger exposure time or decrease the aperture opening.

Problem 5: Light print

Probable Cause:

Print is underexposed, either because the exposure time is too short or because the enlarger lens aperture is too small.

Solution:

Increase your enlarger exposure time or increase the aperture opening.

What Can Go Wrong

Problem 6: Streaked print

Uneven or streaked print.

Probable Cause:

You did not agitate the print sufficiently in the developer.

Solution:

Rock the tray gently but constantly as the print is developing.

Problem 7 (A): Flat print

No contrast between dark and light tones.

Probable Cause:

You may not have developed your print for the recommended length of time; short development times don't allow sufficient blacks to build up on the paper.

Solution (B):

Develop your print for the recommended amount of time; if that isn't the problem, use a higher contrast filter in the enlarger.

A. Problem print

B. Solution print

Good
Read
this

Don't rush through
the process
guanteed way
to get flat looking prints

REVIEW questions ?

1. What are the two basic kinds of paper?

2. What are the characteristics of photographic paper?

3. How should photographic paper be stored?

4. What chemicals are needed in making prints?

5. What does an enlarger do and why is it important in making prints?

6. What is a contact sheet and what is its function?

7. How do you make a test print?

8. How do you make a contact sheet?

9. How do you make a "straight" print?

10. How should photographers care for their hands to avoid harm from chemicals?

more
about **printmaking**

Untitled, by Jerry Uelsmann, 1969

more
about printmaking

Untitled, **by Jerry Uelsmann, 1969**
(Reprinted with permission, Jerry Uelsmann)

Jerry Uelsmann is a master of what many call synthetic photography, images created by combining other images. Uelsmann himself calls his approach "post-visualization," an approach that allows for discovery and surprise in the photographic process.

Many others espouse the "previsualization" mode in which the photographer imagines the finished image before exposing the film, then employs his or her craft and creativity to produce that previsualized image on paper. In this mode, the real act of creativity occurs when the shutter is released.

Uelsmann wants to leave the photographic process open to creativity and decision making at all points. Much of the creative work is done in the darkroom, deciding which images might go with other images to produce an engaging or provocative final result. Many of his images have a dreamlike quality and gain energy because they combine the realism of the photograph with imagery that is obviously unreal.

Beyond the mechanics of making a straight print are the specialized darkroom techniques essential to making an effective print. In some cases, these techniques offer ways of dealing with problem negatives. In a more positive sense, however, they offer ways of interpreting the image on the negative.

As you print, you should consider what it is you want the print to convey. What is essential to the print? What can safely be eliminated? What should be emphasized? And what subdued? A photographic print is a form of communication. In the darkroom, you can make your prints speak as eloquently as possible.

CONTROLLING CONTRAST IN PRINTING

A crucial characteristic of a good print is its contrast. A print with **proper contrast** will usually contain a solid black, a bright white, and the full range of tones between. A print lacking contrast is said to be muddy or flat. A **flat print** contains dark grays instead of black and light grays instead of white. A print with too much contrast is said to be hard or contrasty. A **contrasty print** contains solid blacks and whites, but at the expense of shadow or highlight detail. Shadows are blocked up to a solid black and show no details. Highlights are bleached out and lack detail.

The best way to control print contrast is by controlling negative contrast. Negative contrast is best controlled by keeping developing temperatures consistent and by adjusting **film development time.** If your negatives are consistently too flat, you can increase your developing time. If they are consistently too contrasty, you can decrease the developing time. But even if you use a proper developing time, some frames on the film may still be too flat or too contrasty and you will need to correct them in printing.

Contrast filters

Contrast filters and variable-contrast paper can be used to correct contrast in a print. Contrast filters are usually numbered 1, 1 1/2, 2, 2 1/2, 3, 3 1/2, 4, 4 1/2 and 5. The whole numbers (1, 2, 3, 4, 5) correspond to grades of paper. Thus, with variable-contrast paper and contrast filters, you can make prints in between paper grade contrasts.

As in paper grades, the contrast filter numbers range from least contrasty (#1) to the most contrasty (#5). As you go from a #1 filter to a #5 filter, the whites get whiter and the blacks get blacker. Using a higher numbered filter with variable-contrast paper often requires more exposure. Additional exposure is achieved by increasing time or by using a larger aperture, or a combination of both.

If a contrast filter is not used, variable-contrast paper reacts as if a #2 filter had been used. You can obtain a more limited range of tones on the print by using a lower numbered contrast filter (#1 or #1 1/2). Conversely, you can achieve a greater range of tones by using the highest numbered contrast filter (#5). To give the print only slightly more sparkle or contrast, you can use a #3 filter.

If the negative itself is too contrasty, you can try using one of the lower filters (#1 or #1 1/2) to compensate and achieve a normal print. If the negative is flat, a #4 or #5 filter will improve the contrast in the print. (If you are using graded papers, you can achieve the same result by changing paper grades.) Inspecting a test print or contact sheet helps you select the proper filter or the proper grade of paper to use for your final print.

CROPPING YOUR PRINTS

Cropping is nothing more than selecting a portion of the negative frame to appear in the finished print (Figure 6.1). You make framing decisions when first shooting the photograph. You decide where to stand, how close to get to the subject, what to include, and what to exclude from the frame. Cropping at the enlarger allows you to refine that frame.

FIGURE 6.1. Cropping. When you make an enlargement, you can select only a portion of the original to appear in the final print. Cropping allows you to refine the original composition and correct framing errors.

A. Full frame print

B. Cropped print

FIGURE 6.2. Croppers. These L-shaped masks allow you to visualize how your image would appear if cropped in various ways.

L-shaped guides can help you visualize how a certain crop will look. You can make two **L-shaped croppers** out of cardboard and hold them together to form an adjustable "picture frame." You can put the croppers over various parts of a test print to see how different crops look before actually cropping at the enlarger. If you make small guides, you can do much the same thing directly on the contact sheet (Figure 6.2). Then, when you are working at the enlarger, you adjust the magnification and the easel to match your crop

Cropping techniques

▸▸ **Improve your composition by cropping to change the placement of the subject.** You can decide more precisely where to place the subject in order to develop a focal point in the composition. You can also make the image more interesting by moving the subject out of the center and placing it according to the "rule of thirds" discussed in Chapter 3.

▸▸ **Make your photographs more dramatic by cropping them to emphasize patterns and lines.** For example, you can turn a dull square photo into a more interesting horizontal or vertical one by following the patterns and lines of the subject in the photo. You can also crop to "straighten out" a tilted horizon or a leaning telephone pole.

▸▸ **Make your photographs more meaningful by cropping as tightly as possible.** Try to eliminate anything in the photograph that isn't the subject or doesn't contribute to the subject. In this way, you can make the meaning of your picture clearer.

▸ **Salvage a scratched or damaged negative by cropping out such areas.** Sometimes you can eliminate a scratch by cropping more tightly. Occasionally, your image may turn out to be more interesting because you were forced to eliminate a blemish in the negative.

It's a good rule to crop tightly, but it can't be applied mechanically. You must be careful not to sacrifice the meaning of the photograph. For instance, a photograph intended to depict the isolation of a subject probably can't be cropped close to the subject. If it were, a viewer couldn't tell the subject was alone. Such a photograph is likely to be stronger if a large expanse of emptiness surrounds the subject. To frame effectively when shooting the picture and when cropping the print, you must understand what your picture is about.

MANIPULATING LIGHTS AND DARKS IN PRINTING

If parts of your enlargement are too light or too dark, you can make adjustments in the print by **dodging** and **burning** (Figures 6.3 and 6.4). These two darkroom techniques allow you to give different exposures to different parts of a print. They are not special techniques; nearly every print you make will require some dodging and burning.

Dodging and burning techniques

Dodging entails covering a dark area during the exposure to limit the amount of light it receives relative to the rest of the print. Dodging is best accomplished with a dodging tool—a piece of cardboard attached to the end of a wire (Figure 6.5). You can also use your hand, a finger, or a small piece of cardboard.

▸ **To dodge a print, you simply shade the portion of the print you want to lighten during part of the exposure time.** The longer you shade the area, the lighter it will be. In order to blend the lightened area in with the rest of the print,

---

A Note on

The Limitations of Cropping

One limitation on cropping is the degree you can magnify the negative. If you crop a small portion out of the negative and then magnify it a great deal to make a normal size print, you will lose print quality. The grain in the negative will be magnified and more obvious. Any slight unsharpness in the picture will be increased. In general, the more of the original frame you can use, the better the print will be, at least technically. It's an old photographic truism that if you wanted it cropped that tightly, you should have taken it that way in the first place. Cropping at the enlarger should be a matter of refinement, not wholesale revision.

BEST TO CROP WHILE YOU SHOOT

handwritten: lightening
handwritten: Bad example

FIGURE 6.3. Dodging. By casting a shadow on the photographic paper while enlarging, you can selectively reduce exposure and lighten specific areas of the print without affecting other areas.

A. Unmanipulated print

B. Dodged print

handwritten: darking
handwritten: Good example

SIX

FIGURE 6.4. Burning. By exposing certain parts of your print longer than other areas, you can selectively darken them.

A. Unmanipulated print

B. Burned print

FIGURE 6.5. Dodging tool. The dodging tool is used to cast a shadow on the area you wish to lighten during exposure. You can make a simple dodging tool yourself by taping a piece of cardboard to the end of an unbent paper clip.

FIGURE 6.6. Burning tool. The burning tool protects most of the print while you give selected areas added exposure to darken them. A light sheet of cardboard works well, but it must be opaque enough to block the light completely.

you hold the dodging tool or your hand several inches above the easel and keep it moving slightly during the exposure.

▸▸ **Burning** involves giving more exposure time to a light area to darken it while protecting other areas from receiving too much exposure. Burning in large areas like a sky is best done with a piece of cardboard (Figure 6.6). For burning in smaller areas, you can cut a hole in the cardboard. You can also use your hands by cupping or spreading them to keep enlarger light away from all areas on the paper except where the picture is too light. Again, you need to keep the cardboard or your hand above the paper and keep moving it in order to blend the burned area into the rest of the print.

Dodging and burning techniques make printmaking a two-stage exposure process. The first stage is the "base" exposure—that is, the exposure for the time you selected from the test print. The base exposure creates the overall image on the paper. During the base exposure, you do any dodging needed to lighten the dark areas of the print. The second stage consists of giving light areas of the print additional exposure to burn in and darken them. Experience improves dodging and burning. Practice will help you get a feel for how long to dodge or burn to achieve a certain print density.

▶▶ **Timing**. You may find it helpful to think about dodging and burning in terms of exposure stops. In this case, one stop is equivalent to opening or closing the enlarger aperture lens one stop or changing the exposure time by half or double. If you burn in an area for a second "base" exposure, you will have increased exposure in that area by one stop. If you dodge for half the "base" exposure, you will decrease exposure in the dodged area by one stop.

For example, if your base exposure is 20 seconds and you dodge a certain area for 10 seconds out of the 20, you will have given the dodged area one stop less than the rest of the print. If you burn in another area for a second full 20-second exposure (40 seconds total), you will have given it one stop more exposure.

In order to increase the exposure in the burned area by two stops, you must double the total exposure again. Thus, it would be necessary to burn it in three times in addition to the base exposure—that is, to increase burning time to 60 seconds and total exposure time for the burned area to 80 seconds. On the other hand, to cut the exposure in a dodged area a full two stops, you would increase the dodging time by half—from 10 seconds to 15 seconds. You should note that dodging affects print density more quickly than burning.

Inspecting a test print will help you to visualize what difference a one stop exposure increase or decrease makes. Keep in mind that it is difficult to see exposure differences of less than about 1/3 stop. Thus, if your base exposure were 15 seconds, burning for less than about 5 seconds would have a negligible effect. At the same time, dodging for less than about 2 1/2 seconds would hardly be noticeable.

SIX

A Note on

Dodging and Burning

A viewer's eye tends to be drawn to the brighter areas of a print. As a result, photographers commonly burn down the edges and corners of a print very slightly to focus attention more on the center, where the subject is likely to be. This isn't a rule, so you shouldn't feel bound by it. But it does point up how dodging and burning can be used as interpretive techniques to control emphasis in a print. But they should be employed subtly. Prints that are obviously manipulated generally have an artificial, mechanical look to them. Instead of strengthening the image, heavy-handed manipulation distracts from it.

FIGURE 6.7. Bleaching. Chemical bleach, potassium ferricyanide, was used to completely remove the background from the image at left. Much more subtle effects are possible by using dilute solutions of bleach and carefully lightening selected areas of the print.

A. Unbleached print   B. Bleached print

Bleaching darks in your prints

Occasionally areas of a print need to be lightened, but dodging would be too complicated or awkward. This can happen if too many areas need to be dodged at once or if the areas to be dodged are too intricate. Dodging is a way of rough hewing the print; bleaching the print gives you more precision.

Bleaching involves chemically lightening—or even removing—dark areas on a print (Figure 6.7). Special products are available for bleaching (Figure 6.8). "Spot Off" is a convenient, already prepared set of two chemicals, an accelerator and a bleacher. Farmer's reducer, an old photographic recipe, is available in packets. But a dilute solution of potassium ferricyanide works about as well as anything else. A pinch of the ferricyanide crystals added to water makes a light yellow bleach. A more dilute solution bleaches more slowly; a stronger solution, more quickly.

All of the bleach products work by converting the metallic silver that forms the photographic image back into silver halide salts. You then remove the silver salts by fixing again.

➤ **Bleaching technique.** Done well, bleaching is a slow and rather painstaking process requiring a lot of patience. It's a good idea to practice bleaching on a waste print first to help get the feel, especially if you haven't done it before.

You begin by wetting the print in a tray of fixer. Then you blow the excess fixer away from the area you plan to bleach and apply the bleach carefully to that area. If it's a large area, you can use a cotton swab. For very small areas, you can use a small watercolor brush. After about 20 seconds, you place the print back in the fixer for 15 seconds or so. You can rub your finger or the print tongs very gently over the bleached area to remove the yellow stain. If necessary, repeat the process to lighten the area even more. It helps to keep a second print handy for reference to see how things are progressing. After you have bleached the area as intended, you must fully fix and wash the print again.

CORRECTING SPOTS ON YOUR PRINTS

Perhaps Lady Macbeth said it best: "Out, damned spot. Out, I say." No matter how carefully you clean the dust off your negatives, no matter how clean you keep your darkroom (more about that later), no matter how carefully you handle your negatives, no matter that you follow all the directions in the book, you will still—sometimes—get spots on your prints.

White spots

The tiniest piece of dust, sitting quietly on your negative in the enlarger, is magnified along with the negative and becomes an unsightly white blemish. Don't despair. You can remove it via a process called, logically enough, spotting.

Spotting involves adding dye to the print until the tone of the spotted area corresponds to the tone of the part of the print adjacent to it. You use a small,

FIGURE 6.8. Photographic bleaches. A number of commercial products are available to bleach photographs, but most photographers simply use a dilute solution of potassium ferricyanide.

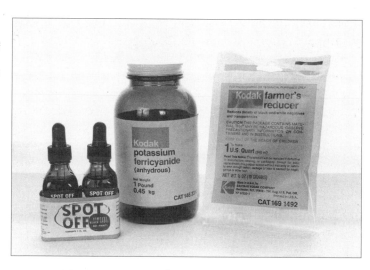

FIGURE 6.9. Spotting prints. Use a very fine watercolor brush and diluted Spotone to fill in white spots on prints. This is painstaking work, but necessary if white dust marks are not to distract from your image.

pointed brush and liquid photographic dye, called Spotone (Figure 6.9). The dye comes in several different colors, and you may need to mix it to get the tone that matches the tone of the print to be spotted. The directions that come with the dye give the proportions to use for the paper you are using. A number 0000 watercolor brush works well for applying the dye.

▶ **Spotting technique.** Once you've mixed the dye to obtain the correct tone, you'll need to dilute a small amount to match the shade of gray that surrounds the spot. It's best to mix a drop of the dye with a few drops of water and test it on a scrap print. The dye should be just a bit lighter than the area you will spot. It is very important to get the excess dye off the brush and to work with an almost dry brush on a dry print. You start from the center of the spot and work outward, stippling the dye into the white spot. You must work carefully so that the dye does not overlap tones around the spot.

Spotting, like bleaching, is a painstaking process. Unlike bleaching, however, if something goes wrong, you can usually just rewash the print to remove the dye and start over.

Black spots

Very occasionally, you will encounter a black spot on your print. Black spots are usually caused by small nicks or scratches in the negative. They almost invariably end up in the middle of someone's forehead or as a blob in an expanse of open sky, looking very much like a flying saucer. They are always difficult to remove.

➤ **Bleaching.** Often the best solution, but not an attractive prospect, is to bleach out the spot. However, that will leave a white halo on the print, which you must then spot in to match the surrounding area. By the time you are finished, you'll feel much more like a painter than a photographer.

➤ **Reprinting techniques.** Reprinting can eliminate or subdue the spot. Sometimes you can reprint the photograph and take some steps to eliminate or subdue the spot. Frequently, a small scratch in the negative can be hidden by evenly coating the negative frame with an oily substance. The oil fills in the scratched area so it is less likely to refract light and cause a dark scratch mark on the print.

You can buy commercial products for this purpose. But you can often get by with what photographers inelegantly refer to as "nose grease." Most of us spent our early teen years worrying about oily skin. Now you can use it to advantage: Smear a bit of skin oil from beside your nose over the entire surface of the negative frame. (If you wear makeup, you can use skin oil from behind your ear.) When you make the print, you will usually find the scratch mark has disappeared or, at least, isn't as apparent. When you finish printing, be sure to clean the oil from the negative with negative cleaner.

Not to rub it in, of course, but the best solution would have been to store the negatives carefully in the first place so they didn't get scratched.

MOUNTING YOUR PRINTS

You can preserve your prints and best display them by mounting them onto cardboard. **Dry mounting** the print onto special mounting board by heating the

---

A Note on

Darkroom Cleanliness

No discussion about printmaking would be complete without a word about darkroom cleanliness. A photographer's darkroom should be immaculate at all times. You should clean the trays and sink to prevent chemical deposits from building up. If necessary, you should scrub them down with a non-abrasive cleanser periodically. Every few months you should mop down all walls and the ceiling with a damp sponge to remove collected dust. If possible, blow out the enlarger periodically with compressed air to remove dust. It goes without saying (but we'll say it anyway) that there should be no chemical spills on the enlarger baseboard or adjacent counters.

Remember, dust and dirt are your mortal enemies. A darkroom should be as clean as an operating room.

print, adhesive, and cardboard under pressure is the best way to preserve prints permanently. For this process, you need drymount tissue, a paper cover sheet, mounting board, a cutter (a metal straightedge and mat knife work well), a tacking iron, and a heated mounting press.

The dry mount tissue is saturated with adhesive that melts and forms a bond when it is heated. When heated under pressure, the adhesive penetrates the fibers of the board and the print and bonds them together. Many photographers prefer to use acid-free mounting board; it is more expensive than other types, but desirable where permanence is needed. Other less neutral boards may eventually cause stains on the mounted print.

Dry mounting techniques

Before you begin, make sure everything is free of dust and dirt. Dirt particles can cause permanent bumps on the mounted print. You also need to decide on a size for the mounting board. You can mount the print on a board that is several inches larger than the print and leave a border between the edge of the print and the edge of the board. The width of the border can vary according to your preference, but you generally have better visual balance if the bottom border is wider than that at the top and sides. You can also **bleed mount** the print—that is, let the photo extend to all four edges of the board, with no border. In this case, you can begin with a board that is the same size or only slightly larger than the print.

▶▶ **With a press.** You preheat the mounting press and the tacking iron to the temperature recommended by the paper manufacturer. RC papers cannot stand high temperatures, and if you do not follow the manufacturer's instructions, the plastic coating on the paper may melt and blister. After the press is heated, preheat the mounting board in the press to remove moisture from it.

Next, with the print face down on a clean, flat surface, use the heated tacking iron to tack the tissue to the back of the print on each of the four sides. The tissue must be the same size or larger than the print, and it must be the correct type for the paper you used to make the print.

Once the tissue is tacked to the print, turn the print face up and trim off excess tissue—or even portions of the print if you wish to crop it—with a mat knife and a metal straightedge. Then, using a soft cloth to protect the print from fingerprints, position the print backed with tissue on the mounting board and carefully lift the corners of the print to tack the tissue to the board.

Put a cover sheet over the print to protect it from the heating surface in the top of the press. You should never use newsprint or anything with printing on it as a cover sheet because the words may become imprinted on your print. Although you can purchase special cover sheets, a smooth, high-gloss butcher paper works well.

Place the assembled board, tissue, print, and cover sheet into the heated press. When you take it out of the press, apply pressure to the cover sheet with a book or your hands so the edges won't curl up as it cools.

If you mounted your print on a large board to leave a border, you might find mounting tissue protruding from the edges of the print. This tissue can be removed if you are careful by using a straightedge and a small utility knife or razor blade. If you don't hold the straightedge down tightly, however, the blade may slip and cause you to cut into the print or the board and ruin your work. If you bleed-mounted the print, you use a mat knife to trim the board and print to be flush along all four edges.

▸▸ **With a household iron.** If you do not have a mounting press and tacking iron, you can mount your prints with a regular household flatiron. In this method, you set the control for synthetic fibers. When you tack the tissue to the back of the print, you can't press too hard or you will crease the print. Working on a hard, flat surface minimizes the danger of creases.

Trim the print and the tissue in the same manner as before and position the tissue, print, and cover sheet on the mounting board. Then seal the print to the board by ironing it with light strokes.

You should iron the print from the center outward to avoid getting air bubbles between print and board. If you do get bubbles, you can try working them out by ironing. If that doesn't work, you can prick the print with a small needle to allow the air to escape, then iron over the surface. Mounting with a household iron always holds some risk of causing creases on the print. It's good insurance to make one or two backup prints—just in case.

▸▸ **Alternatives.** One alternative if you lack a dry mount press is to use one of the positionable **cold mount tissues** now available. Simple pressure, without heat, is enough to bond the print to its backing. The print can usually be lifted off and mounted again if mistakes are made. This type of tissue is more expensive than dry mount tissue, but surer to use in the absence of a press. Another alternative is to matte the print. This involves fastening the print to the back of a cardboard window. This method is preferable when the print is to be framed.

How to

Mount Prints

Step 1: Turn on the mounting press, and preheat it to between 180°F and 210°F to mount a print on RC paper. Then turn on the tacking iron to preheat it as well.

Step 2: Place the mounting board in the press for 30 seconds to remove moisture from it.

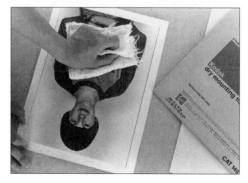

Step 3: With a soft cloth, clean the print, and make sure that everything else you use is free from dirt and dust. Any dirt particles will cause lumps in the mounted print that can't be removed.

Mount Prints

Step 4: Place the print face down on a clean, flat surface with the mounting tissue on top, and use the preheated tacking iron to tack the tissue to the print on all four sides.

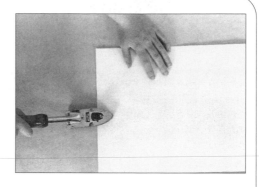

Step 5: Use the metal straightedge and the mat knife to trim the print and the tissue flush to size.

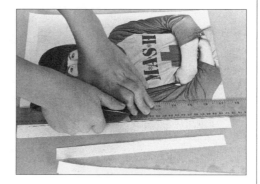

Step 6: Position the print and the tissue, face up, on the mounting board. Using a soft cloth to protect the print from fingerprints, carefully lift the corners of the print and tack the tissue to the board at the corners.

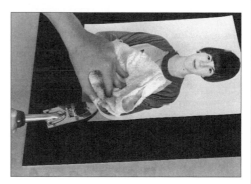

SIX

How to

Mount Prints

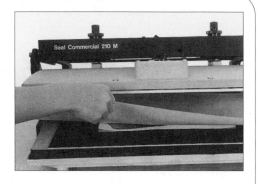

Step 7: Place the board, the tissue, the print, and the cover sheet into the heated press for 30 to 45 seconds.

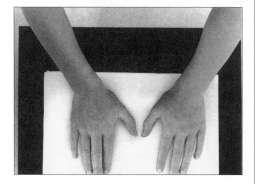

Step 8: Pull the mounted print out of the press, and apply pressure to the cover sheet so the edges don't curl up as it cools.

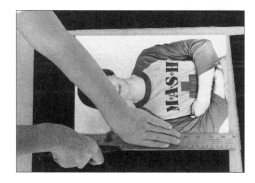

Step 9: If the print is to be bleed-mounted flush to the edges of the board, trim the board and print with the mat knife and straightedge.

What Can Go Wrong

Even experienced printers find that things do go wrong in the darkroom. Some problems just can't be avoided all of the time. Fortunately, there are things that you can do when, despite your best efforts, you have a problem print.

Problem 1: White spots on print

White spots or scratches on the print.

dust & scratch

SIX

Probable Cause:

You did not thoroughly clean the negative, or in the case of scratches, you did not handle the negative or wet print carefully enough.

Solution:

Make a new print being more careful, or use a photographic dye such as Spotone, to touch up the print you already have.

Problem 2 (A): Black spots on print

Black spots or scratches on the print.

Probable Cause:

You may have deep nicks or scratches on the negative or pinholes caused by air bubbles on the film during development.

Solution (B):

Make a new print, cropping away the damaged area on the negative, or use photographic bleach to lighten the dark spot or scratch.

Airbubbles

A. Problem print

B. Solution print

What Can Go Wrong

Problem 3 (A): Part of image too dark

Probable Cause:

The area needed less exposure than the rest of the image.

Solution (B):

Dodge the area by using your hand or a dodging tool to limit the amount of light that it receives from the enlarger relative to the rest of the print.

A. Problem print

B. Solution print

REVIEW questions ?

1. Why is contrast so important to a successful print?

2. What are contrast filters?

3. How do contrast filters improve a print?

4. What is cropping and how does it improve a print?

5. What techniques are used to crop a print?

6. What is "dodging" and how does it improve a print?

7. What is "burning" and how does it improve a print?

8. What is "bleaching" and when can it help a print?

9. How can spots—both black and white—be eliminated on a final print?

10. What techniques should be used in mounting finished prints?

SIX

handling light and color

"*Camera lens, film, developer and printing paper have but one purpose:*

to capture and present light. Yet for

all its place of importance in the

photographic scheme, light is too often

unknown, unstudied, and abused by photographers...."

Edward Weston

lighting

SEVEN

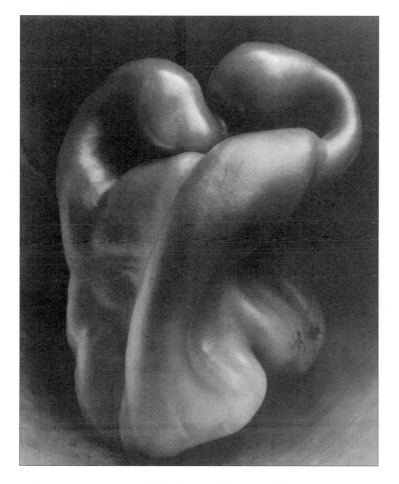

Pepper #30, by Edward Weston, 1930

lighting

***Pepper #30,* by Edward Weston, 1930**

(© 1981 Center for Creative Photography, Arizona Board of Regents)

Edward Weston made a career out of photographing natural objects in a provocative way, often through the unique use of light. Although he began his career in 1911 as a studio photographer taking portraits, he later disdained artificial light and started doing more of his work outside where he concentrated on the problems of using natural light. After four years in Mexico, Weston returned to the United States in 1927 and started photographing the subjects that would make him famous: single, ordinary objects like vegetables, fruits, rocks, tree roots, shells, even toilets. One of his most noted images was of a bell pepper, which Weston spent weeks shooting, constantly experimenting with light.

Photography is the language of light. The word itself derives from Greek words meaning light writing. Most of the equipment photographers use deals with light: Lenses focus it. Film records it. Meters measure it. Darkrooms keep it out until needed. Cameras are miniature darkrooms that protect film from light until exposure.

Light in photography comes from a variety of sources, and it has various qualities and characteristics that affect the entire process—from setting up the camera to making the final print. Using light effectively can make the difference between a mediocre photograph and an eloquent one.

QUALITIES OF LIGHT

▶▶ **Intensity.** Intensity is the brightness or dimness of the light reaching your subject. It is what your light meter measures. If you make meter readings carefully,

[handwritten: INTENSITY OF Light effects: depth of field motion]

FIGURE 7.1. Effect of light intensity. Proper exposure neutralizes the direct effects of lighting intensity. No matter whether the scene is bright or dim, about the same amount of light will reach and expose the film because shutter and aperture settings will compensate. However, because the shutter and aperture settings will vary, differences in light intensity will indirectly affect the depth of field and how the camera records motion. Compare this pair of photographs with Figure 2.12, where there is a trade-off between depth of field and shutter speed.

[margin: SEVEN]

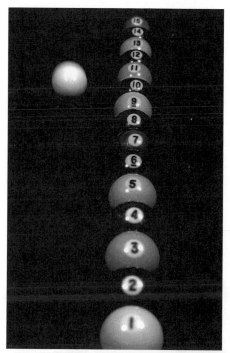

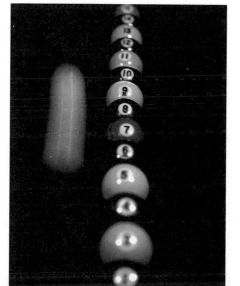

A. In bright light, fast shutter speeds and small apertures increase overall image sharpness.

B. In dim light, slow shutter speeds and large apertures limit overall image sharpness.

[handwritten: Bright Light • Stops action • Greater Depth of Field]

[handwritten: Dim light • narrow depth • Blurs action]

the intensity of the light shouldn't directly affect the brightness or dimness of the final photograph because you adjust shutter speed and aperture to match light levels. However, the intensity of the light influences your choice of film (fast, medium, or slow). Light intensity and film speed, in turn, fix the range of shutter speeds and apertures you can use. Thus, light intensity has an indirect, but very definite, impact on depth of field and the action-stopping ability of the shutter, as shown in Figure 7.1.

▸ **Contrast.** Lighting contrast is the difference in illumination levels between the fully lit areas of the subject (the highlights) and the areas that are not directly lit (the shadows). Contrasty scenes will have very brightly lit highlight areas and only dimly lit shadow areas. Flatly lit scenes will have relatively less difference between illumination levels in highlight versus shadow areas, as shown in Figure 7.2. Lighting contrast is usually expressed as a lighting ratio, the arithmetic ratio of the illumination levels in the highlight areas to those in the shadow areas. For example, a lighting ratio of 1:2 means that the highlights are illuminated twice as brightly as the shadows, that is, that there is a one-

FIGURE 7.2. Lighting contrast. The relative difference between the illumination of the highlight and shadow areas is the lighting contrast, usually given as the lighting ratio. Contrasty scenes, which have high lighting ratios, exhibit a large difference between highlight and shadow illumination. Flat scenes have much less difference.

A. Contrasty lighting: a lighting ratio of 1:8, or three stops difference between highlights and shadows.

B. Flat lighting: a lighting ratio of 1:2, or one stop difference between highlights and shadows.

highlights 8 times as light or shadow

highlights twice as bright as shadows

FIGURE 7.3. Specularity. Large light sources placed relatively near the subject produce diffuse light, which creates soft-edged shadows that usually contain considerable shadow detail. Small or distant light sources create specular light and harsher shadows with more defined edges and less shadow detail.

A. Diffuse light produced by a large light source near the subject.

B. Specular light produced by a small, distant light source.

stop difference between the two. A lighting ratio of 1:4 means the highlights are lit four times more strongly than the shadows, or that there is a two-stop difference. As a photographer, you can often influence or control the lighting contrast through the introduction of additional light sources, reflectors, and shades that alter the relative illumination of highlights and shadows and thus alter lighting contrast. Lighting contrast is only one type of contrast that photographers need to be aware of. See the Note below.

A Note on

Contrast in Photography

Lighting contrast is only one of the factors that determines the overall contrast in your final print. Subject contrast, the difference in values between light tones and dark tones in subject matter, also plays a role. For example a white egg photographed against a white background will have less subject contrast than a lump of black coal photographed against the same white background. Secondly, the photographic materials you use will influence final contrast. You might select an inherently contrasty lithographic film for its ability to create extreme highlights and shadows with few midtones. Or you might use a #1 enlarging paper because it minimizes print contrast. A third important factor is negative contrast, which you can control to a large degree by film development, as discussed in Chapter 4. The Zone System approach to photography, in fact, uses film development as a systematic control over other forms of contrast so the photographer can produce a print that echoes the scene as the photographer interprets it.

▸ **Specularity.** Light can be focused and very sharp, or at the other extreme, it can be very soft and diffuse. Sharp, or **specular**, light usually produces harsh, well-defined shadows. It generally comes from a single point, such as a flash unit or the sun in a cloudless sky. Diffuse light, on the other hand, gives hazy, ill-defined shadows or no shadows at all. Diffuse light emanates from large light sources, like sun being filtered and diffused through clouds on an overcast day, or from several light sources. Figure 7.3 shows the same subject photographed with both specular and diffuse lighting. The degree of diffusion of the light also affects the contrast of your negatives: More specular light produces more contrasty negatives. To compensate, some photographers shorten developing times for film shot in specular light (like direct sun) and extend developing times for film shot in very diffuse light (like haze or fog).

▸ **Direction.** The direction of light is the angle at which the light strikes your subject. It affects the way texture and shape are depicted in the photograph. Sidelight, which rakes across the subject at right angles, tends to enhance texture. Frontlight minimizes texture and creates few shadows. As a result, the subject usually appears rather flat. See Figure 7.4 for an example of frontlight and sidelight. Backlight throws shadows to the front of the subject and lends depth to the

FIGURE 7.4. Effect of light direction. The angle at which the light strikes the subject determines how shadows will fall. Frontlight drives the shadows toward the background and minimizes the appearance of texture. Sidelight pushes shadows toward the edge of the frame and enhances texture.

A. Frontlight "erases" texture in the roof and front of the building.

B. Sidelight emphasizes the stucco siding and tile roof.

FIGURE 7.5. Natural light. Sunlight outdoors is the sole light source here. Natural light changes with the time of day, the weather, and the season.

picture. It often gives the photograph a hazy appearance and may result in a silhouette. Light that comes from above the subject looks "natural" because that's where sunlight comes from. Light that comes from below the subject tends to appear unnatural and sinister; photographers often refer to it as "ghoul lighting."

▶ **Color.** Different light sources emit different colors of light. Light may be cool (bluish) or warm (reddish-yellowish). In black-and-white photography, the color of the light usually is not of concern. In color photography, it is crucial, as discussed in Chapter 9.

KINDS OF LIGHT

A true mastery of light requires years of experience. Your mastery can perhaps begin with an understanding of three broad categories photographers often use to distinguish common lighting situations: natural, existing, and artificial.

FIGURE 7.6. Existing light. Light that is part of the scene, but not sunlight, can be visually compelling and gives the image a sense of authenticity.

A. Artificial lights at night create dramatic contrasts in shadow and highlight areas.

B. Indoor sports like gymnastics are almost always photographed with existing light.
(Photograph courtesy of Karl Maasdam.)

FIGURE 7.7. Subject photographed in artificial light. The lighting is carefully controlled in the studio, but mimics the general characteristics of diffused daylight.

Natural light

Natural light is the light from the sun, usually outdoors. It takes many forms, from the soft, diffuse light of an overcast day to the harsh, contrasty light of bright direct sun. Natural light may create no shadows, soft shadows, or deep shadows. Shadows may be longer or shorter depending on time of day and season of the year. The specularity of natural light is often influenced by the weather.

Sunlight is rich in possibilities, sometimes unpredictable, and always impossible to control directly. Still, however, it is usually possible to anticipate or at least work around outdoor lighting conditions. Sometimes, it is a matter of waiting—for the angle of the light to change, for the clouds to shield and diffuse the sun's light, or for another day when conditions are more to your liking. Sometimes, it is a matter of moving—to shade your subject from the direct sun and its harsh shadows or to establish the desired direction of the sunlight relative to the subject. Figure 7.5 shows two subjects in natural light.

Existing light

Existing light is the light found at the location of your photograph, usually indoors to distinguish it from natural sunlight, but also outdoors at night when sunlight yields to other exterior light sources. Existing light is often created from a variety of light sources—that is, a mixture of window light, light fixtures, and reflections. It is often uneven: Some portions of the scene may be brightly lit while others are cast in deep shadow. The effect can be fascinating when captured on film, but it requires you to take careful readings on your light meter and learn to gauge light as you survey the scene. Figure 7.6 shows two subjects photographed using existing light.

The most common problem with existing light is that light intensity is often low. Even with fast films, you may have to shoot at very slow shutter speeds and with a wide-open lens aperture. You may need to brace the camera or use a tripod and focus very carefully if you want reasonably sharp pictures.

Artificial light

Artificial light refers to the light you add to the existing light on the scene. It may be as simple as a single flash or as complex as banks of studio lights. Given proper equipment, you can create just about any lighting effect you wish. Normally, however, photographers attempt to add light in a way that looks as natural as possible. That way, attention is focused on the subject rather than the lighting itself. Figure 7.7 shows a subject in artificial light. Photographers use two basic types of artificial light: that from continuous light sources and that from flash units.

▶▶ **Continuous light** is steady, uninterrupted light from an electric light source. Sources of continuous light include, of course, the ordinary tungsten household light bulb. Photography, however, frequently demands a more powerful light source. **Floodlights,** or **photofloods,** are simply strong, frosted tungsten bulbs, usually 250 or 500 watts. **Spotlights** are similar, but the bulbs are not frosted and are designed to focus light in a smaller area. Both are intense, but shorter lived than household bulbs. Photofloods generally burn out after only a few hours of use. Although photofloods or spotlights can be screwed into normal light bulb sockets, you can purchase inexpensive clamp fixtures and reflectors to allow you more flexibility in placing the lights.

More intense and more expensive continuous light sources are available. Quartz-halogen lights are small and portable, but extremely intense. They are often used with movie cameras. For most black-and-white photography, however, the less expensive photoflood and spotlight are usually quite adequate.

The advantage of continuous light is that you can preview the lighting effect as you set the lights. You can see the shadows—their direction, shape, and intensity—before taking the picture. That makes it easier to create specific lighting effects. While continuous light sources can be relatively inexpensive, they have the disadvantages of not being as portable or as powerful as flash units.

FIGURE 7.8. Photoflood lamp. This type of fixture can be put on a light stand or clamped to any sturdy support.

▸▸ **Flash light** is a brief, intense burst of light from a flash unit. Most flash units are portable and usually powerful for their size. Nearly all flash sources used today are battery-powered electronic flashes, or strobes. As electronic flash units have gotten cheaper, they have all but replaced the less-convenient flash bulb.

The electronic flash has many advantages. The gas-filled flash tube can be used repeatedly without needing to be replaced. The flash is portable and lightweight. Compared to continuous light sources, a strobe delivers a lot of light. Its very brief duration makes for sharper negatives. It is correctly balanced for daylight color film. Indeed, with a flash unit, a photographer is ready to take pictures nearly anywhere.

However, because the light is so brief (a few ten-thousandths of a second), the effect of the light cannot be seen until the photograph is processed. As a result, photos made with a strobe can be horrendous. Intelligent use of flash requires a bit of experience and a sensitivity to how the light will look in the finished photograph. Thus, it is best if you first experiment with continuous light sources to develop a feel for lighting.

USING CONTINUOUS LIGHT

Because they require a source of electricity, photofloods are rarely used outside a studio or room. You can manage with any normal light fixture simply by switching from a household bulb to a photoflood. (Be sure that the light fixture can withstand the heat generated by the stronger photoflood.) It is more convenient, however, to use specialized photographic lighting equipment. You can choose between a fixture that clamps to some support or one that attaches to the top of a light stand (Figure 7.8). Light stands offer flexibility because they can be placed where you wish and their height adjusted.

Whatever fixture you use, the important factor to keep in mind with studio lighting is the effect of the intensity, contrast, specularity, and direction of the light on the final photograph. It's a good idea to take the time to experiment with light. If you can find a patient subject to sit for a portrait shooting, you can learn much about how lighting affects the final image. Or you can set up still life subjects and experiment with different lighting arrangements.

Lighting for portraits

Because a portrait subject usually sits still, you can use relatively slow shutter speeds; in fact, you may be forced to use them because continuous light sources are typically not powerful. You determine the aperture setting by using a conventional light meter to take a reading off the person's face after you have set up the lights.

When setting up for portraits, you should look at the features of your subject— shape of head, texture of skin, facial expression, and personality—and take them into consideration when lighting. You can achieve different effects by changing the angle of light, the height of light, and the qualities of light, as well as by using more than one light source.

➡ **Change the angle between the light, subject, and camera** (Figure 7.9). Front lighting, where the camera and light are side by side facing the subject is, sometimes called "flat lighting." The subject's face tends to be rather flat, or two dimensional, because no significant shadows are produced. Side lighting, on the other hand, where the camera faces the subject and the light is at a right angle to the subject, tends to produce many strong shadows because of the cross lighting. While hair and clothing textures are enhanced, side lighting tends to divide the subject's face in half and is thus sometimes called "hatchet lighting." Back lighting, where the light is behind the subject, but positioned so that it does not shine into the camera lens, produces what is called a "halo" effect. Back lighting alone can sometimes be effectively used for silhouettes, but it is mostly used with other lights in portrait work where the halo effect helps to separate the head and shoulders from the background and thus give the portrait dimension.

➡ **Alter the height of the light** (Figure 7.10). Bottom lighting, where the light is placed very low in front of the subject and aimed upward, is often called "ghoul lighting." The shadows produced are exaggerated and unnatural, and they tend to give a sinister or evil look to the subject's face. Top lighting, where the light is high above the subject's head and aimed downward, tends to create dominant shadows that are not unlike those created by the sun at high noon. Top lighting can be useful for highlighting the subject's hair, but it can be unflattering to the subject's face in that the eye sockets are often in deep shadow while the nose and chin seem more prominent because of the shadows underneath. High side lighting, where the light is placed high to the side of the subject and aimed downward at a 45° angle, is often called "classic" lighting. It produces natural-looking shadows and creates a pleasing three-dimensional effect.

FIGURE 7.9. Angle of light

A. Front lighting emphasizes surface detail.

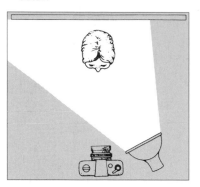

B. Side lighting emphasizes texture and three-dimensionality.

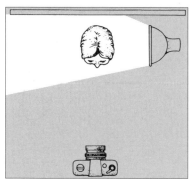

C. Back lighting emphasizes shape, the outline of the subject.

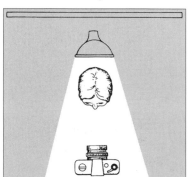

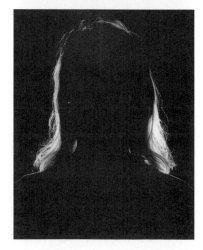

FIGURE 7.10. Height of light

A. Bottom lighting creates an unnatural and dramatic appearance.

unflattering shadow

B. Top lighting can create a skulllike appearance.

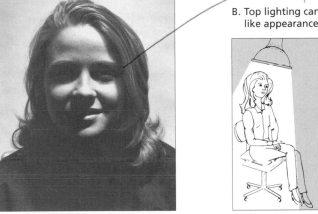

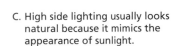

C. High side lighting usually looks natural because it mimics the appearance of sunlight.

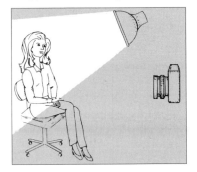

FIGURE 7.11. Specularity of light

A. Specular light creates hard-edged shadows.

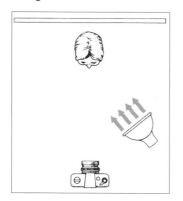

B. Diffused bounce light creates soft-edged shadows.

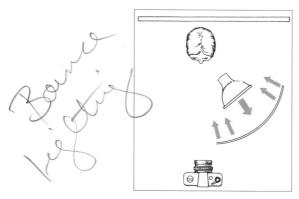

▸▸ **Change the specularity of the light** (Figure 7.11). A single, concentrated light produces strong harsh shadows and a contrasty look. For a softer look, you can diffuse the light. You can diffuse light by bouncing it off a wall, the ceiling, a white sheet of cardboard, or an umbrella with a silvered or white interior. You can also purchase diffusers made of spun glass that attach to the front of the reflector.

You can alter the relative intensity of the light (and thus adjust the lighting ratio) simply by moving the light closer to or further from the subject. You can also vary the light position to change the direction of the light and thus create different shadow patterns.

FIGURE 7.12. Multiple sources of light

A. Main light establishes the overall shadow pattern.

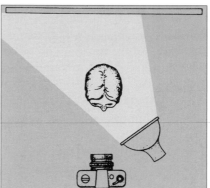

Maina Key light

B. Adding the fill light creates more detail in the shadows.

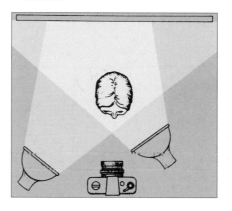

Fill light

SEVEN

C. Adding the background light separates the subject from the background.

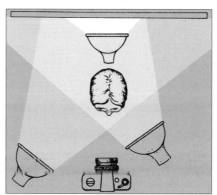

Fill Key Back

▶▶ **Use more than one light**. A common approach for portraits is to use a single light, called the **main light** or "key light," to create the main shadows and another less intense light, the **fill light**, to make the shadows less harsh. A common two-light setup for portraits places the main light high and at the side. The fill light is positioned lower and placed further back from the subject, just next to the camera on the side opposite the main light. Because it is less intense than the main light, the fill light does not eliminate the shadows created by the main light; it merely fills them in.

In a three-light setup, another light is positioned to illuminate the background. The purpose of the **background light** is to separate the subject from the background by increasing the contrast between the two. Professional portrait photographers will often add a fourth light, an **accent light,** which is a spot light placed high above and to the rear of the subject to highlight the subject's hair. Figure 7.12 illustrates two-light and three-light setups, but you needn't be a slave to them. See what happens when you vary the pattern.

FIGURE 7.13. Use of a simple reflector.
A white sheet of cardboard can take the place of a second light. Position it just out of camera view and angle the reflector to aim the fill light where you want it. For more efficient fill, you can buy metallicized reflectors or cover a sheet of cardboard with tin foil.

A. No fill. This version is lit solely by one large light source coming from the right side.

B. Filled with reflected light. Note the lightened shadow areas and the large highlight on the left side of the tea ball.

You can obtain much of the effect of a second light by using a simple reflector, like a sheet of white cardboard. Position the reflector as close as possible to the subject, but just outside the camera frame, and angle it to reflect the main light source back into the shadows. You can back off the reflector to reduce the amount of fill light. Or you can fasten tinfoil to the reflector to make it more efficient and create more fill. Figure 7.13 illustrates the use of a simple reflector.

Lighting for still life subjects

When you work with continuous light, the subjects for your photographs do not always have to be living, breathing beings. You can make interesting photographs of various still life subjects.

Translucent objects, like glassware (Figure 7.14), as well as highly polished shiny objects are fascinating subjects that provide unlimited opportunities for experimenting with light. Lit from the front or from the sides, they are reflective. Lit diffusely from the rear, they become light sources themselves. If you fill a glass with water, it becomes a lens and can magnify other objects in your photograph.

SEVEN

FIGURE 7.14. Translucent still life subject

A. Backlit glassware shot against a white background. The lighting challenge is to define the edge of the glassware against the white background.

B. Setup used to produce the image at left. Black reflectors create a dark edge on the glass so it does not blend into the white background.

FIGURE 7.15. Flash connections using camera hot shoe and sychronization cord.

A. Flash synchronized via the camera's hot shoe connection.

B. Flash connected to the camera with a synchronization cord, in this case long enough to move the flash away from the camera and create shadows that model the subject as three-dimensional.

Highly textured objects are also interesting still life subjects. For example, terry cloth towels, baskets, or stitcheries are very sensitive to the angle of light—that is, whether front lit or side lit.

You can sharpen your compositional skills by careful choice of subject, background, camera angle, and angle of light. In photographs of still life subjects, simplicity will get you off to the best start.

USING FLASH UNITS

Once you have had some experience with continuous light sources, you will be better prepared to move into the momentary world of flash photography. Flash does add a few complications to your picture taking. You need to make certain the flash goes off when the camera's shutter is open. If you have a 35 mm camera with a focal plane shutter, you are limited in the shutter speeds you can use with flash. And because ordinary light meters cannot measure the brief burst of flash light, you need to determine the aperture setting in some other manner.

Flash synchronization

Synchronization involves coordinating the timing of the flash firing and the camera shutter opening. Mechanically, synchronization is achieved by connecting the flash and camera electrically. Some strobes are connected with a "sync" cord; others are designed to be mounted directly on the camera's "hot" (electrical) shoe (Figure 7.15). In either case, a set of electrical contacts in the camera acts as a switch to set off the flash at the proper moment.

In addition to the mechanical connection, many cameras have synchronization settings. Two settings have been used over the years to synchronize the shutter with various types of flash. Most common today is an "X" synchronization, which is used with electronic flash, or strobe, lights. Sometimes, the "X" synchronization setting will be marked with a small lightning bolt, rather than an "X." In "X" synchronization, the shutter is allowed to open completely, then the flash is fired.

This timing works well with electronic flash because it fires almost instantaneously, as shown in Figure 7.16A.

"M" synchronization, on the other hand, fires the flash a short time before the shutter opens. It is used with flash bulbs, and the early firing allows the bulb time to warm up and reach peak intensity while the shutter is open. The light from the bulb is thereby used more efficiently, as shown in Figure 7.16B.

Because flash bulbs have all but disappeared from common use, most newer cameras have only "X" synchronization or set the proper synchronization

FIGURE 7.16. Flash synchronization. Synchronization involves coordinating the firing of the flash with the opening of the shutter.

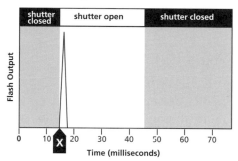

A. "X" synchronization used with a strobe: The flash is fired just as the shutter is fully open. This timing works well with strobe because it fires almost instantaneously.

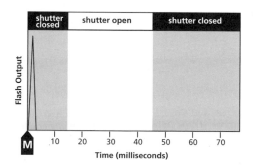

B. "M" sychronization used with a flash bulb: The flash is fired shortly before the shutter opens. That allows the bulb some lead time to reach reasonable light output. As a result, more of the output capacity of the bulb is actually used.

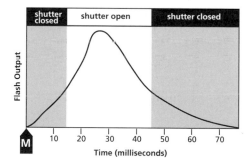

C. "M" synchronization used with a strobe: The strobe is fired and extinguishes before the shutter even opens. The strobe appears to be working normally, but it makes no contribution to exposure because the shutter is closed while it is firing.

FIGURE 7.17. Flash connections. "X" synchronization should be used with electronic flash. "M" synchronization is used with flash bulbs. Nearly all hot shoes are "X" synchronization, even if not so marked.

A. Separate sockets for "X" and "M" sychronization

B. Hot shoe marked for "X" sychronization

automatically. In older cameras you may need to select the synchronization mode. In some, you select the desired synchronization mode by flipping a switch. Others have separate plug-ins for the synchronization cord that connects camera and flash (Figure 7.17). Cameras that have just one unmarked connection are usually "X" synchronization. Virtually all "hot shoe" connections use "X" synchronization.

Since electronic flash is nearly instantaneous, if you mistakenly use the "M" synchronization setting with it, the flash will be set off (and peak and die down) before the shutter opens. The net result will be the same as if you had not used flash at all, as shown in Figure 7.16C.

Shutter speeds with flash

A focal plane shutter restricts the shutter speeds that can be used with electronic flash because of the way the shutter operates. Remember that a focal plane shutter works through the operation of two curtains that open and close to admit light to the film. At slow shutter speeds, the first curtain is released to open the shutter. A short time later, the second curtain releases and follows the first to close the shutter. The slower the shutter speed, the longer is the delay between the time the first curtain opens and the second closes.

Because the shutter curtains can only travel so fast, fast shutter speeds entail releasing the second curtain before the first has completely traveled across the film frame. It is as if exposure takes place through a moving slit. That's fine for continuous light sources since all portions of the film frame will receive equal amounts of light during exposure. But with an extremely brief light source, like strobe, the flash light will reach only the part of the frame that is behind the open slit at the moment the flash fires. Thus, shutter speeds have to be restricted to those that leave the entire frame uncovered at some instant. The maximum shutter speed that can be used with flash is usually marked in some distinctive color on the camera's shutter speed dial, as shown in Figure 7.18. It is generally 1/60, 1/125, or 1/250 of a second, depending on the design of the focal plane shutter in the camera. Slower speeds can also be used because the shutter curtains will not block the strobe light during exposure.

Flash exposure settings

Setting the shutter speed and aperture for a flash exposure has a few peculiarities. Because the light from the flash is so brief, you can't determine exposure settings in the usual way. Conventional light meters cannot read the brief, nearly instantaneous, burst of light.

In addition, the shutter speed no longer affects the light reaching the film during exposure, at least not the amount of light due to the flash itself. The electronic flash is so much faster than any shutter speed you can use that the shutter can't effectively "trim" the light coming from the flash. Slowing down the shutter speed will not increase the strobe exposure, but will allow more ambient light to register on the film. Speeding up the shutter may cut off part of the frame, but will not reduce the intensity of the strobe light that does reach the film.

Another complication in flash exposure is that, because a flash unit acts as a concentrated, point light source, the illumination on the subject rapidly gets weaker as the flash is moved further from it. That is, the distance from the flash to the subject directly affects the aperture setting. Exposure is thus determined by the camera aperture and the distance from the flash to the subject, not the aperture and shutter speed.

If you have a manual flash you will need to calculate the aperture setting using a **guide number.** The guide number is the product of the flash-to-subject distance (in feet) times the aperture number that gives correct exposure at that distance:

Guide Number = Flash-to-Subject Distance × f-stop

SEVEN

FIGURE 7.18. Shutter speed dial showing maximum flash speed. On this camera, the "x" beside the 1/60 second shutter speed signifies that this is the fastest speed that can be used with flash. On some cameras, the maximum flash speed may be marked in a distinctive color or by a small lightning bolt symbol.

The guide number is a constant for a certain speed of film used with a certain flash output. Most strobes come with a table of guide numbers for various film speeds, so you can find out the guide number without making tests. Often the guide number table is printed on the back of the flash unit or incorporated into a built-in calculator dial.

In practice, it works this way: With the flash unit attached to your camera, you focus on the subject. Then you look at the focusing scale on the lens to determine flash-to-subject distance. You now know two components of the equation, the guide number and the flash-to-subject distance, so you can calculate the third, the aperture setting:

f-stop = Guide Number ÷ Flash-to-Subject Distance

Usually it's even simpler than that. Most flash units have a calculator dial built in that does the computation for you. You dial in film speed and flash-to-subject distance; it tells you the aperture to use.

Because the distance from the flash to the subject directly affects the aperture setting, you must reset the aperture each time the flash-to-subject distance is changed. To simplify things, most current flash units are automatic. They have a built-in light sensor that monitors the amount of light reflected back from the subject and shuts the flash off as soon as adequate exposure is indicated. With this type of flash, you have only to set the aperture once, to an aperture setting determined by settings on the flash and the speed of the film you are using. After that, you can simply keep shooting. The sensor will automatically compensate for differences in the distance between the flash and the subject.

A somewhat more sophisticated version of the automatic flash is the dedicated flash. As its name suggests, this is a flash unit specifically dedicated to use with a certain type of camera. The flash communicates electronically with the metering system in the camera to determine proper exposure. The flash will usually set the shutter speed automatically, often makes use of the behind-the-lens meter built into the camera, and will display a ready light in the viewfinder.

Keep in mind, however, that the light sensor on either an automatic or dedicated flash is essentially a reflected light meter. Lighting situations that fool a reflected light meter will also fool the sensor. For instance, a highly reflective surface like a window or mirror will reflect light from the flash directly back at the sensor, causing underexposure of the subject. Placing a small subject against a large and very dark background will have an opposite effect because insufficient light will be reflected back at the sensor.

Strong ambient light may also influence exposure. **Ambient light** is the continuous light that already exists apart from the light from the flash. Ambient light might be strong window light or powerful artificial lighting sources. Unlike the light from the flash, you can control ambient light using the camera's shutter. In some situations, you may want to use a very slow shutter speed to allow ambient light to fill in the scene with existing light. That technique may allow moving objects or light sources to create a blur, because in effect you are creating a double exposure: a sharp image created by the flash superimposed over a somewhat blurry image created by the ambient light. You will need to decide whether that effect is desirable. If you use the fastest shutter speed allowable with flash for your camera, however, you will usually find that the flash is much more powerful than any other light source present and that you can ignore ambient light.

Flash techniques

It is probably obvious that the most convenient way to use a flash unit is simply to mount it on the camera. That makes it easy to determine the flash-to-subject distance by just focusing the camera. Unfortunately, this method rarely yields the most pleasing lighting. Because the flash and the camera see the subject from the same vantage point, you get extremely flat lighting. The shadows created are very thin and create a flat, two-dimensional image.

Because the flash unit is a concentrated light source, the light it creates is very contrasty. It tends to burn out the areas it does light and creates dense, thin shadows in others. Both problems can be overcome with a little extra work.

The problem of flat lighting can be solved by getting the flash unit off the camera, usually off to one side. Since the synchronization cord must remain attached to the camera, you may need an extension synchronization cord. They are available in lengths up to 25 feet. But a coiled cord, approximately 4 feet long, also works well. You can hold the flash in one hand and the camera in the other. Even more convenient is a light stand or clamp that allows you to mount the flash unit so you can concentrate on the subject and operating the camera. Once you get the flash unit off the camera, you will find your subjects take on a more three-dimensional appearance because you are now creating useful shadows.

▶▶ **Bounce flash.** The harsh quality created by strobe light can be overcome by diffusing the light (Figure 7.19). A common method is to bounce it off a reflective surface, like a wall or ceiling. Some flash units are made so that you can tilt the flash head in such a way that the light will bounce off a wall or ceiling and onto the subject. Other reflective devices also work well. A large sheet of white cardboard is inexpensive and allows more control than fixed walls and ceilings. Special studio **umbrellas** (Figure 7.20), although more expensive, are very convenient to use and deliver a diffuse, even light.

The only difficulty with bounce flash is determining the aperture setting. Best results are obtained using automatic flash units. Most are designed so that the flash head can be bounced off a ceiling or wall while the sensor remains pointed at the subject. If you don't have an automatic flash, experience is probably the best guide to bounce flash exposure.

SEVEN

FIGURE 7.19. Subject photographed with flash

Bounce lighting

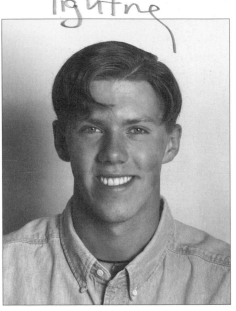

A. Direct flash is highly specular and creates strong, hard-edged shadows.

B. Bounce flash is diffuse and creates softer shadows, but retains a three-dimensional effect.

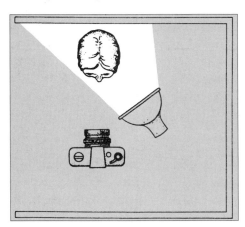

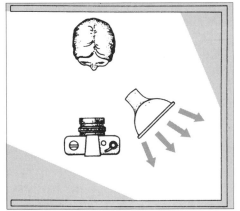

If your flash cannot be used for bounce flash, you can try the old handkerchief trick: Place a clean white handkerchief over the flash head to diffuse the light. You will need to make some exposure compensation. A common rule of thumb is that one layer of the "standard white handkerchief" requires one additional stop of exposure.

▸▸ **Multiple flash.** Another method for dealing with the harsh light from strobes involves the use of light from more than one flash unit (Figure 7.21). It's done in

FIGURE 7.20. Studio umbrella for bouncing or diffusing light. Lighting umbrellas like this should be used as close to the subject as possible for maximum diffusion.

essentially the same way as with continuous light sources. In a two-flash light setup, for instance, one flash acts as the main light and the other as the fill light.

One problem unique to multiple flash, however, is synchronizing them all to the camera. Adapters are available so that more than one cord may be directly connected to the camera. This is not a good practice, however, because it is possible to overload and damage the flash contacts inside the camera that way. Safer, and much more convenient, is the use of a so-called "slave" trigger. A slave is a light-sensing device that, when triggered by a strong flash of light, sets off the flash to which it is attached. In use, the master strobe is connected directly to the camera by a conventional sychronization cord. When the camera shutter is released, the master strobe is fired. The light from the master flash then triggers the slave strobes. It all happens almost instantaneously. The camera's flash contacts are protected and you don't have several sychronization cords underfoot.

A remaining problem is how to calculate the aperture setting. If all the strobe units used are automatic models, their sensors usually take care of the problem. The best alternative, although much more expensive, is the purchase of a reliable flash meter. It is especially designed to measure strobe light intensity.

▶▶ **Fill flash.** Another useful application of flash in multiple lighting is the use of a strobe as a fill light when the main light is the sun. The technique is called fill flash, because the strobe is used to fill in the harsh shadows created by the sun. Some people may think you're crazy to be using a flash in full sun, but other photographers will know you are crazy like a fox. Used well, fill flash gives much more pleasing results than direct sun alone (Figure 7.22), and you will probably save yourself much burning and dodging when it comes time to print the photographs.

FIGURE 7.21. Multiple flash. More than one flash can be used to control lighting contrast.

 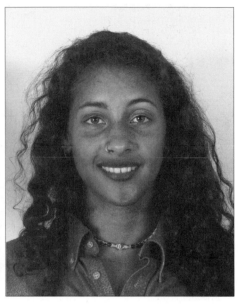

A. A single flash unit on the left creates a high
   lighting contrast.

B. Adding a second flash on the right fills in the
   shadow side and decreases the lighting ratio.

The fill flash technique requires calculations similar to those you make for conventional flash exposures. But for fill flash, you calculate how far away from the subject to set the flash in order to obtain the strength of the fill you want.

Begin by making a conventional meter reading of the sunlight exposure and set your aperture and shutter speed accordingly. Next, decide how much fill you want. If you want the strobe fill light to be half as intense as the sunlight (which will give a lighting ratio of 1:2), pretend for purposes of calculation that the aperture is a stop more open than it actually is. Then use the guide number to determine how far from the subject the flash would have to be for that aperture:

Flash-to-Subject Distance = Guide Number ÷ f-stop (opened by 1 stop)

This calculation will tell you how far back to place the flash to obtain fill light that is half as intense as the main sunlight. Keep in mind when working outdoors with a flash that if you are using a focal plane shutter, you are still restricted to slower shutter speeds.

One last warning about flash: Be careful to avoid unwanted reflections as you shoot. Because the flash is so brief, you probably won't see the glare of the flash in the window behind the subject. Or the harsh reflection off your subject's glasses. If you properly anticipate the problem, careful choice of camera and lighting angles will usually avoid it.

FIGURE 7.22. Fill flash. The flash is used to fill in shadow areas created by direct sun.

A. Without fill flash: The sun acts as a main light.   B. With fill flash: The flash acts as a fill light.

What Can Go Wrong

Because lighting is such a complex part of photography, many things can go wrong. No one becomes skilled at lighting without some trial and error. You should experiment with various types of light and various lighting setups to become familiar with it. Here are some common pitfalls.

Problem 1: Harsh shadows on the subject

Probable Cause:

You are using only a single light source coming from one direction.

Solution:

Fill the shadows with a second light source, use a fill reflector, or diffuse the main light by bouncing it.

Common
Sense

What Can Go Wrong

Problem 2: Reflections from the background

Probable Cause:

You are standing in the wrong position.

Solution:

Reposition camera or light so reflection is outside frame or so that subject obscures the reflection.

Problem 3: Shadows behind subject

Shadows on the wall behind the subject.

Probable Cause:

Subject is too close to the wall.

Solution:

Move the subject away from the background, and/or raise the light and angle it downward.

Problem 4: Overexposed foreground

Probable Cause:

You were standing too close to the subject or figured the wrong aperture setting.

Solution:

Use bounce flash to spread the light and even out exposure, or if that is not possible, plan to burn and dodge the print.

What Can Go Wrong

Problem 5 (A): Reflections from a subject's glasses

Probable Cause:

You are standing in the wrong position.

Solution (B):

Angle the subject slightly away from the camera, tilt the glasses down a bit, or use a polarizing filter.

A. Problem print

B. Solution print

Problem 6: Entire frame underexposed

Probable Cause:

Shutter speed set much too fast or synchronization incorrectly set; it is also possible that the flash may be too far away from the subject to light it properly or that the aperture is set incorrectly.

Solution:

Synchronization should be set to X for electronic flash. Recheck flash exposure settings.

What Can Go Wrong

Problem 7: Part of frame underexposed

Probable Cause:

Shutter speed is probably set too fast, cutting off part of the frame during flash exposure.

Solution:

Don't exceed the maximum flash speed for your camera's shutter.

REVIEW questions ?

1. What are the principal qualities of light?

2. What are the different kinds of light?

3. When is the use of natural light appropriate?

4. When does existing light work well?

5. What is artificial light and when is it necessary?

6. What is continuous light?

7. What is flash sychronization and how should it be set for electronic flash?

8. What shutter speeds can your camera use with strobe?

9. How can you determine exposure when using an electronic flash?

10. What techniques help avoid the two-dimensional, contrasty quality associated with the use of direct flash?

1. Take a series of portraits or still life studies using artificial lighting (either strobes or continuous lighting). Begin by using a single light source and varying the direction of the light: high, low, eye-level, front, side, back. Then compare specular light with diffuse light. You can diffuse the light by bouncing it off a large white surface (wall or ceiling) or by using a diffusion screen (a white piece of fabric will work well if you're careful not to let it get too hot). Finally adjust the lighting ratio using a second light source or a reflector. Shoot several frames with a lighting ratio of about 1:2 and several more at a lighting ratio of between 1:8 and 1:12. Develop the film and make a contact sheet. Study the frames and identify which lighting technique produced which result. Were some lighting strategies more successful with this subject than others? Would some strategies have worked better with other types of subject matter?

2. Take a series of urban landscapes at night. Look for interesting arrangements of artificial light. The nighttime landscape will photograph completely differently from its daytime counterpart. Surface detail will all but disappear, while shapes and planes will become more prominent. Reflections will act as light sources and shooting after a rain will often add interest. You'll need to use fast film or a tripod to get sharp results. Metering is relatively subjective because it will be difficult to find subject matter of a middle gray value. A good rule of thumb for street scenes is to shoot at an aperture of f/4 and a shutter speed of 1/60 for an ISO 400 film. And don't forget to bracket, usually at least two stops above and below your predicted exposure. Don't be surprised if your negatives look unusual after you've developed them. Night light is often extremely contrasty and very uneven, so your negatives will seem strange. Wait until you have a contact sheet to judge your results.

SEVEN

CHAPTER 8

lenses,
filters,
and accessories

Monolith, the Face of Half Dome, Yosemite National Park, 1927, **by Ansel Adams**

lenses, filters, and accessories

Monolith, the Face of Half Dome, Yosemite National Park, 1927, by Ansel Adams

(Photograph by Ansel Adams. ©2000 by the Trustees of The Ansel Adams Publishing Rights Trust. All Rights Reserved)

Ansel Adams first read about Yosemite National Park in April 1916 while he recuperated from a childhood illness. He noted in his autobiography that he became "hopelessly enthralled" with descriptions of the park and begged his mother and father to take him there. The boy and his parents traveled there the next year and the 14-year-old saw for the first time a region that would form the center of his later career as the foremost nature photographer in the country. Adams got his first camera on that trip too—a Kodak Box Brownie. He would return to the park again and again for inspiration and subject matter up until his death in 1984.

In taking "Monolith," Adams wrote that he needed to use a red filter to give him in the photo the effect he felt emotionally: "I had only one plate left. I attached my other filter, a Wratten #29 (F), increased the exposure by the sixteen times factor required, and released the shutter. I felt I had accomplished something, but did not realize its significance until I developed the plate that evening. I had achieved my first true visualization."

f you've been to a well-stocked photo shop, you know that you could buy accessories for your camera for the rest of your life and still not have purchased everything available. There are lots of things to spend your money on when you are a photographer. The trick is to spend it on things that are useful and help you improve your photographs.

First on most photographers' lists of useful equipment would be a selection of lenses. Different lenses expand your photographic capabilities by allowing your camera to envision the world in new ways. Other items that will help you improve your photography include filters to control tonalities, tripods to improve sharpness, viewfinders to aid composition and focusing, or motor drives to allow more rapid shooting. You will also want to consider things to protect your equipment and help you carry it with you: camera cases, bags, and straps.

TYPES OF LENSES

Lenses gather the rays of light coming from the scene to be photographed and project them as reversed images onto the film at the back of the camera (Figure 8.1). It sounds rather simple, yet lenses are probably the most powerful part of a camera system. To many photographers, a camera body is just something to which you attach your lenses. Lenses are what give you creative control over the look of your photograph.

Many cameras use interchangeable lenses. The difference in lenses comes from their **focal length**—that is, the distance between the optical center of the lens and the point where it focuses (plane of focus). Focal length determines the size of the image formed by the lens, called **magnification**, and how much of the scene is included in the image, called the **angle of view** (Figure 8.2). In practice, focal length also controls the perspective of the image—that is, the relationship between the sizes of foreground and background subjects.

Photographers also speak of the "speed" of a lens. It is a measure of how much light it transmits to the film. A fast lens has a larger maximum aperture and lets

EIGHT

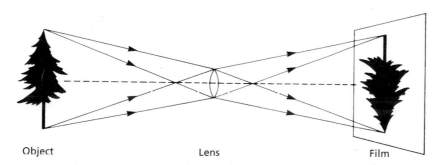

Object   Lens   Film

FIGURE 8.1. Diagram of a lens transmitting reflected light. The lens projects an inverted image of the subject onto the surface of the film. The focal length of the lens determines how large the film image will be.

FIGURE 8.2. Focal length and angle of view. The longer the focal length of a lens, the narrower its angle of view. Lenses with shorter focal lengths are generally referred to as wide angle lenses.

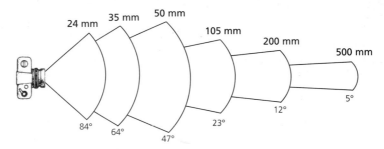

through more light. A slower lens has a smaller aperture and lets through less light. Faster lenses are larger in diameter and generally more expensive than slower lenses of the same focal length.

Depending on their focal lengths, lenses are generally classified as normal, telephoto, or wide angle. In addition, there are special-purpose lenses; use of these is dictated by features other than focal length.

▸▸ **Normal lenses** have a focal length that is the same as (or very close to) the diagonal measurement of the film size with which they are used. For 35 mm film, the normal focal length is 50 mm. For 2 1/4" x 2 1/4" film, it is between 75 and 85 mm. For 4" x 5" film, it is 135 to 165 mm. The normal lens is the center point in the spectrum of focal lengths. It "sees" the subject in roughly the same way a person does when looking straight ahead (Figure 8.3B). A normal lens is the one most often purchased with a camera and it is a useful general-purpose lens.

▸▸ **Wide angle lenses** have focal lengths shorter than a normal lens. Common sizes in 35 mm photography include the 35 mm, 28 mm, 24 mm, and 20 mm. Lenses shorter than 20 mm are commonly called "fish-eyes" because they usually produce a distorted circular image. Wide angles, as the name suggests, capture a wider angle of view than a normal lens (Figure 8.3A). They have less magnification than a normal lens and tend to push background further away from foreground. As a result, they appear to add depth to the image.

Wide angle lenses are useful for photographing scenery where a panoramic view is desired. They are also frequently used in tight quarters where no other lens offers a sufficient angle of view. Because they distort the image, the shorter "fish eyes" are sometimes used to create interesting graphic effects in the photograph. Many photographers prefer wide angles for candids of people because they force the photographer to work close to the subject, producing a look of immediacy and intimacy that often adds power to the picture.

▸▸ **Telephoto lenses** have focal lengths longer than the normal lens. Common telephoto focal lengths in 35 mm photography include 85 mm, 105 mm, 135 mm,

FIGURE 8.3. Photographs taken from the same vantage point with different lenses. Because the position of the camera does not change, the perspective (relative size of foreground and background objects) remains constant. The longer the focal length of the lens, however, the more the subject is magnified.

A. Taken with wide angle lens (20 mm)

— wide but far away

B. Taken with normal lens (55 mm)

EIGHT

C. Taken with telephoto lens (105 mm)

D. Taken with telephoto lens (180 mm)

Close but very narrow

200 mm, 300 mm, 400 mm, 500 mm, 600 mm, 1,000 mm, and 1,200 mm. The telephoto gives a narrow angle of view and magnifies the subject by bringing it closer to the camera (Figures 8.3C and D). The longer the focal length, the narrower the view and the greater the magnification. Telephotos also exhibit a perspective effect often referred to as "telephoto compression." A telephoto tends to reduce differences in size between foreground and background objects, thus seemingly forcing foreground and background into one plane, as though they were compressed.

Telephoto lenses are most frequently used when it is impossible to get close to the subject. Common applications include wildlife photography, sports photography, theater photography, or candid shots of people where the photographer wishes to remain unnoticed. They are also commonly used in portraiture, where they maintain a pleasing perspective. The 105 mm, for instance, is often used for head-and-shoulders portraits.

Perspective can be controlled by using different lenses. Perspective is the relative size of foreground versus background objects. If you were to shoot the same picture using a variety of focal length lenses and move the camera each time to keep the foreground subject the same size, you would find that background objects would change size in the photograph (Figure 8.4). Wide angle lenses emphasize the foreground and the distance between foreground and background. Telephoto lenses emphasize the background and compress the distance between foreground and background.

▸▸ **Zoom lenses** do not have a fixed focal length. The focal length of the lens can instead be adjusted over a range of focal lengths. A commonly found model allows adjustment from 35 mm to 135 mm. In effect, the photographer owns a 35 mm lens, a 135 mm lens, and all lenses between. Many zoom lenses also offer a macro mode, which allows close-up photography. While zoom lenses offer a great deal of flexibility in a single package, they are not the answer to everyone's need for lenses. Zoom lenses tend to be bulkier than fixed focal length lenses. They are not quite as sharp unless a very high quality model is used. And they are usually slower than an equivalent fixed lens.

▸▸ **Autofocus lenses** can be electronically focused by circuitry built into the camera body. In use, you superimpose a tiny viewfinder autofocus spot over the subject, press a button on the camera, and the lens automatically rotates to the sharpest point of focus. Like most things automatic, autofocus lenses do have limitations. If your subject is standing behind a wire fence that the autofocus mechanism can confuse for the subject, for instance, it may focus on the fence rather than your subject. In addition, the autofocusing mechanism may not operate well with low-contrast subjects or strongly backlit subjects. However, most autofocus cameras allow you to switch to manual focus mode, so these are usually simple problems to correct.

FIGURE 8.4. Using different lenses to control perspective. In this series, the camera is moved back as the focal length is increased so that the person with the umbrella in the foreground remains the same size. Note how the background sculpture increases in relative size as the focal length increases, creating the phenomenon known as "telephoto compression."

A. Taken with wide angle lens (20 mm)

B. Taken with normal lens (55 mm)

EIGHT

C. Taken with telephoto lens (105 mm)

D. Taken with telephoto lens (180 mm)

▸▸ **Special-purpose lenses** are also available. Macro lenses, for example, are designed for close-up work. A true macro lens allows you to focus close enough to make a negative image that is the same size as the subject itself. Thus, you can take a picture of a paper clip and the negative image will be as large as the paper clip itself. Most macro lenses are 50 mm or 100 mm focal lengths and can be used as any lens of the same focal length. They are not as fast as a non-macro lens of equivalent focal length, however.

Other special-purpose lenses have built-in flash units for technical and scientific use. Some can shift up and down or from side to side to allow more control in architectural photography. Others have special optical corrections for use in copying flat subjects like paintings or printed pages.

CHOICE OF A LENS

Buying lenses is like buying cameras: Your choice depends on your needs and the amount of money you have to spend. As with cameras, it is a good idea to start simply and add lenses as your needs require them.

Talk to fellow students, your instructor, and advanced photographers for advice on what lens or lenses to buy initially. Although most people begin with a normal lens, it is often not the ideal choice. You may want to begin with a zoom lens that offers a variety of focal lengths. Or, if your budget allows buying more than one lens, you may want to get both a telephoto and a wide angle to begin with.

Frequently, the speed of the lens (its maximum aperture) is as important a consideration as its focal length. Many focal lengths are available in two or more maximum apertures. If you often shoot in low-light levels, or need a brighter viewfinder to make focusing easier, then a faster lens is probably your best choice.

GUIDE TO FILTERS

A **filter** is nothing more than a piece of optical glass, plastic, or gelatin (often colored) that attaches to the camera's lens and is used to modify the light before it reaches and exposes the film.

When you use a filter on your camera, you increase your ability to control the final image. For example, you can make clouds in the sky more distinct. Or you can eliminate distracting reflections on the surface of glass or water. Or you can create a very limited depth of field even on bright, sunny days when you would ordinarily have to use a small aperture (and be content with its large depth of field). Different filters accomplish different tasks.

Types of filters

▸▸ **Contrast filters** control how colors are rendered in black and white. Will a red apple photograph as a light or a dark gray? The film you are using will render it one way. Contrast filters allow you to control the shade of gray more directly.

Contrast filters are themselves colored red, yellow, orange, green, or blue, for instance. They follow a simple rule: A colored filter tends to transmit light of its own color and block other colors. Thus, a red filter allows red light to pass through it more readily than other colors. (That's why it looks red.)

If you use a red filter to take a picture of a bright red apple sitting next to a green artichoke, the red apple will be exposed more than usual because the red light reflected from it passes easily through the red filter to the film (Figure 8.5). In the final print, the red apple will be lighter than normal. On the other hand, the green light reflected from the artichoke will have more difficulty passing through the red filter and the artichoke will be exposed less than normal. When using a filter, the photographer usually compensates for this underexposure, so the artichoke is rendered nearly normally. Thus, we can modify the rule to read: A colored filter lightens objects of its own color and darkens others.

Although contrast filters potentially offer great flexibility in controlling tonal rendition in the final black-and-white photograph, they tend to have rather standard uses. A common application is to make clouds stand out against a blue sky. If you shoot a picture that includes fluffy white clouds against a blue sky and don't use a filter, you're likely to find that the clouds and sky simply wash together into a white haze (Figure 8.6A). A medium yellow filter can be used to create contrast between sky and clouds; it darkens the blue sky so the white clouds stand out better against it (Figure 8.6B). An orange filter serves much the same purpose, but darkens the sky slightly more. The most dramatic of the so-called cloud filters is a deep red, which can darken the sky to an almost black tone (Figure 8.6C).

An orange filter is also often used in shooting around bodies of water. If you want the whitecaps at the beach to stand out in the final photograph, the orange filter is your answer.

FIGURE 8.5. Using a contrast filter. Compared to the photograph taken with no filter, the photograph shot with a red filter shows that the red filter makes the red apple appear lighter. Filters lighten objects of their own color and darken others. In this case, exposure compensation rendered the artichoke nearly the same value.

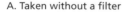

A. Taken without a filter   B. A red filter makes the red apple appear lighter.

FIGURE 8.6. Using cloud filters. A yellow filter creates cloud contrast by darkening the blue sky compared to a photograph shot with no filter. A red filter gives even more dramatic clouds by darkening the blue sky even more. A blue filter "erases" clouds by decreasing contrast between cloud and sky.

A. Taken without a filter

B. Taken with a yellow filter

C. Taken with a red filter

D. Taken with a blue filter

A blue filter is a cloud filter in reverse. It decreases the contrast between sky and clouds by lightening the tone of the sky (Figure 8.6D). It finds its primary use as a way to accentuate haze or fog in the photograph.

⏵ **Ultraviolet and skylight filters** are carefully designed for very specialized purposes. The ultraviolet filter, called a "UV" or "haze filter," cuts out unwanted ultraviolet light, and the skylight filter can be used in color photography to "warm" bluish shadows. Yet most photographers buy the filters for another, distinctly different reason: lens protection. (See the Note opposite.)

The UV filter cuts out haze by eliminating ultraviolet light from the light exposing the film. The UV filter can be quite useful when shooting distant landscapes or doing aerial photography. It is also helpful when shooting at high altitudes, where there is a lot of ultraviolet light. Ultraviolet light exposes film, but focuses at a slightly different distance than visible light. Without a filter, then, the result is a secondary, out-of-focus "ghost" image on the film. The UV filter absorbs the ultraviolet light, eliminating the secondary image, so that only the sharp visible light image is recorded.

The skylight filter is really intended for use in color photography. Color photographs taken in the shade typically pick up a bluish cast from light reflected from the sky (skylight). Bluish tinted people aren't very appealing, so the skylight filter is used to restore a warmer color. For the black-and-white photographer, the filter is useful only for lens protection.

▸▸ **Polarizing filters** absorb glare and reflections by removing polarized light. As light is reflected off a shiny surface, it is polarized in the process. Without going into great detail, that means the reflected light vibrates only in one direction. The polarizing filter allows you to select the vibrational direction of light that passes through the filter to expose the film. By adjusting the filter, you can eliminate reflected light. A polarizing filter does not affect the coloration of the light passing through it, however. It is color neutral. As a result, it can be used with color films without distorting the color.

You might use a polarizing filter to photograph objects in a display case that creates distracting reflections (Figure 8.7). Polarizing filters are constructed so that, even after the filter is mounted on the lens, the filter can be rotated to orient the polarizing material. In practice, you rotate the filter to "dial out" reflections on the case and create a clearer view of the objects inside.

A polarizing filter can also be used to reduce glare from water or polished, non-metallic surfaces. The polarizer also makes an effective cloud filter. (It is the only cloud filter that can be used with color film.) If you want the dramatic sky

EIGHT

A Note on

Protecting Your Lens

The UV and skylight filters are often used for an important, but less sophisticated, purpose than originally intended. Both filters look like clear optical glass in a filter mount. Neither filter costs you anything in exposure: They don't cut out enough light to make any appreciable difference in film exposure. But, if mounted on the lens and left there, they will protect it against dust, water, sand, and scratches. It is much cheaper to buy and replace a damaged filter than the front element of your lens. Most photographers keep one of the two filters mounted on the front of each lens they own, removing it only to mount another filter in its place.

FIGURE 8.7. Using a polarizing filter. The filter is rotated to orient the polarizing material so that it absorbs the light reflections on the surface of the display case, giving a clearer view of the camera inside.

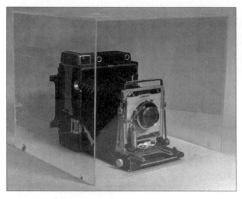 

A. Taken without a filter   B. Taken with a polarizing filter

usually found only in Dracula movies, you can use a deep red and a polarizing filter at the same time.

A polarizer takes some trouble to use. The direction of polarization depends on the angle between your camera, the subject, and the light source. So you must readjust the polarizer every time your camera angle changes. The amount of the light loss due to the filter depends on its manufacture, and you should consult the manufacturer's recommendations for exposure adjustments.

▸▸ **Neutral density filters** are sunglasses for your camera. They cut down on the brightness of a scene, but they are "neutral" in that they don't alter color rendition. They are most useful when you want a very limited depth of field or want subject blur, but have too much light to use an open aperture or to slow the shutter speed. By cutting down the amount of light reaching the lens, a neutral density filter allows you to use the settings you wish. The filters are available in various densities. Some cut exposure by a fraction of a stop, others by several stops.

▸▸ **Correction filters** compensate for differences between the type of light a film is designed for and the type of light actually used. Most often, they are used with color films. A color film intended to be shot in daylight produces a yellow-orange cast if shot indoors under tungsten light. A bluish filter is available to correct this problem. Color film shot under fluorescent light produces a greenish cast, but another filter is available to correct that problem. In fact, dozens of correction filters are available to match certain color films to certain light sources.

Correction filters are rarely used in black-and-white photography, even though, strictly speaking, they probably should be. Most black-and-white film is designed to be shot outdoors. If shot under tungsten light, which has relatively more red light, red objects will be somewhat lighter than they should be and green objects, somewhat darker. It is possible to correct this problem with a light green filter. But in practice, most photographers just ignore the difference. In addition to the problem of packing another filter around, the filter would cost exposure. And if you are working with tungsten light, you probably have precious little light to begin with, and using a filter would just aggravate the problem.

Using filters

Since filters seem so useful, why not use them all the time? One very good reason is that they cost you light. They cut down the light reaching the film, often by two stops or more. This effective loss of light can force you to use slower shutter speeds than desirable or limit depth of field when you want more sharpness. The UV and skylight filters do not reduce exposure, but when using nearly any other filter, you need to make some exposure compensation.

If your camera has a built-in, behind-the-lens meter, needed exposure compensation is taken care of automatically for many filters. But, because the sensors in light meters are not equally sensitive to all colors, this method is not always as accurate as it is convenient. For the most accurate exposure, remove the filter, make a meter reading, and adjust the exposure (speed and/or aperture)

EIGHT

TABLE 8.1. Filters for black-and-white photography

Color	Wratten number	In daylight		In tungsten light	
		Filter factor	f-stop increase	Filter factor	f-stop increase
Medium yellow	8	2	1	1.5	$^2/_3$
Results: Normal-looking clouds against sky; slightly lighter skin tones; darker green foliage					
Yellow-green	11	4	2	3	$1^2/_3$
Results: Natural-looking skin tones and sky in outdoor portraits					
Orange	15	3	$1^2/_3$	2	1
Results: Whiter clouds against darker sky; exaggerated contrast with snow or sand; reduced atmospheric haze; darker water					
Medium red	25	8	3	4	2
Results: Very white clouds against dark sky; reduced haze; enhanced contrast with snow or sand; often used with infrared film					
Deep blue	47	8	3	16	4
Results: Increased haze in scenics; darkened skin tones					
Polarizing	—	2.5	$1^1/_3$	2.5	$1^1/_3$
Results: Reflections eliminated; increased cloud contrast					

Note: If your camera has a built-in, behind-the-lens meter, you will not need to make any special exposure compensation for filters.

according to a "filter factor" recommended by the filter manufacturer. After setting the corrected exposure, replace the filter to take the pictures.

Table 8.1 lists some filters commonly used in black-and-white photography. In the table, the various colors of filters are identified by their **Wratten number—** Kodak's system for numbering filters, used by many filter manufacturers.

The filter factor indicated for each filter is used to calculate the exposure increase needed to compensate for the loss of light reaching the film when you have the filter on your camera lens. The filter factor, which is often engraved on the filter mounting rim, indicates the reduction in the amount of light that will be transmitted through the filter and lens to the film. A filter factor of 2 means that half the light is transmitted; 3 means that a third of the light is transmitted; 4 means that a fourth of the light is transmitted; and so forth.

For example, if you decide to use a medium yellow (Wratten #8) filter with a filter factor of 2, you would need to double your exposure to compensate for the loss of half the light. You double the exposure by opening up the aperture one step or by cutting your speed in half. For example, let's say your light meter indicates the correct exposure under daylight conditions is 1/125th of a second at f/16. Your new camera settings would be either 1/125 at f/11 (if you change the aperture) or 1/60 at f/16 (if you change the speed).

It is important to keep in mind that each time you open up the aperture one stop, you double the exposure. Thus, when you use a filter with a factor of 4 (1/4 of the light is transmitted), you need to open the aperture two stops. The first time you open up, you double the light from 1/4 to 1/2; the second time you open up, you double again from 1/2 to 1. You can do the same thing with shutter speed. To compensate for 1/4 the amount of light, you halve the speed twice.

You can also compensate for filters by adjusting both the aperture and the speed. For example, with a yellow-green (Wratten #11) filter with a filter factor of 4, you could open up the aperture one stop and halve the shutter speed and achieve the same results as changing either the aperture or the speed twice. Accordingly, if your light meter indicates 1/125 at f/16, the following would all give the same results when you have a filter factor of 4:

1/125 at f/8 (aperture adjusted two stops),
1/30 at f/16 (speed adjusted two times),
1/60 at f/11 (speed and aperture each adjusted once).

Calculating the exposure for some filters requires fractional changes in the aperture. For example, a filter factor of 3 requires 1 2/3 increase in the f-stop. On most cameras, you can make between-stop settings. But if your camera does not allow you to make settings between f-stops, you can come as close as possible and then bracket the exposures to allow for variances.

One additional note: If you use two filters at one time, the new filter factor becomes a multiple of the two filter factors. For example, if the two filter factors are 2 and 3, the new filter factor becomes 6. In certain filter combinations, you could come up with exceedingly long exposures.

Another problem with filters is that not all the tonal modifications made by the filter are helpful. For instance, a red filter plays havoc with Caucasian skin. The filter eliminates the red pigmentation in healthy skin, making people appear as sickly, white ghosts. A yellow-green filter is a better choice if you need a cloud filter that works well with white skin. Table 8.1 also summarizes the effects of the commonly used filters in black-and-white photography.

BUYING AND USING OTHER ACCESSORIES

In addition to filters, there are a number of other accessories that you can buy to augment your camera and lenses. While not absolutely necessary, these items will help you as you become more skilled and able to take on more demanding photographic assignments.

Tripods

A **tripod** is a three-legged support for your camera that can be folded and carried along for use when your camera must be perfectly steady. When using a tripod, you extend the legs down and out and attach the camera to the top where it can be aimed as needed. If necessary, you can hang your camera bag or some other weight from the top of the tripod to make it steadier.

If you are using a slow shutter speed, the camera must be steady during the entire exposure time if you want sharp results. It is difficult or impossible to hand-hold the camera when your shutter speed is much below 1/60th of a second; even your heartbeat is enough to shake the camera. If you are using a long focal length lens, even moderate shutter speeds may be too slow because camera vibration is magnified right along with the image. At other times, you may have to hold lights and not be able to hold your camera. The tripod helps solve all of these problems.

Tripods are available in various styles (Figure 8.8). You should pick one that best fits your needs: large and durable for studio use or small and compact for field use. You should test several before buying one. The tripod should be steady when you press down on the top. It should be tall enough for your purposes and lightweight enough if you plan to carry it along on assignment.

If Murphy had made laws about photography, surely the first would have been that when a tripod is needed most, it is home in the closet. If you have only an occasional, unpredictable need for a camera support, there are alternatives to full-size tripods. One is a very small, so-called **tabletop tripod.** They are steady, yet small enough to fit in your camera bag. Another alternative is a **clamp camera support**. You screw the clamp into the tripod socket of the camera, then attach the clamp to something steady, and you're in business.

EIGHT

FIGURE 8.8. Tripod alternatives. Full size tripods are sturdy enough to hold even large cameras steady, but they can be heavy and cumbersome. The table top tripod and the tripod clamp are not as sturdy as a full size tripod, but can be carried in a camera bag so they are available when needed. The monopod is useful if you need to move camera position quickly.

A. Conventional tripods are sturdy and can support large cameras very steadily.

B. Tabletop tripods are easily stored in a camera bag for use whenever needed.

C. Clamp camera supports let you attach your camera to a sturdy base, in this case a car.

D. Monopods can be used to support long telephoto lenses and allow quick changes in location.

Some photographers use a **monopod,** a one-legged stand. Although not freestanding, they are much steadier than hand-holding the camera and allow you to move the camera quickly from one place to another. An alternative to the monopod is a five- or six-foot length of lightweight chain with a tripod socket at one end attached to the camera. You step on one end of the chain, pull the camera up to bring the chain taut, and you have a reverse monopod.

Perhaps the least elegant, but still very serviceable, alternative is a bean bag. You simply place the bean bag on something steady and nestle the camera down into it. Your camera will be as steady as the surface supporting the bean bag.

The advantage to any of the alternatives to a full-size tripod is their portability. You are thus more likely to have them with you when needed.

Cable releases and motor drives

Cable releases are a good idea if you use a tripod or other camera support. A cable release is a flexible cable with a plunger at one end and a socket at the other that attaches to the shutter release of the camera. Pressing the plunger allows you to trip the shutter without jarring the camera (Figure 8.9). Some cable releases have a locking mechanism so you can keep the shutter release depressed for long exposures using the "B" shutter speed. This technique can be useful in certain types of flash photography.

Motor drives automatically advance the film and cock the shutter after each exposure is made. Motor drives and their slightly less expensive cousin, the **autowinder,** allow photographers to expose up to five frames per second (about two frames per second with the autowinder). These accessories enable you to concentrate on the subject, say a fast-moving sports event or an action-filled news scene, without having to advance the film manually after each exposure.

Although it can be a useful tool, the motor drive can be overkill for many photographers. Motor drives are expensive. They are heavy. They are noisy. Probably more than half the motor drives sold are purchased, not because they are really needed, but because they seem to confer a bit of status on the photographer. If you have money to spend and don't really need a motor drive, you would do better to buy another lens. It will do much more for your photography than a motor drive you don't really need.

EIGHT

FIGURE 8.9. Using a cable release to trip the shutter. The cable is flexible so movement in your hand does not shake the camera when using a slow shutter speed.

FIGURE 8.10. **Camera bags.** Soft bags are more flexible and often store more equipment. The hard bags offer better protection and can usually be locked for security when travelling.

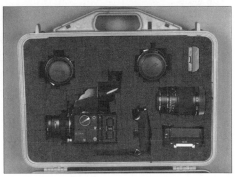

A. Soft camera bag

B. Hard camera bag

Viewfinder attachments

Viewfinder attachments augment the regular viewfinder of a camera when you are using it on a tripod or in an awkward position. Many cameras accept interchangeable viewfinders to give a better look at scenes from waist-level, from above, from awkward angles, or to give a magnified view.

You can often buy interchangeable viewing screens. Some camera manufacturers offer dozens of different screens: various split-image rangefinders, various microprism grid patterns, just plain ground glass for unobstructed viewing, any of the above ruled with reference lines to make it easier to line things up in architectural photography or copy work. It is usually only the more expensive camera models, however, that can accept the interchangeable screens.

Many cameras will, however, accept eyepiece correction lenses. If you wear glasses and find them bothersome when shooting, one of these lenses may well make it possible for you to photograph without your glasses. Another handy addition for eyeglass wearers, and others as well, is an eye cup. It is a small rubber cup that fits over the eyepiece of the viewfinder, shading it and making it easier to study the scene in front of you.

Camera cases, bags, and straps

Camera cases, bags, and straps protect your camera from harm and allow you to carry it around. Neither task is trivial. Your camera is a costly instrument and may be the source of your income so you need to protect it.

Camera cases are one way of protecting your camera, especially the lens, when you use it or when you place it in your car or on a shelf. Cases come in soft or hard varieties with a front, or lens hood, that swings down, out of the way when you are shooting. A hard case is particularly useful if you carry your camera with you on a bicycle. If you fall or accidentally drop the camera, the hard case may save you expensive repairs.

Cases may not cover cameras with large lenses, and the lens hoods sometimes get in the way when you are photographing. For these reasons, many photographers do not buy cases. They carry and protect their cameras in special bags instead.

Camera bags allow you to carry several cameras, lenses, other attachments, and film. What you can carry is limited only by the size of the bag. A soft bag usually holds more equipment for its size and allows the photographer to stuff into it whatever might be needed for a particular assignment (Figure 8.10A). The soft bag is a favorite of photojournalists, who need its flexibility and portability. A hard camera bag offers more protection than a soft case (Figure 8.10B). They are usually lined with foam which can be custom cut to hold lenses, camera bodies, and other accessories. They can often be locked and are a favorite of photographers who travel frequently and need the extra protection and security.

One problem with camera cases is that they usually look like camera cases. They mark you as a photographer and the equipment you carry as expensive. Your equipment becomes a visible target for thieves. One very accomplished professional photographer always carries his equipment in grocery bags for that reason. That may not be the best solution, but you do need to be cautious. The best security seems to be to keep equipment out of sight when not being used. If you leave equipment in a car, lock it in the trunk, out of sight. If they don't know it's there, they probably won't steal it.

A Note on

"Software"

We've looked now at several categories of camera hardware. All of it can be useful, even essential at times. But the topic of equipment needs perspective. No amount of hardware will make you a good photographer.

It's not what's in your camera bag that really counts, but what's in your mind. People who work with computers have a word for it—"software," which boils down to ideas, thoughts, and perceptions. These are the things that make the difference between an adequate photographer and a truly good one. Outstanding photographers both think and feel photography.

Of course you can't buy this kind of software off the shelf. But you can expose yourself to it. Look at photographic magazines. Look at the work of good photographers. Talk to other photographers—about photographs, not equipment. Think. Shoot. Analyze. Reshoot.

Whether you use a camera case or keep your equipment in a bag, you will need a **camera strap** to hold the camera around your neck. Nearly all cameras come with one, but they are generally thin and begin to saw through your neck if you wear them long. A broader strap is an inexpensive accessory that may make shooting for long periods much more comfortable. They are especially useful if you carry several cameras, or a particularly heavy camera, say one with a large lens or a motor drive attached.

Camera straps may be responsible for more damage and camera repair than any other single item. In some instances, the metal "O" ring that attaches the strap to the camera may chafe against the camera and damage its finish. Many straps come with a plastic or leather shield to protect the camera. In more serious cases, the "O" ring itself wears through, the strap breaks loose, and the camera falls free. Another of Murphy's photographic laws says that this is most likely to happen when you are standing on concrete pavement where your camera will sustain maximum damage when it hits. You should check your camera strap, the "O" ring, and the mounting lug in the camera periodically to make certain they are secure and in good shape.

You must also be careful of camera straps if you store your camera with other equipment on a shelf. The strap can get tangled with other items, and you could accidentally pull the camera off the shelf and drop it to the floor.

REVIEW questions ?

1. What are the main types of camera lenses?

2. How does the focal length of a lens affect how perspective is rendered in a photograph?

3. What are the most important considerations in choosing a lens?

4. What does a filter do and why is that useful in photography?

5. What are the principal types of filters?

6. What filters can be used in photographing clouds in the sky?

7. What two filters can be used for mechanical lens protection?

8. What is a tripod and when should it be used?

9. What is a cable release and when should it be used?

10. What is a motor drive and how does it aid the photographer?

try it YOURSELF

The discussion on filters in this chapter deliberately omitted special effects filters. Too often, photographers rely on gimmicks to compensate for an otherwise shallow image. However, if you want to try out a simple special effect, see what you can do with some petroleum jelly and a clear filter (like a skylight or UV filter). Smear a thin coat on the filter to get a diffused, soft-focus effect. A thicker coat will give more diffusion. You can leave a clear area in the center of the filter for soft edges, or cover the filter evenly for even diffusion. You can also streak the jelly on the filter to achieve effects that resemble blurred motion. The creative possibilities are virtually endless. So is the trouble you will have cleaning the jelly off the filter—be sure to use a spare filter.

CHAPTER 9

color photography

Alfried Krupp, by Arnold Newman, 1963

color photography

Alfried Krupp, by Arnold Newman, 1963

(© Arnold Newman/Liaison Agency)

Arnold Newman is an undisputed master of the photographic portrait. Most of his portraits—of statesmen, artists, musicians, scientists—are celebrations of the human spirit and imagination. His image of Alfried Krupp, however, is testimony that there is human evil as well.

In the early 1960s, Newman was asked by *Look* magazine to photograph Krupp, head of one of the largest industrial corporations in Germany. At first, Newman refused, complaining that he did not want to glorify a man who had been a personal ally to Adolf Hitler and a convicted war criminal. The *Look* editors replied that they did not want him to glorify Krupp at all. So Newman set off for Germany, obtaining the reluctant cooperation of Krupp. Unbeknownst to Krupp, Newman used his mastery of photographic technique to portray Krupp as the devil incarnate. He used harsh side light to define Krupp's head as a skull with grotesque features. The symmetrical composition creates a cavernous stage for a character seemingly out of Goethe's *Faust*. And Newman knew the fluorescent lights in the factory background, left uncorrected, would create a dull green cast against which Krupp's head would seem to be lit by fire. The result is one of Newman's most popular portraits and the photograph by which we have come to remember the inglorious Krupp.

Color photography is technically more complex than black-and-white for a number of reasons. Despite the additional technical complexity, however, color photography is in some ways actually easier than black-and-white.

You've probably discovered by now that black-and-white photography requires you to adapt your normal way of seeing things. What you originally see as hues of color will be translated into shades of gray on black-and-white film. A deep red rose will be rendered as a dark gray. The subtle yellow of an egg yolk will become a light gray. Black-and-white photography is more abstract than color and requires you to develop a sense of how colors will translate to gray values on film. Color photography is more realistic; what you see is what you get (more or less, as we shall see).

SHOOTING COLOR

Color balance

Although color photography does not require you to make the same mental adjustment that you must make with black-and-white photography, your perception of color is still not as literal as that of color film. The human brain automatically makes adjustments in color perception for differences in the color of light sources. Light from a household tungsten light bulb is yellow-orange compared to daylight, but our color perception makes an automatic correction for the difference. Color film does not make the same adjustment (Figure 9.1). Color film designed to be shot outdoors in daylight will exhibit a yellow-orange cast if used instead indoors with tungsten lights and will be greenish when used with fluorescent light. While we see a flesh tone as normal in all three types of

FIGURE 9.1. Color balance. Daylight film used with strobe gives correct color balance. But daylight film shot with tungsten or fluorescent light has a pronounced color cast.

A. Strobe   B. Tungsten   C. Fluorescent

Conventional light bulb

light, our perception does not extend to making that same correction when we look at an off-color print or slide. The yellow-orange or greenish cast will be readily apparent.

The overall coloration of a light source is measured by its **color temperature**. Many light sources emit light from a glowing filament. In a tungsten household light bulb, for instance, electricity heats the filament and causes it to glow brightly. The color of light given off by the filament depends on how hot it is heated. At lower temperatures it glows bright red but as the temperature increases it progressively becomes yellow, then white hot, and eventually blue. The overall coloration of the light source is thus linked to the temperature scale, given in degrees Kelvin (Figure 9.2). (The Kelvin scale is a temperature scale like the Fahrenheit scale or the Celsius scale except that the Kelvin scale adds 273 degrees to the Celsius temperature scale, so 0°K is absolute zero and 273°K is the freezing point of water.) The color temperature of a household light bulb is about 2,800°K. The color temperature of sunlight is about 5,000°K. In a sometimes confusing

FIGURE 9.2. Color temperature. The color of light given off by a glowing filament changes as it is heated or cooled. Color temperature is measured in degrees Kelvin (°K). On this scale, noon daylight is 5,000°K, very close to the color balance of daylight color film (5,500°K). If the color balance of the light source and film don't closely match, color distortions result.

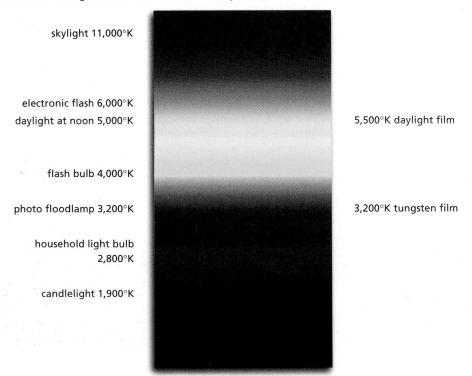

skylight 11,000°K

electronic flash 6,000°K
daylight at noon 5,000°K   5,500°K daylight film

flash bulb 4,000°K

photo floodlamp 3,200°K   3,200°K tungsten film

household light bulb
2,800°K

candlelight 1,900°K

twist of nomenclature, what we normally refer to as warmer colors like red and yellow are actually colors lower on the color temperature scale while a cooler color like blue is higher on the scale.

In color photography, the issue is to match the color temperature of the light source to the expectations of the color film you are using. The general subject of matching light source to film is called **color balance.** You must somehow balance the color of the light to the type of light expected by the film. The simplest way to achieve correct color balance is to use a film designed for the light you will use. Nearly all color films are available in a version balanced for daylight. Some are also available in a tungsten version.

Daylight film is designed to be used with light that has a color temperature of 5,500°K. Ideally, the film could be used in any daylight situation with perfect accuracy. In practice, however, it's not quite that simple. The color of daylight shifts according to the time of day. Daylight film is most accurate from about 10 in the morning to about 3 in the afternoon. Before and after that period, daylight is slightly warmer than usual. Photographs taken in early morning or late afternoon will exhibit a slight reddish-orange cast (Figure 9.3). Many photographers find this warm light—often called "sweet light"—very desirable for color portraiture and attempt to shoot during those times. If unwanted, however, the warm cast can be removed with a pale blue filter. Daylight film can also be used safely with electronic flash, which has a color temperature of 6,000°K, nearly identical to daylight, and doesn't vary with the time of day.

Tungsten film is intended to be used with light bulbs. Actually, two types of tungsten film are available—type A and type B. Both are designed for use with

Kelvin

FIGURE 9.3. Color temperature of sunlight at various times of day. The color temperature of daylight is usually very close to 5,000°K at noon on a sunny day. Early and late in the day it is noticeably warmer. Weather and atmospheric conditions may also influence the actual color temperature of daylight and how it will record on color film.

A. Sunrise   B. Noon   C. Sunset

NINE

photoflood lamps. Type A is balanced for the standard 3,400°K photoflood. Type B is balanced for a 3,200°K photoflood. If used with daylight, both type A and type B films will result in images with a bluish cast.

Both daylight and tungsten films, when you use them with fluorescent lights, yield a greenish looking photograph. To correct for this color imbalance, you must use a special color correction filter on your camera—for instance, an FL-D filter for daylight film. Filters are available to balance daylight film to fluorescent light or tungsten film to fluorescent light. In fact, filters are available to match many types of light sources to color films (Figure 9.4). For example, an 80A filter allows you to use daylight film with 3,200°K tungsten lights. An 85 filter balances type A tungsten film with daylight. In general, you can usually find a filter that will match any type of color film to almost any standard light source (Table 9.1).

Fluorescent light presents something of a special problem in color balance. Part of the problem is due to the fact that a fluorescent tube emits a discontinuous spectrum, so some colors are far more prominent than other colors. The other problem is that fluorescent tubes vary widely in their color balance. In an effort to improve on the tendency of older tubes to produce only a cool light that many people found depressing, manufacturers have developed newer tubes that are warmer. The photographer usually doesn't know what sort of fluorescent lighting he or she is working with and, to complicate matters, different types of tubes will often be mixed together in the same room. As a result, fluorescent filters rarely completely correct for color imbalance, but will almost always give more pleasing results than shooting without the filter.

Color balance is an important consideration in color photography. But don't pass up an otherwise effective color photograph simply because you happen to have the wrong film in your camera or because you don't have (or can't afford) the correct color correction filter. In many cases, an imbalance in color can be corrected when making a print. In other cases, the imbalance isn't all that bothersome and, in fact, may sometimes make the color image more interesting if less accurate. Remember, the essence of 35 mm photography is experimentation. If you're not sure, try it. Although experimentation in color is a little more expensive than in black and white, it is still cheaper in 35 mm than larger formats. The image that is technically correct and literally accurate may not always be the most effective and interesting. Be aware of color balance, but don't let it paralyze you.

FIGURE 9.4. Color correction filters. A variety of filters are available to correct for an imbalance between color film and nearly any common light source. Shown here are FL-D, 85, 80A filters.

TABLE 9.1. Color correction filters

Light source	Daylight film	Filter number Tungsten film Type A	Type B
Daylight/electronic flash	—	85	85B
Sunrise/sunset	82A	—	—
Clear flash bulbs	80C	81C	81C
Photoflood (3400 K)	80B	none	81A
3200 K lamp	80A	82A	none
Household bulb (2900 K)	80A+ 82B	82C	82B
Fluorescent lights	FL-D	—	FL-B

[handwritten: 3,400 K 3,1 3200K indoor]

[handwritten: Professional film]

Consumer and professional films

If you go shopping for color film, you'll probably notice that some films are marked "Professional" while others are not. The difference has to do with the fact that color films "age"—their color balance shifts over time. Consumers will typically buy a roll of film, shoot it over a long period of time, finish it off at someone's birthday party or Thanksgiving dinner, and eventually take it in to be processed. Films intended for consumers are expected to age for some time before they are processed and are designed to reach optimum color balance weeks or months after purchase. It is assumed that consumers will not be as critical of color balance as a professional photographer producing a color photograph for a food advertisement, where slight imbalances could ruin the image. Professional films are manufactured at optimum color balance and, it is assumed, will be refrigerated until exposed, then quickly processed. Refrigeration essentially arrests the aging process so the professional photographer knows the film is at optimum color balance when it is exposed. If you buy color film marked "Professional," be sure to keep it refrigerated until you use it. Keep it in its original moisture-proof packaging until you take it out of the refrigerator, then give it time to warm to room temperature before breaking the moisture barrier. A roll of film needs about an hour to adjust from normal refrigeration and about an hour and a half to adjust from the freezer.

Exposure

Color films are generally more sensitive to exposure errors than black-and-white films. Many black-and-white films tolerate exposure errors of two or three stops, and in spite of the error, will still yield negatives from which you can make acceptable prints. These black-and-white films are said to have a wider exposure **latitude**. Color films do not have as much latitude as black-and-white films. Color negative films tolerate errors of about 1 1/2 stops and color transparency films, of one stop or less (Figure 9.5).

The most serious danger with transparency films is overexposure, which can render highlight areas as clear film devoid of detail. Because of their low tolerance for error, color slide films are often bracketed. To bracket a shot, you first expose one frame at the exposure indicated by the meter, then make second and third exposures, one underexposed a stop, the other overexposed a stop. Bracketing gives you some insurance against exposure error. By bracketing, you will also discover that exposure is not always an exact science. Exposure of color slide film affects how the colors are rendered. Slight overexposure tends to wash the colors out a bit, creating a pastel image on the slide. Slight underexposure creates more intense, more **saturated** colors. Because many photographers find saturated colors desirable, they routinely underexpose slide film slightly by inflating the ISO speed rating by 1/3 stop. For example, they rate an ISO 64 slide film at 80 by setting their light meter dial to 80. (The opposite is true of color negative films, where slight overexposure gives better color saturation.) More saturation is not always better, however. A photograph with a fragile mood may be enhanced by a pastel rendition, while another requires the more intense look of deeply saturated colors.

You can learn a great deal about how exposure affects color slide film by bracketing routinely at first and studying the results to see how exposure affects the final image. You will learn that exposure is a powerful interpretive technique with color transparencies. The exposure that is technically correct does not always yield the most effective picture.

Red eye

Nearly everyone has taken flash pictures of friends, family, or pets where the eyes seem to glow red like a frame out of a cheap horror film. The problem, called red eye, is caused by light reflecting off the blood vessels at the back of the

FIGURE 9.5. Exposure variation in color transparency film. Color slide films have very little latitude, or tolerance for exposure error. Many photographers protect against this problem by bracketing—that is, taking several frames of film and varying the exposure each time to be sure that one gets optimum exposure.

A. Underexposed one stop   B. Normal exposure   C. Overexposed one stop

subject's eye. Eyes adjust to dim light by opening the pupil to allow more light in, just as we open the aperture on a camera lens, and light from a flash bounces off the back of the eye and records as bright red on the film. One solution is to move the flash far enough away from the lens so the light can't bounce directly back into the lens. Usually just moving the flash only a few inches will solve the problem. For flash units built into the camera body that can't be moved, some camera manufacturers include a red eye prevention setting that fires the flash several times prior to exposure. The bright flashes proceeding exposure close the subject's pupils down far enough to eliminate or reduce red eye.

Filters for color photography

Many of the filters you use with black-and-white materials aren't very helpful with color films. A red filter might increase cloud contrast with black-and-white film, but with color film it just turns everything red. This can sometimes be used for special effect (Figure 9.6), but normally you'll want to avoid colored filters with color films.

As noted in Chapter 8, there are some filters that can be useful with color films. A skylight filter, which you may have on your lens for scratch and dust protection anyway, will help warm bluish shadows when shooting outdoors. Neutral density filters are color neutral, but can reduce exposure, allowing the use of slower shutter speeds or wider apertures. Another useful filter is the polarizer. It is color neutral and can be used to increase cloud contrast, cut reflections, and increase color saturation (Figure 9.7).

COLOR THEORY

Two major systems for achieving full-color renditions are in common use. One, the additive system, is used primarily in color television. The other, the

NINE

FIGURE 9.6. Using a contrast filter for special effect. Colored filters used to create contrast effects in black-and-white photography will simply photograph as colors on color film. Sometimes this can produce an interesting special effect, but black-and-white filters are generally not useful in color photography.

A. Without filter

B. With red filter

see next page for Polarizing!

FIGURE 9.7. Polarizing filter. The polarizing filter produces greater color saturation in color photography by eliminating the surface glare from subject matter. It is the only cloud filter that does not shift color balance.

A. No polarizer   B. Polarizing filter used

subtractive system, is used in photography and in graphic arts. Both systems use various mixtures of but three colors to generate all other colors.

Additive primaries

The **additive system** is based on the principle that adding together equal parts of red, green, and blue light creates white light. For instance, if you take three light sources—one red, one green, and one blue—and direct all of them at a projection screen, they create white light where the beams of colored light overlap (Figure 9.8). Where the red and green beams overlap, you get yellow light. Other combinations of the additive primaries yield still other colors. In general, nearly all other visible colors in the spectrum can be created by mixing the three additive primaries in various proportions and intensities.

A color television tube contains three electron guns, each corresponding to one additive primary. The guns excite red, blue, or green phosphors on the screen to create various combinations of the three additive primaries and, thus, the various colors you see on the television screen. The additive system is ideal for television and computer monitors because the screen creates and emits light, much as the three colored light sources. In the computer world, this approach to color generation is called RGB color, discussed in detail in Chapter 11.

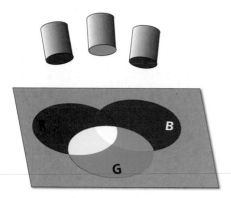

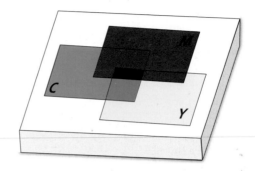

FIGURE 9.8. Additive primary colors. When you add together equal amounts of red, blue, and green light, you get white light. By mixing the three additive primaries in different ways, you can create nearly all other colors. This approach is used in color television and computer monitors.

FIGURE 9.9. Subtractive primary colors. The subtractive system starts with white light and modifies its color by filtering. If you use full-strength cyan, magenta, and yellow filters, all of the light is blocked. Other colors result from different combinations and strengths of filters.

Subtractive primaries

The **subtractive system** is something of the reverse of the additive system in that you begin with white light and use filters to subtract colors from it. Three filters are used—one yellow, one magenta, and one cyan. These are the three subtractive primary colors. If you begin with white light and pass it successively through various combinations of the subtractive primary filters, you can create other colors.

For instance, if you take a light box and lay yellow, magenta, and cyan filters on top of it, you get red where the magenta and yellow filters overlap (Figure 9.9). Where all three filters overlap, you get no light at all, or what appears to be black or neutral gray. By using subtractive primary filters of various strengths in various proportions, it is possible to modify white light to produce nearly any visible color in the spectrum.

The subtractive system is used both in photography and full-color printing where you view the photograph or printed image with white light reflected off the page. The transparent photographic dyes or colored printing inks act like subtractive primary filters that modify the white light and produce the full range of colors we see. In the computer realm, this system is known as CMYK color and is widely used in computer printers that produce color images.

Many combinations and interactions between the additive and subtractive primaries are possible. They can all be conveniently summarized in a simple **color wheel** (Figure 9.10). Any color can be formed by combining its two most immediate neighbors. For instance, red is flanked on one side by magenta and,

NINE

on the other, by yellow: Red equals magenta plus yellow. Yellow and cyan make green; cyan and magenta make blue, and so on.

Colors opposite one another on the color wheel are called **color complements.** There are three pairs of complements: yellow and blue, magenta and green, and cyan and red. These color opposites interact to form white or black, depending on whether you are working subtractively or additively. If you begin with light the color of one member in a complementary pair (say blue) and pass it through a filter of the other color in the pair (yellow in this case), the filter absorbs the light and you get nothing, black. On the other hand, if you begin with blue light and add yellow light, you get an equal mixture of blue, red, and green light, or white light.

The color relationships between the additive and subtractive primaries lie at the heart of the technology that makes color photography possible and can be helpful in considering the aesthetics of color photography. Many people, however, find it easier to think of color in terms of hue, saturation, and value.

Hue, saturation, and value

In this color system, **hue** is the color itself, **saturation** is the purity of the color, and **value** is the lightness or darkness of the color (Figure 9.11). It might help to think about color in terms of the physics of light: Hue is the wavelength of the light, saturation is a measure of whether the wavelength is contaminated by other wavelengths, and value is the amplitude or energy of the light. Thus hue would refer to a particular blue as opposed to a red or a yellow. Saturation, also called chroma, would refer to the strength of the color and whether it has been dulled due to contamination by other colors. Desaturated colors become increasingly gray. Value refers to the brightness of the color. In many computer applications, this color approach is referred to as the HSB model, for hue, saturation, and brightness.

FIGURE 9.10. The color wheel. The wheel shows the relationships between the additive and subtractive primaries. Any color on the wheel can be formed by combining the two adjacent colors (for example, red is made of equal parts of yellow and magenta). Color opposites on the wheel (like blue and yellow) are complementary pairs.

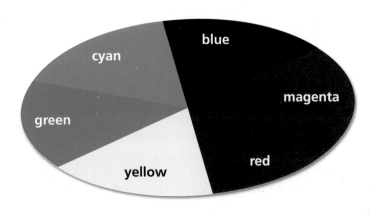

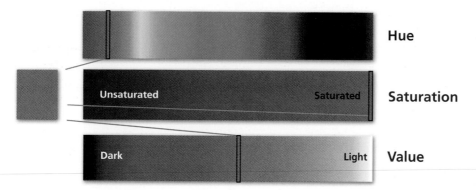

FIGURE 9.11. Hue, saturation, and value. Color can be described in terms of its hue, saturation, and value. Hue is the color itself, green or red, for instance. Saturation is the purity of the color, a measure of whether the color is contaminated by other colors. Value is the lightness or darkness of the color. In this example, the particular orange color on the left is described by a specific hue in the red/yellow region of the spectrum, a high degree of saturation, and a medium value.

COMPOSITION FOR COLOR

There is an old photographic proverb that says if a photograph wouldn't be good in black and white, the addition of color isn't going to make it any better. And while it is true that content and composition are as important in color as they are in black-and-white photography, it is equally true that the color photographer must also pay attention to color; it is, after all, what forms the image. The relationships among the colors in your color photographs are as important as the relationships among the gray tones in your black-and-white work.

Placing contrasting colors next to one another will accentuate their differences (Figure 9.12). The contrasting colors might be color complements, colors opposite one another on the color wheel, or warm colors contrasted with cool colors. Using a mixture of colors that are closely related, on the other hand, will create color harmony in the image and give a less energetic result (Figure 9.13). This approach is also known as limited palette color. You can achieve a similar effect by shooting monochromatic subjects where all the colors are essentially the same (Figure 9.14). Monochromatic images usually work very subtly with color and sometimes are enhanced by adding a color accent, an isolated color that becomes a strong focal point in the image (Figure 9.15).

COLOR FORMATION

Most color materials—films and papers—use one of two methods to create the colors you see in the image. One method creates color dyes during processing and is called a **chromogenic system**. The other method, which begins with a

NINE

Figure 9.12. Contrasting colors. The blue color of the colander is the complement of the yellow-orange persimmons. Contrasted here, the two colors seem to intensify one another.

Figure 9.13. Color harmony. The closely related browns and yellows in this image create a quiet mood. This approach is often referred to as limited palette color.

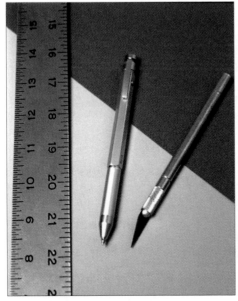

Figure 9.14. Monochromatic color. This image is a uniform hue, with variation primarily in value, like a black-and-white photograph.

Figure 9.15. Color accent. The red ribbon becomes a strong focal point in this otherwise monochromatic image.

complete set of color dyes and then removes those that are not needed to form the image, is called the **dye-destruction system.**

Two types of chromogenic systems are in common use. The **dye-injection system** uses a separate development step for each of the three film emulsion layers. During each development step, dyes are injected into the film to form the color image in that layer. The process is very complex and requires expensive, specialized equipment for accurate processing. Kodachrome is the only common dye-injection film and only eight processing laboratories in the world can process Kodachrome film.

The **dye-incorporated system,** by contrast, creates dyes in all three emulsion layers at once. When a dye-incorporated film is manufactured, chemicals called color couplers are included in each emulsion layer that can form dyes when the film is processed. The color couplers in the blue-sensitive layer will form yellow dye; in the green-sensitive layer, magenta dye; and in the red-sensitive layer, cyan dye. Although dye-incorporated films are themselves more complex to manufacture, processing is much simpler than with dye-injection films. Dye-incorporated films can be processed in almost any darkroom using appropriate chemicals. With the exception of Kodachrome, nearly all other color films use the dye-incorporated color formation system. Most color printing papers also use the dye-incorporated system.

A dye-destruction color material is black to begin with. Color dyes are already formed in all three emulsion layers. Exposure makes some of the dyes vulnerable to processing chemicals. Those chemicals then remove the dyes that are not necessary in the final color image. The process is not unlike the job of a sculptor who begins with a block of marble and removes everything that isn't needed to form the statue. The advantage of the dye-destruction method is that the dyes used are very stable. As a result, the final product is relatively permanent and unaffected by exposure to sunlight. By contrast, dyes generated from color couplers are usually vulnerable to sunlight and will fade eventually. The most common color material that employs the dye-destruction process is Ilfochrome (formerly known as Cibachrome), used to make prints from color transparencies. This process, like the dye-incorporated system, can be used in nearly any standard darkroom.

THE C-41 PROCESS: COLOR NEGATIVES

The C-41 process is universally used for color negative films. The C-41 process is similar to black-and-white processing, although it uses a different set of chemicals. You can process C-41 film in almost any darkroom. The process requires six steps, completed in just over 24 minutes. Specific steps for the process are as follows:

NINE

(handwritten margin notes)
- Additional Chemicals needed
- time & temperature very critical

Step	Time*	Notes
Developer	3:15	Temperature is 100 ± 0.25°F (37.8 ± 0.15°C). Agitate for 8 inversions during the first 15 seconds, then 2 inversions at 30-second intervals thereafter
Bleach	6:30	Agitate for the first 30 seconds, then for 5 seconds at 30-second intervals
Wash	3:15	Running water
Fixer	6:30	Same agitation as bleach step
Wash	3:15	Running water
Stabilizer	1:30	Agitate for the first 30 seconds
Dry		

*These are the processing times recommended for the Kodak Flexicolor process. Be sure to read and follow the instructions that come with the chemicals you use.

You can use the same processing tanks and reels for C-41 that you use for black-and-white processing. There is really only one dramatic difference in darkroom procedures for the C-41 process: The processing temperature should be 100°F rather than the usual 68°F used for black-and-white processes. Temperature is especially critical for the developer step, where you must keep it within a quarter of a degree for the full developing time. To make this easier, many photographers use a water bath and place the chemicals and tank in it to help hold the temperature constant (Figure 9.16). You must also time the steps very precisely, especially the developer step, and you may need to adjust the developer time depending on how many rolls you've already developed. Color film will typically look somewhat opalescent and bluish until it dries.

Chromogenic black-and-white films

To understand how the C-41 process works, it's easiest to begin by looking at black-and-white films designed to be processed alongside color films

Figure 9.16. Water bath. Because temperature control is so critical in color film processing, use of a heated water bath is recommended.

(Figure 9.17). These films are called **chromogenic black-and-white films** because they use color couplers to form the final film image. They yield a monochromatic negative that can be used to make black-and-white prints. Chromogenic black-and-white films were originally marketed to help conserve silver by reclaiming it from the film and reusing it. They are often used today by photographers who want the convenience of having their black-and-white film processed by their local one-hour photo processor.

Chromogenic black-and-white films have an emulsion layer that contains both light-sensitive silver salts and associated color couplers. Sensitivity centers form on the silver halide salts that are exposed to light (Figure 9.18). The development step converts those exposed silver halides to metallic silver, just as in black-and-white film development, and at the same time the color couplers immediately adjacent to the developing silver salts are converted into a color dye. Thus color dyes form in exposed areas but not in areas of the film that were not exposed to light. Following development, the emulsion contains two negative images: one a conventional silver image and the other a monochromatic dye image. The bleach step converts all the developed silver metal back into silver salts and the fixing step removes the silver salts from the film, leaving only the dye image. The silver can be reclaimed from the fixing solution and used again. The negative is usually more brownish-red than neutral gray, but that doesn't affect its usefulness. It can be enlarged like conventional black-and-white films.

Tri-pack film construction

Since the C-41 process can yield black-and-white negatives, it is obviously not just the process alone that is responsible for the color images we get from

Figure 9.17. Chromogenic black-and-white films. Films like Kodak's T400CN and Ilford's XP2 are processed just like color negative films, but result in a monochrome negative that can be printed like an ordinary black-and-white negative.

Figure 9.18. Chromogenic black-and-white film. When process C-41 black-and-white films are developed, a conventional silver-based negative image is formed which simultaneously creates a negative dye image. The silver image is bleached and removed from the film using fixer, leaving only the negative dye image. The silver can be reclaimed from processing solutions and used again.

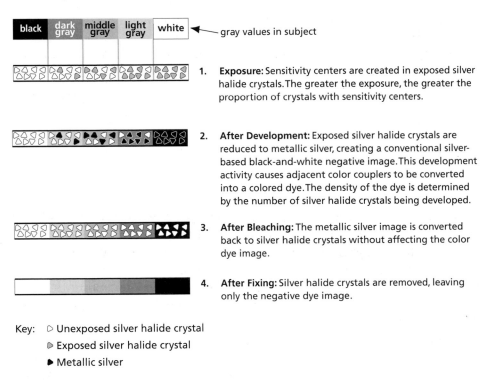

gray values in subject

1. **Exposure:** Sensitivity centers are created in exposed silver halide crystals. The greater the exposure, the greater the proportion of crystals with sensitivity centers.

2. **After Development:** Exposed silver halide crystals are reduced to metallic silver, creating a conventional silver-based black-and-white negative image. This development activity causes adjacent color couplers to be converted into a colored dye. The density of the dye is determined by the number of silver halide crystals being developed.

3. **After Bleaching:** The metallic silver image is converted back to silver halide crystals without affecting the color dye image.

4. **After Fixing:** Silver halide crystals are removed, leaving only the negative dye image.

Key: ▷ Unexposed silver halide crystal
       ▷ Exposed silver halide crystal
       ▶ Metallic silver

color film. In fact, it is really the construction of the film itself, the way it incorporates the additive and subtractive primary systems, that creates full color images. Nearly all modern color materials—negative and positive films and papers—employ a **tri-pack** construction. The film or paper has three emulsion layers, one for each of the three complementary color pairs. Each layer records one additive primary component of the original scene. In the final print or transparency, the layers are combined subtractively to recreate the original scene in full color.

Color negative films employ the tri-pack construction (Figure 9.19). Three emulsion layers, each sensitive to one of the additive primaries, are coated over a transparent film base. As with black-and-white film, an anti-scratch coating of hard gelatin is placed on top of the emulsion to protect it from abrasion. Also like black-and-white film, color film is coated on the back side with an anti-halation layer to prevent light from being reflected up off the back surface of the film and exposing it a second time. The anti-halation backing is dissolved during film processing.

Figure 9.19. Tri-pack construction of color film. Color film is coated with three emulsion layers. Each layer is sensitive to one of the additive primary colors and will be dyed its complementary subtractive primary color during processing. For instance, the top layer records the blue component of the scene being photographed and will be dyed yellow during processing.

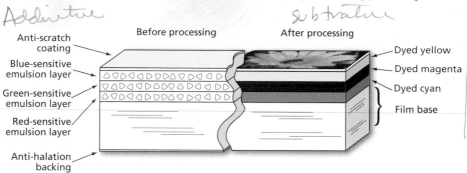

Color negative films

Say you take a picture of a red fire hydrant against green grass. The red light reflected from the hydrant exposes the layer of film sensitive to red light. The green light from the grass exposes the green-sensitive film layer. After the negative is developed, the portion of the film exposed by the red hydrant is dyed cyan, the color complement of red. The portion of the negative exposed by the green grass is dyed magenta, the color complement of green. Your negative thus shows a cyan hydrant on magenta grass. Just as black-and-white tones in a black-and-white negative are reversed, everything in a color negative appears as its color complement, or color opposite (Figure 9.20 A and B). In actuality, a color negative appears orangish overall because it has a built-in orange mask to make printing the negative easier (Figure 9.20 C). When a print is made from the negative, the orange cast disappears and the original colors are restored (Figure 9.20D).

Figure 9.20. Complementary colors in color film. The red hydrant is recorded as cyan, the color complement of red. The green grass is recorded as magenta, the color complement of green. In an actual color negative an orange printing mask often makes it difficult to see the color complements. During printing, the cyan hydrant prints as the color complement of cyan and again becomes red. Dogs everywhere are happier.

A. Positive image   B. Negative image   C. Masked image   D. Image on print

Color negative film undergoes the same processing steps as chromogenic black-and-white films. The difference is that the process creates dyes of different colors in the three emulsion layers. In color films the blue-sensitive emulsion layer contains color couplers that yield a yellow dye image (Figure 9.21). At the same time, a magenta dye image is created in the green-sensitive layer and a cyan dye image in the red-sensitive layer. After development, all the silver is removed from the film by bleaching and fixing, leaving only the three-color dye image.

Color papers used to print color negatives work on the same principle as color negative film. It has a similar tri-pack emulsion construction. Each emulsion layer is sensitive to one of the additive primaries and each will be dyed one of the subtractive primaries. The emulsion layers are coated onto a white paper base instead of a transparent film base, however, and the processing chemicals are

Figure 9.21. Color negative film. Each of the three emulsion layers is sensitive to a different additive primary and contains color couplers that can be converted to the subtractive complementary color. C-41 development creates a silver-based negative which simultaneously forms a color dye image. The silver is bleached and removed from the film, leaving only the color dye negative.

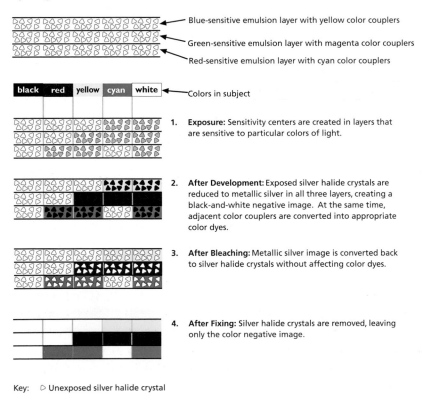

Blue-sensitive emulsion layer with yellow color couplers

Green-sensitive emulsion layer with magenta color couplers

Red-sensitive emulsion layer with cyan color couplers

black | red | yellow | cyan | white — Colors in subject

1. **Exposure:** Sensitivity centers are created in layers that are sensitive to particular colors of light.

2. **After Development:** Exposed silver halide crystals are reduced to metallic silver in all three layers, creating a black-and-white negative image. At the same time, adjacent color couplers are converted into appropriate color dyes.

3. **After Bleaching:** Metallic silver image is converted back to silver halide crystals without affecting color dyes.

4. **After Fixing:** Silver halide crystals are removed, leaving only the color negative image.

Key: ▷ Unexposed silver halide crystal
      ▷ Exposed silver halide crystal
      ▶ Metallic silver

different. During printing, the colors on the negative are again reversed, back to their original hues. The cyan hydrant and magenta grass in the color negative reverse to their color complements: a red hydrant against green grass.

THE E-6 PROCESS: COLOR TRANSPARENCIES

Nearly all black-and-white photography uses negatives. But in color work, color positives are almost as popular as color negatives, in fact preferred in much serious 35 mm color photography. Color positive films use basically the same construction as color negative films. Each of three emulsion layers records one of the additive primaries and will later be dyed one of the subtractive primaries. The real differences between the color negatives and color positives occur in the E-6 process itself. The E-6 process is used to develop all color transparency films except Kodachrome.

Figure 9.22 shows how positive processing first creates a negative image and then develops the film a second time to create a positive color image. The steps and times are as follows:

Step	Time	Notes
First Developer	6:30	Temperature is 100 ± 0.25°F (37.8 ± 0.15°C). Agitate for 8 inversions during the first 15 seconds, then 2 inversions at 30-second intervals thereafter
Wash	3:00	Running water or four fill-and-dump cycles
Color Developer	6:00	Temperature and agitation same as first developer
Wash	3:00	Running water or four fill-and-dump cycles
Bleach/Fix	10:00	Same agitation as first developer
Wash	4:00	Running water or six fill-and-dump cycles
Stabilizer	1:00	Agitate for the first 15 seconds only
Dry		

Time and temperature are most critical for the first developer, but you should use a water bath to keep the temperature as consistent as possible throughout the series of steps.

After the film is developed, you view the three superimposed images in white light to see the reconstructed full-color scene. If you hold a color slide up to white light, you are in effect looking through three filters; each emulsion layer acts as either a yellow, magenta, or cyan filter. The strength of each subtractive filter varies in various places on the film to modify the white light and recreate the original scene in full color. Because of technical characteristics of the positive process, the resulting slides tend to be finer grained than corresponding negative images. This added sharpness makes them preferred in 35 mm color work because the small slide can be enlarged greatly and still result in a sharp and detailed likeness.

COLOR REPRODUCTION

Printed reproduction of color photographs in newspapers and magazines uses the same approach as tri-pack color films and papers. The original full-color

Figure 9.22. Color positive film. Like color negative film, each of the three emulsion layers in color slide film is sensitive to a different additive primary and contains color couplers that can be converted to the subtractive complementary color. E-6 development first creates a silver-based negative without affecting the color couplers. The film then undergoes a second development which develops the remaining silver halides and simultaneously forms a color dye positive. The silver is subsequently bleached and removed from the film, leaving only the color dye positive.

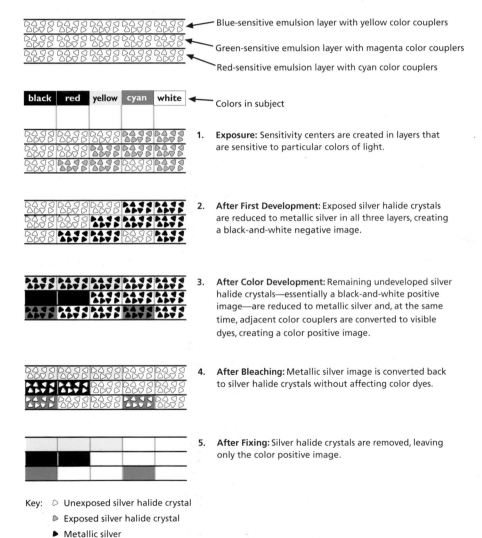

Blue-sensitive emulsion layer with yellow color couplers

Green-sensitive emulsion layer with magenta color couplers

Red-sensitive emulsion layer with cyan color couplers

| black | red | yellow | cyan | white |

Colors in subject

1. **Exposure:** Sensitivity centers are created in layers that are sensitive to particular colors of light.

2. **After First Development:** Exposed silver halide crystals are reduced to metallic silver in all three layers, creating a black-and-white negative image.

3. **After Color Development:** Remaining undeveloped silver halide crystals—essentially a black-and-white positive image—are reduced to metallic silver and, at the same time, adjacent color couplers are converted to visible dyes, creating a color positive image.

4. **After Bleaching:** Metallic silver image is converted back to silver halide crystals without affecting color dyes.

5. **After Fixing:** Silver halide crystals are removed, leaving only the color positive image.

Key: ▷ Unexposed silver halide crystal
  ▶ Exposed silver halide crystal
  ▶ Metallic silver

image is first separated into its yellow, magenta, and cyan components. This can be done by rephotographing the image through special color filters, but is more often done today by scanning the photograph into a computer and having the computer make the color separations. To improve sharpness and contrast, the full set of color separations usually includes a fourth, black component. The printer then makes a set of four printing plates, one for each of the subtractive

Figure 9.23. Full-color reproduction of a color photograph. Printing color photographs involves first separating the color image into its subtractive primary components—yellow, magenta, cyan—with a neutral gray/black component added. On the printing press, each separate component is printed over top of the others using yellow, cyan, magenta, and black printing inks.

Yellow printing plate

Yellow image

Magenta printing plate

Yellow Image overprinted with magenta image

Cyan printing plate

Yellow and magenta images overprinted with cyan image

Black printing plate

Yellow, magenta, and cyan images overprinted with black image

NINE

primaries and one for the black component. The plate representing the yellow component is inked with yellow ink and printed onto a sheet of paper. The plate representing the magenta component is inked with magenta ink and printed over the yellow image. Then the cyan and black images are added, forming a full-color image (Figure 9.23). Because of the expense involved in making the color separations and the precision needed to superimpose the color images one over the other, color reproduction is comparatively costly and time-consuming.

NON-CONVENTIONAL COLOR PROCESSES

For a different look to your photographs, you'll want to explore color materials besides the usual color negative and transparency films.

Infrared color film gives "false color." Trees and other foliage will be colored magenta rather than green because they reflect a lot of infrared light. Skies and water will be a deep blue (Figure 9.24). Infrared color is usually shot using a deep yellow filter (Wratten number 12) to absorb violet and blue light, although other yellow or orange filters will also yield interesting effects.

If you compare Polacolor film with conventional slides or prints, you'll notice that it renders colors very differently from conventional emulsions. Colors tend to be more subtle and somewhat warmer. Compare the images shot with conventional film and Polaroid film in Figure 9.25 A and B. For a distinctly different look, photographers have discovered how to take a partially developed Polaroid image and transfer it to paper or fabrics—a process known as Polaroid image transfer (Figure 9.25 C). It is even possible to take an already developed Polaroid image, soak the emulsion layer loose in hot water, and recapture the emulsion on some sort of support like paper or glass, a process known as Polaroid emulsion transfer (Figure 9.25 D).

FIGURE 9.24. Infrared film. Infrared film is sensitive to wavelengths of light beyond human vision. Vegetation is usually rendered in magenta tones while skies and water take on a deeper blue cast. The film is usually exposed using a deep yellow filter.

A. Conventional film   B. Infrared film

FIGURE 9.25. Color Polaroid film. Polaroid films are known primarily for their convenience and the instant results they produce. They are also known among serious photographers for the distinctive way they render colors and for their ability to transfer images to non-photographic papers.

A. Conventional film

B. Polapan color Polaroid film. Polaroid color tends to be more subtle, less brilliant than conventional film.

C. Polaroid image transfer. Here, the Polaroid image was transferred to watercolor paper rather than the built-in receiver sheet. The process is detailed in the How To section that follows.

D. Polaroid emulsion transfer. A processed Polaroid is soaked in very hot water to separate the emulsion layer. This thin and fragile image is then captured on a sheet of paper, glass, or plastic.

How to

Create a
Polaroid Image Transfer

Step 1: Expose the Polaroid film. Here a Polaroid back on a 4 x 5 camera is being used, but you can also expose positive transparencies (slides) using a Polaroid Daylab or using an enlarger with a Polaroid back.

Step 2: After the film is exposed, switch the back to its "Processing" setting and pull the Polaroid film packet to begin processing.

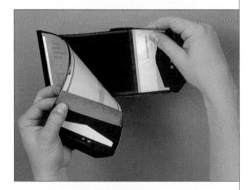

Step 3: About 5 to 10 seconds after pulling the sheet, separate the film packet so the image does not fully transfer to the receiver sheet. Be careful not to get any of the caustic processing jelly on your hands.

Step 4: Carefully tear apart the contents of the Polaroid packet to separate the sheet with the negative image. This sheet has a metal strip attached to one end. Remove the metal strip and the remnants of the processing pod.

How to

*Create a
Polaroid Image Transfer*

Step 5: Carefully position the film portion of the packet on a sheet of watercolor paper. You can experiment with whether the paper is damp or dry and whether you use hot or cold press watercolor paper.

Step 6: Use a small roller to make firm contact between the film and the paper. You can experiment with how long you continue to roll, but the image will usually transfer in about a minute.

Step 7: Carefully lift the film away from the paper. Dark areas in the image will have a tendency to pull loose and tear. Most people who make Polaroid transfers accept this as part of the process.

Step 8: The finished product is an image that is a photograph but has some of the qualities of a watercolor image. The colors are more muted than a normal Polaroid and the image is somewhat diffuse. You can experiment with different types of paper and can even transfer to silk and some types of wood.

NINE

REVIEW questions ?

1. What is color balance? What happens if color is off-balance and how do you correct for it?

2. What is color temperature?

3. Describe how to bracket exposures.

4. What is the additive system of color formation and where is it used?

5. What is the subtractive system of color formation and where is it used?

6. What is chromogenic color formation? What is a chromogenic black-and-white film?

7. What is tri-pack construction in color film?

8. What is the C-41 process used for?

9. What is the E-6 process used for?

10. What is color infrared film?

try it YOURSELF

1. Here's a way to improve your eye for color and find out how color film reacts to different colors and color relationships. First, take a series of shots of different subjects, all of them the same color. Try yellow, for instance: a banana, a lemon, someone in a yellow rain slicker, the center line of a street, yellow pencils. They are all colors of the same name, but do they appear the same in the finished photograph? Next, see how the background affects the appearance of the color. Does an orange on a blue background seem different from an orange on a yellow background? Last, compare limited palette color with "circus" color. Take some shots of subjects containing a limited number of related hues, say all earth colors—browns, greens, oranges, yellows. Take other shots of subjects that contain clashing colors—mixtures of greens and reds, and oranges and blues, and yellows and purples, and so on. Compare the two approaches to color. What subjects are most successful with limited palette color? Which images seem most energetic?

2. Experiment with color film under different light sources and using daylight at different times of day. Use daylight balanced color slide film. (Using color negative film will tend to negate your experiments because color casts will be corrected during the printing process and you won't be able to see the effect of the differing color temperatures of the light sources.) If possible, use the same or similar subject matter in all your shots. Take a series of exposures using sunlight, tungsten light, fluorescent light, street light, window light, candle light, firelight, neon light, flashlight—whatever light sources you can find that you think might be interesting. Next, take several photographs at different times of day: sunrise just as the sun breaks the horizon, noon, and sunset just as the sun hits the horizon. You'll have only about 5-10 minutes of warm light at sunrise and sunset, so you need to anticipate your exposures. You'll see the effect most clearly with light subject matter. After the slides are processed, lay them out on a light table to compare the results from both series. In many instances, you would want to correct for the color imbalances you'll see, but sometimes the effects can be interesting and effective.

NINE

digital photography

"*There is no doubt that computerized image-making processes are rapidly replacing or supplementing traditional still-camera images in many commercial situations, especially in advertising and photojournalism. Given the economies involved, there will probably come a time when almost all silver-based photographies are superseded by computer-driven processes.*"

Geoffrey Batchen

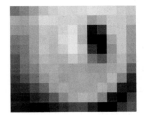

capturing
digital images

Sonata in Blue iii, by John Paul Caponigro, 1999

capturing
digital images

Sonata in Blue iii, by John Paul Caponigro, 1999
(Copyright © 1999 by John Paul Caponigro)

"While I make single images that stand on their own, I tend to work in series," says John Paul Caponigro, one of a new generation of photographers who use the computer to produce images. "The series acts as a container, binding together a number of similar themes and pointing the way to correlations with work in other series. This image belongs to the suite *Sonatas,* which is one of the interlocking sub-sets of the *Waterways* series.

"While I look forward to the day when I use purely digital capture for my imagery, today I use color transparency film, which is then scanned. All of the image editing is done with Adobe Photoshop. I then make giclée (state-of-the-art inkjet) prints. Recent advances in printing technologies have enabled me to refine the final prints I make of this image, almost on a yearly basis. What's more, the new prints, once fugitive, now last many times longer than conventional color prints. The coatings on new papers are particularly bright and smooth, which allows the highlights to be exceptionally clean, holding detail without sacrificing the velvety surface of giclée printing. I prefer to print on the sensual, matte surfaces of rag papers."

You can see more of Caponigro's work in color on his Web site at www.johnpaulcaponigro.com.

The principles of photography have remained essentially unchanged for the past 125 years, since Daguerre and Talbot first began experimenting with the photosensitive properties of silver. It is not that the electronic revolution didn't make an early mark on photography. As new technology developed in the 1980s, electronics were applied to making conventional processes more accurate, more efficient, and more convenient. Cameras began to sport autofocus lenses, electronic shutters, and programmed exposure. Darkroom timers went electronic. Exposure meters became more sophisticated and more precise. But the imaging system itself remained essentially unchanged: the only way we could create a photograph was to direct light at a silver-based emulsion which was then chemically developed to create a visible image.

All that has changed. Rapid advances in the past decade now make it possible to capture images in electronic form, process them electronically, and produce printed versions of them. In digital cameras, light is converted directly to an electronic pattern, which is stored like any other computer data. Currently, images from digital cameras are rarely as detailed as those from conventional cameras, but digital cameras offer offsetting advantages of their own—in speed, delivery, and flexibility. Many photographers combine the high resolution of conventional film with the strengths of digital processing to get the best of both technologies.

In many ways, the job of the photographer changes very little with electronic photography. The digital camera is simply a new tool in the hands of someone who seeks to communicate visually. Digital photographers will continue to be concerned about composition, about working with subjects, about getting images that tell a story, make a point, express a vision, or create a fantasy. They will need to know about lens focal length and depth of field. Most fundamentally, they will always need to understand and appreciate the qualities of light and shadow.

In other ways, however, the new electronic technology is revolutionary. In electronic photography, computers replace processing tanks, and photographers can exert much greater control over the final image in their new digital darkrooms. Photographs can be transmitted from one point to another over telephone lines or via satellite almost instantaneously—a tremendous advantage to photojournalists especially. Electronic methods free the photographer from reliance on costly silver materials and put an end to handling, storing, and disposing of hazardous chemicals. New output devices create fresh visions of the photographic image and offer intriguing new avenues for the art photographer to explore.

THE ELECTRONIC IMAGE

At the heart of what makes digital photography different from conventional silver-based photography is the way in which the two technologies represent light and shadow. If you ignore the subject matter of any black-and-white photograph and simply look at it as an abstract pattern, you will see an

TEN

organization of tones that range from pure white through a series of increasingly darker gray values to dense black. Photographers call this series of tones the **gray scale** (Figure 10.1). In any photograph, conventional or digital, the pattern of gray tones is produced by the direct action of light.

In a conventional silver image, the gray scale is created by variations in exposure on light-sensitive silver salts, as discussed in Chapter 4, "Developing the Film." In a silver-based photographic print, dark shadows are represented by dense areas of black silver. Midtone grays are represented by a mixture of black silver and white paper. Bright highlights are represented by primarily white paper with occasional specks of black developed silver. In an electronic image, however, variations in the brightness of light are translated into an electronic signal which is digitized and stored in numerical form. The image area of a digitized photograph is divided into a grid pattern, something like a checkerboard, but with thousands or even millions of tiny squares. Each square in the picture is called a picture element, or **pixel** for short. Each pixel represents a particular gray value (Figure 10.2). On close inspection, a conventional photographic print consists of randomly dispersed specks of black silver against white paper. The specks of silver vary in size and number, and the proportion of black silver to white paper creates the gray values in the print. A digital photograph, by contrast, is an orderly pattern of pixels, with each tiny pixel representing a specific gray level (Figure 10.3).

SEE EXAMPLES

Figure 10.1. The photographic gray scale. From a technical point of view, a photograph is simply a pattern of tones, gray values that range from white to black.

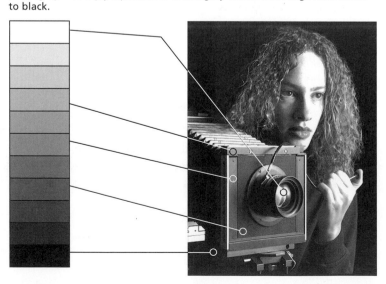

Figure 10.2. Pixel structure of a digital photograph. The image space of a digital photograph is subdivided into a checkerboard pattern of tiny cells called picture elements, or pixels for short. Each pixel holds a certain value of gray.

CONVERTING LIGHT TO AN ELECTRONIC IMAGE

You can convert light into pixels using a variety of strategies (Figure 10.4). The most direct is the digital camera, which provides a digital image without further processing, although the images tend to have relatively low resolution except for the most expensive cameras. Many digital photographers combine conventional photographic processes with film scanners and reflection scanners to take advantage of the high resolution of film. This strategy adds more steps to the process but results in higher quality for about the same investment in equipment.

At the heart of all three types of equipment—digital cameras, film scanners, and reflection scanners—is a special electronic sensor, in most cases a charge-coupled device, or **CCD** for short. A CCD contains thousands of tiny light sensing elements and each element can convert varying levels of light into an electrical signal. The brighter the light, the stronger the electrical signal. This signal is then digitized and stored in numerical form for later use.

The digital camera

In a digital camera the CCD is a two-dimensional checkerboard array of individual photosensitive receptors, each one representing one pixel in the final image. The CCD array is usually slightly smaller than a 35 mm film frame but contains thousands, even millions, of sensing elements. In a digital camera, the CCD array is positioned at the focal plane, where the film would be exposed in a conventional camera. Light coming through the camera lens is focused on the CCD, which converts it into a pixelized image (Figure 10.5). The image data is either stored in digital memory built into the camera or transmitted to an external storage device.

TEN

Conventional photograph

Digital photograph

highlight

midtone

shadow

highlight

midtone

shadow

Figure 10.3. Highlight and shadow in conventional and digital photographs. Both conventional and digital photographs are patterns of various gray values. In a conventional photograph, the gray values are represented by varying densities of silver metal against white paper. In a digital photograph, the gray values are produced by varying the gray value of individual pixels.

The overall resolution of a digital camera is determined by how many elements its CCD contains. Array CCDs with millions of light-sensing elements are difficult to manufacture. As a result, high-end digital cameras capable of producing images with a million or more pixels are very expensive compared with conventional film cameras. Despite the expense, digital cameras can be invaluable to the photojournalist on a tight deadline at a news scene far from home. Not only does the digital camera eliminate film processing and printing, but the photographer can plug the camera into a modem and transmit the image over telephone wires back to the newsroom. It is thus possible to have pictures in the newsroom only seconds after they are taken.

The disadvantages of digital cameras are their current high price and low sharpness compared to conventional film cameras. As this book is going to press in mid-2001, a simple digital camera costs between $500 and $1,000 and can't match the image quality of a conventional 35 mm camera costing a fraction as much. Digital cameras that even begin to approach the quality of conventional 35 mm film cost between $5,000 and $10,000 and are slower to use than conventional cameras. But the world of digital photography changes rapidly. Improvements in CCDs bring cameras with higher resolutions and the increasing popularity of digital imaging brings prices down.

Because of the current high cost of digital cameras capable of producing high resolution images, many—perhaps most—professional photographers working in the digital realm combine old and new technologies, shooting their

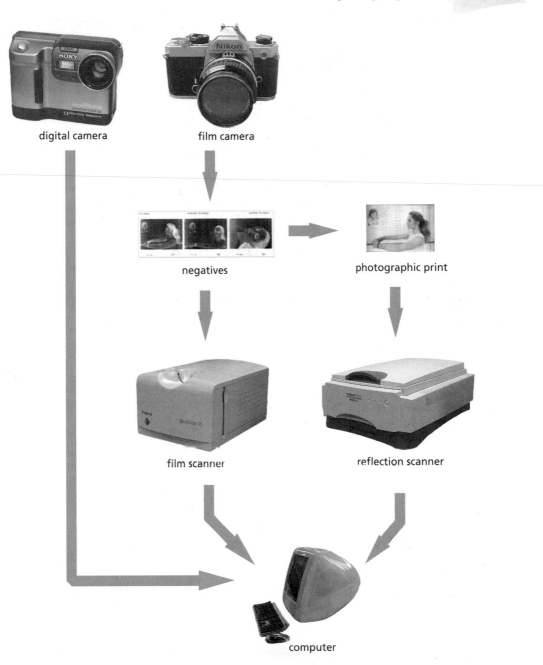

digital camera

film camera

negatives

photographic print

film scanner

reflection scanner

TEN

computer

Figure 10.4. Capturing digital images. Digital cameras provide the most direct pathway to digitized images, but resolution is usually not as high as with conventional film cameras. Many photographers use a combination of the old and the new, combining conventional film with either film or reflection scanners.

Figure 10.5. Digital camera. The "film" in a digital camera is a charge-coupled device (CCD) which converts light into an electrical signal that is then digitized. Because the camera must capture the entire frame in an instant, the CCD is a two-dimensional array like the digital image itself.

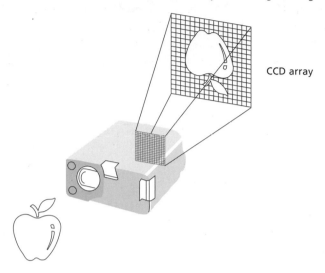

CCD array

photographs with conventional cameras and film, then digitizing the film image using a film scanner.

The film scanner

Film scanners are the digital analog of the photographic enlarger. Film scanners use a linear CCD, in which sensor cells are arranged in one long row rather than a two-dimensional grid. This type of CCD is simpler to build and much less expensive than an array CCD. In the film scanner, light shines through the film

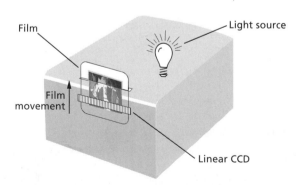

Film

Light source

Film movement

Linear CCD

Figure 10.6. Film scanner. Light shines through the negative or color transparency and is digitized using a linear CCD which captures the image one row of pixels at a time as it scans across the surface of the film. It may take from a few seconds to several minutes to complete the scan but very high resolutions are possible.

and hits a linear CCD. As the film slowly passes across its face, the CCD samples the transmitted light, building an overall composite electronic representation one row at a time (Figure 10.6). By moving the film very slowly, it is possible to obtain high-resolution images with many millions of pixels. Film scanners are capable of producing much higher quality images than are digital cameras, and are much less expensive. The disadvantage is that you have to process the film and it can take from several seconds to many minutes to completely scan one frame of film.

Some studio photographers use medium and large format cameras that employ digital camera backs based on scanning linear CCDs rather than array CCDs. In essence, this approach combines the digital camera and the film scanner into one device. The scanner is part of a back that attaches to the camera and positions the linear CCD where conventional film would ordinarily be located. The back captures the pixels one row at a time as the linear CCD moves across the image area in the camera back. Because the scans, and thus the exposures, take several minutes, this scanning approach works only for still life subjects. But for such applications as catalog and advertising photography, the scanning digital camera makes it possible to capture high quality images without the need for film and processing. Images can be previewed immediately and adjustments in lighting or composition made if needed.

Film scanning is accessible even if you don't have a film scanner—if you have a CD-ROM drive on your computer. Many photofinishers can take your slides or negatives and scan them onto a Kodak Photo-CD for a nominal charge. You get back a CD with each image stored in several sizes. Most image processing software, like Photoshop for example, can read Photo-CD image files and you can work with them as though you produced the scans on your own film scanner.

TEN

Figure 10.7. Reflection scanner. Like a film scanner, the reflection scanner (or flatbed scanner) creates a digitized image one row of pixels at a time. Light reflected off the photograph being scanned registers on a linear CCD as it travels along the length of the photograph.

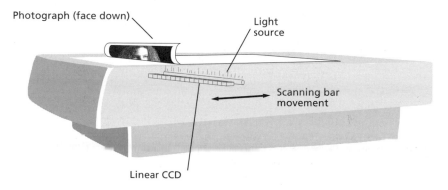

Photograph (face down)

Light source

Scanning bar movement

Linear CCD

The flatbed scanner

A flatbed scanner is used to digitize photographic prints and other reflective materials. Flatbed scanners look and behave much like a simple office copier. The basic principle is the same as a film scanner: a linear CCD gathers light intensity information from the print one row at a time and builds a pattern of pixels representing the image. In the flatbed scanner, light reflected off the print hits a mirror as it moves across the image and the light is directed through a lens to the linear CCD (Figure 10.7).

Flatbed scanners are relatively inexpensive, easy to use, and capable of producing quality digitized images, although usually not as high quality as those from a film scanner. Their principal disadvantage in digital photography is that you must develop your film and make prints before digitizing the image, so the flatbed scanner offers no savings in processing time. On the other hand, flatbed scanners are readily available and will accept nearly any kind of printed material, not just photographs.

The drum scanner

The highest quality scans are produced by drum scanners, which use a different technology than the CCD. Drum scanners use photomultiplier tubes (PMTs) to translate light into a digitized signal. PMTs are more sensitive to light than CCDs and usually yield a greater range of detail in the scanned image, particularly in the shadow areas. Drum scanners are used primarily by printers and service bureaus to prepare photographs for publication, and can scan film negatives, positives, and prints. The scanners are very expensive, with production models costing from $100,000 to more than $1 million. Even tabletop drum scanners cost more than $25,000. In addition, drum scanners require a skilled operator to calibrate the scanner and operate it.

THE STRUCTURE OF A DIGITAL IMAGE

Each pixel in a black-and-white digital photograph is represented by a numerical value that indicates the gray level for that tiny part of the image. For example, absolute black might be level 0 and absolute white, level 15. Lower numbers would represent darker pixels and higher numbers would represent lighter pixels. Middle gray would be about level 7 or 8. In effect a digitized photographic image is a table of numbers, and computers are used to store and manipulate the numbers—and thus the image itself (Figure 10.8).

When you are working with a digital camera or computerized image processing software, you don't have to worry about the intricacies of all the thousands of numbers that make up the image. But it does help to know something about how the numbers work in general because this numerical representation defines the characteristics and limitations of the digital process. The properties of a digital

Figure 10.8. Digitized image stored as a table of numbers. A grayscale image contains pixels with a range of tones from black to white. Each tone is represented by a numerical value, for example black might be 0 and white, 15, with middle gray represented by 7. Within the computer, the image data is stored as a series of numbers.

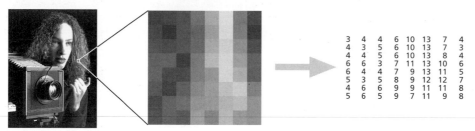

3	4	4	6	10	13	7	4
4	3	5	6	10	13	7	3
4	4	5	6	10	13	8	4
6	6	3	7	11	13	10	6
6	4	4	7	9	13	11	5
5	3	5	8	9	12	12	7
4	6	6	9	9	11	11	8
5	6	5	9	7	11	9	8

image are determined by the number and size of the pixels and by the range of gray values represented by the numbers.

Pixel size

Pixel size determines image resolution. The resolution of any photographic image is essentially its ability to distinguish fine detail. In a digital image, larger pixels give coarser resolution, while smaller pixels allow for finer detail and higher resolution (Figure 10.9). As you might expect, if you have two images of the same size, one with lots of small pixels (higher resolution) and another with fewer larger pixels (lower resolution), the higher resolution image will contain a greater total number of pixels.

Typical sizes for pixels vary from about 1/50 inch to 1/500 inch. A low-resolution image using 1/50-inch pixels has 50 pixels per linear inch. The resolution is said to be 50 pixels per inch, or 50 ppi. In a 50 ppi image it will take 50 x 50, or 2,500 pixels to represent each square inch of the image. A high-resolution image with 500 ppi will require 500 x 500, or 250,000 pixels per square inch. The number of pixels required to represent an image increases with the square of the resolution. Thus higher resolution images require many more pixels than low-resolution images. At the same time, the table of numbers representing the higher resolution image will also grow with the square of the resolution.

Image size

The number of pixels required to represent a digital photograph also depends on the physical size of the photograph. The number of pixels required is directly related to the surface area of the image. If you have two images with the same resolution (same pixel size), but one image is larger than the other, the larger image will require a larger number of pixels. For example, an image with two square inches of image area will require twice the number of pixels as an image with one square inch of image area. And an 8 x 10 image will require four times

Figure 10.9. Pixels and Resolution. Higher image resolution—the capacity to record fine detail—requires smaller pixels. The total number of pixels in the image increases with the square of the resolution.

Pixels per linear inch	10	25	50	100
Pixels per square inch	100	625	2,500	10,000

the number of pixels as a 4 x 5 image because it has four times the surface area (Figure 10.10). At the same time, the table of numbers storing the image information for the 8 x 10 photograph will also need to be four times larger.

Number of gray levels

Each pixel in a digitized black-and-white image is black or white or some gray value in between. The number of gray values that can be represented controls the smoothness of the gray scale. If too few gray values are available, the image will appear not to have a continuous gray scale and will instead jump abruptly from tone to tone. As an extreme example, suppose that only two tones were available: black or white. The result would be what is called a **line-conversion**, where a grayscale image is converted into an image that has no intermediate

Figure 10.10. Pixels and image size. An 8 x 10 photograph has four times the surface area of a 4 x 5 photograph and will require four times as many pixels to represent the image.

grays (Figure 10.11A). With four gray values, you would get a **posterization**, where the image is composed of only a few distinct gray values, in this case black, white, and two intermediate gray values (Figure 10.11B). Line conversions and posterizations can be interesting and useful techniques, but in most cases, abrupt transitions from one gray tone to another rob the photograph of tonal richness and create distracting artifacts. One such problem is **banding**, which can occur in a smooth tonal transition from dark to light (Figure 10.11C). If too few gray tones are available, the transition will appear to jump from one tone to another in a series of stripes or bands. As a result, most black-and-white digital photographs use 256 levels of gray, usually more than enough to eliminate banding and create the illusion of a continuous and uninterrupted gray scale (Figure 10.11D).

The number of gray levels that can be used to represent each pixel in a digital photograph is a function of the **bit depth** of the image. Quantitatively, bit depth is the amount of computer storage allotted to each pixel. The greater the bit depth, the more gray levels that can be stored. Because they are more complex, color images generally require more bit depth than black-and-white images. Bit depth is directly related to the method used by the computer to store grayscale or color information for each pixel.

Storing image information

At the most basic level, computers are binary—they can only work with the numbers 0 and 1. Electronically, computers keep track of 0s and 1s by setting microchip switches to *on* or *off* states. Computers have millions of such switches so they can handle large collections of numbers. Each switch holds the value of one binary digit, or **bit** for short. Grouping switches together makes it possible to store and manipulate larger numbers. For example, three binary switches can be used to represent the decimal numbers 0 through 7 and could represent eight levels of gray in a digital photograph (Figure 10.12).

Personal computers usually work with groups of eight switches, or bits, as a single entity, called a **byte**. One byte can have 256 different values, so it can be used to store the numerical value for one letter of the alphabet in your word processor, or to store numbers between 0 and 255 in your spreadsheet. In a typical black-and-white digital image, the grayscale value for each pixel is contained in one byte. Because each byte can hold 256 different values, each pixel can have 256 distinct levels of gray. That's why a 256-step gray scale is usually used in black-and-white digital images. Such a black-and-white image has a bit depth of 8 bits (or one byte). In a color digital image, three bytes are usually required to represent each pixel, one byte for each of the three additive primaries—red, blue, and green—and the bit depth is 24 bits. (Chapter 11 deals with digital color in more detail.)

see trent on 252

Figure 10.11. Effects of number of gray levels. The bit depth of a digital image is the amount of computer storage allocated to each pixel. The greater the storage space, the greater the tonal range possible.

A. Two gray levels produce a line conversion (bit depth: 1)

C. Sixteen gray levels produce banding in graduated tones (bit depth: 4)

B. Four gray levels produce a posterization (bit depth: 2)

D. 256 gray levels (bit depth: 8)

COMPUTER IMAGE FILES

The computer stores each image as a separate collection of numbers, called a **file**. Every computer file has a unique name so you can find it again, access it, move it, copy it, or delete it. Each image file will store information such as the size of the image, whether it is black-and-white or color, and so on. But most of the file will consist of the pixel values for the image, so the size of the file is largely determined by the number of pixels in the image and the bit depth of each pixel. If you have a black-and-white image containing 1,000 pixels, the file will require about 1,000 bytes of storage. If the same image were in color and each pixel required three bytes of storage, the resulting file would be about 3,000 bytes.

Most image files are much larger than 3,000 bytes and you will find the shorthand terminology for file sizes useful. File sizes are commonly given in kilobytes or megabytes. Strictly speaking, a kilobyte is 1,024 bytes and a megabyte is 1,048,576 bytes, but it may be easier to think of a 1 kilobyte (1 K) file as about one thousand bytes and a 1 megabyte (1,000K, or 1 Mb) file as about one million bytes. Most floppy disks hold between 1.4 and 2 megabytes. ZIP™ disks, used by many digital photographers, hold 100 megabytes. The hard drive in your computer is likely to hold between several hundred megabytes and several gigabytes. Digital image files

Figure 10.12. Computer storage of pixel values. Computers store information in binary digits (or bits) by turning electrical switches on and off. Here, three switches are used to represent eight gray values.

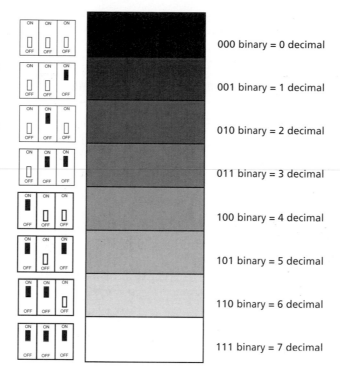

000 binary = 0 decimal

001 binary = 1 decimal

010 binary = 2 decimal

011 binary = 3 decimal

100 binary = 4 decimal

101 binary = 5 decimal

110 binary = 6 decimal

111 binary = 7 decimal

typically vary in size from a few hundred kilobytes on up to nearly 100 megabytes. The exact size will depend on the size of the image, the size of the pixels, the bit depth, and the method used to store the image data.

Computer storage (rounded/exact)

1 bit	the binary digits 0 or 1	
1 byte	8 bits	
1 kilobyte	1,000 bytes	1,024 bytes
1 megabyte	1,000,000 bytes	1,048,576 bytes
1 gigabyte	1,000,000,000 bytes	1,073,741,824 bytes
1 terabyte	1,000,000,000,000 bytes	1,099,511,627,776 bytes

Estimating file size

In a loose sense, the size of an image file is a measure of the technical quality of the image and is an important factor when scanning film or prints. The file size is related both to the resolution (size of each pixel) and the bit depth (number of gray values allowed) of the image. The larger the file, the more image information it contains. You will find it useful to be able to estimate image file sizes and to gauge the relationship between file size and image quality.

As already noted, the size of an image file is primarily determined by the number of pixels in the image and the bit depth for each pixel. The number of pixels in an image, in turn, is determined by the resolution and the size of the image. For example, an image with a resolution of 100 ppi will contain 100 x 100, or 10,000 pixels for each square inch of surface area. If the image size is 4 x 5 inches, its dimensions in pixels will be 400 x 500, or 200,000 pixels total. Now, if each of those pixels has a bit depth of one byte, the computer storage required for the image will be 200,000 bytes (Figure 10.13A).

If you were to increase the size of the image from 4 x 5 to 8 x 10 and keep the resolution at 100 ppi, its dimensions in pixels would become 800 x 1,000, and the total number of pixels would increase to 800,000. At one byte per pixel, the total storage required would be 800,000 bytes (Figure 10.13B).

If you were to leave the size of the image at 4 x 5, but increase the resolution from 100 ppi to 150 ppi, the number of pixels in each square inch would increase from 10,000 to 22,500. The dimensions of the image in pixels would become 600 x 750, or 450,000 pixels in all. The amount of storage for the higher resolution 4 x 5 image would be 450,000 bytes (Figure 10.13C).

Finally, assume you keep the image size at 4 x 5 inches and leave the resolution at 100 ppi, but change the bit depth from one byte (for a black-and-white image with 256 levels of gray) to one bit (for a line conversion containing only black or white pixels and no gray levels). The dimensions of the image in pixels will be 400 x 500, or 200,000 pixels in all. But each pixel will require only one bit (one-eighth of a byte) of storage, so the total storage will be reduced to 25,000 bytes (Figure 10.13D).

In sum, the storage required for a digitized image is the product of the image resolution, the bit depth, and the image size. You can put the factors together in an equation that looks like this:

$$\textit{File size = (height) (width) (resolution}^2\textit{) (bit depth)}$$

The factor for resolution is squared because it affects both height and width.

To find the storage required, for example, for a 5 x 7 inch grayscale image with a resolution of 120 ppi and a bit depth of one byte:

$$\textit{File size = (5 inches) (7 inches) (120 x 120 pixels per square inch) (1 byte per pixel)}$$
$$\textit{= 504,000 bytes}$$

Or, in terms of kilobytes:

$$\textit{File size} = \frac{\textit{504,000 bytes}}{\textit{1,024 bytes per kilobyte}} = \textit{492K}$$

Figure 10.13. Effects of resolution, image size, and bit depth on file size. File size is determined by the number of pixels in an image and the amount of storage allocated to each pixel. The number of pixels depends on the size of the image and its resolution. The image bit depth is the computer storage for each pixel.

A.

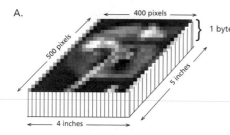

File size = (500 pixels)(400 pixels)(1 byte) = 200,000 bytes

B.

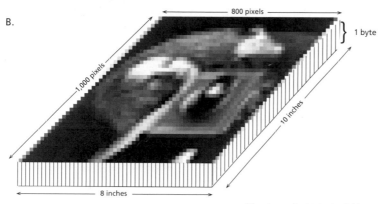

File size = (1,000 pixels)(800 pixels)(1 byte) = 800,000 bytes

C.

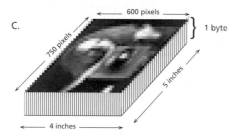

File size = (750 pixels)(600 pixels)(1 byte) = 450,000 bytes

D.

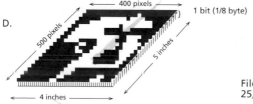

File size = (500 pixels)(400 pixels)(1/8 byte) = 25,000 bytes

TEN

File size and scanning

Most film and flatbed scanners have the capability to scan at different resolutions, producing different file sizes. As a result, before you even begin a scan, you should know how many pixels you will need to sample, that is, how large a file you need to produce. The size of the file depends on what you intend to do with it, most probably on how you intend to print it out.

Chapter 12 deals with printing and displaying digital images in detail, but for now you need only understand that different printers used to produce digital photographs operate at different resolutions. Some printers can produce more detailed, sharper images than other printers. This resolution is measured by the number of halftone dots per inch the printer can produce. Most modern laser printers, for example, can produce about 60 halftone dots per inch, usually expressed as 60 lines per inch, or 60 lpi.

A common rule of thumb is to scan at 1 1/2 to 2 times the resolution of the final image, that is, to sample 1 1/2 to 2 times as many pixels per inch as the printer can produce halftone dots per inch. This oversampling, known as the **halftoning factor,** results in a higher quality final image and is more critical with lower resolution printers. If your printer can produce higher than 133 lpi halftones, you should use a halftoning factor of 1 1/2 times the printer resolution. If your printer only produces 133 lpi or lower halftones, use a halftoning factor of 2 times the printer resolution. For example, if your printer produces 60 lpi halftones and you will be neither enlarging nor reducing the image, then you should scan at twice the printer halftone resolution, or 120 ppi. Scanning fewer pixels will compromise the quality of the final image and it will appear soft and slightly blurred. Scanning more pixels will needlessly increase the size of the image file, tax storage space, and bloat processing times when you are working with the image on the computer—all without increasing the quality of the final print.

If you will be reducing or enlarging the image, you need to adjust the number of pixels you capture accordingly. For example, if you are scanning a 35 mm black-and-white negative but plan to print it out as an 8 x 10, you will need to base the size of the image file on the finished printed image. If your printer produces 60 lpi halftones, then the halftoning factor will be 2, and the 8 x 10 image will require a resolution of 120 ppi. You can calculate the estimated grayscale file size as follows:

File size = (8 inches)(10 inches)(120 x 120 pixels per square inch)(1 byte per pixel)
    = 1,152,000 bytes

Or in terms of kilobytes and megabytes:

$$\text{File size} = \frac{1,152,000 \text{ bytes}}{1,024 \text{ bytes per kilobyte}} = 1,125 \text{ K or } 1.13 \text{ Mb}$$

Note that the scanning resolution of the film scanner will need to be much higher than 120 ppi because it is scanning a single film frame—an area of only a little more than one square inch. You must magnify the number of pixels just as you magnify the image itself. You can calculate the required scanning resolution as follows if you know the width of the original and printed versions:

$$\text{Scanning resolution} = (\text{halftone resolution})(\text{halftoning factor}) \left(\frac{\text{width of printed version}}{\text{width of original}} \right)$$

In the example of the 35 mm black-and-white negative given above, the scanning resolution would be:

$$\text{Scanning resolution} = (60)(2)\left(\frac{8}{0.941} \right) = 1,021 \text{ ppi}$$

Thus to produce an output resolution of 60 lpi, you need to scan at 1,021 ppi because the image is being magnified from a 35 mm frame to an 8 x 10 print. If you were scanning a color image, the estimated file size would increase according to the bit depth for the color information, probably three bytes per pixel. In this instance, the 1.13 Mb grayscale file would grow to a 3.39 Mb color file.

Most scanners are operated using a dialog box on your computer. In many cases the dialog box incorporates settings for the final printed output size and type of printer you plan to use—settings which allow the computer to calculate the required file size and scanning resolution for you automatically. If you depend on the computer for this calculation, be sure you indicate as closely as possible in the scanner preview how the final image will be cropped.

TEN

Checklist for using a film scanner

Step 1:   Turn on the scanner and let it warm up for about 30 minutes to stabilize the light source and CCD.

Step 2:   Open the scanner software. In many cases you can operate the scanner using a Photoshop plug-in (File > Acquire).

Step 3:   Clean the negative just as you would if you were making an enlargement.

Step 4:   Insert the negative into the scanner's film holder. (If you are scanning a mounted transparency, you won't need to use the film holder.)

Step 5:   Insert the film holder or slide into the scanner. Orient the emulsion side of the film according to the manufacturer's directions.

Step 6:   Select the film type to be scanned in the scanner dialog box.

Step 7:   Make a preview scan and crop the image as needed.

Step 8:   Focus the scanner if necessary.

Step 9:   Calculate the required file size and set the final scan resolution accordingly. The scanner software may do this calculation for you if you enter the final printed size and the type of printer you will be using, and if you are sure to crop the photograph in the scanner preview window.

Step 10:   Scan the image and save the resulting image file.

Step 11:   Sharpen the scan using one or two applications of Photoshop's Unsharp Mask filter.

Step 12:   Correct brightness, contrast, and color as needed.

REVIEW **questions** ❓

1. What replaces film in a digital camera?

2. How is the photographic gray scale represented in a digital image?

3. What is a pixel?

4. What device is usually used to convert light to an electronic representation in a digital camera or scanner?

5. What is the relationship between pixel size and digital image resolution?

6. Increasing the size of a digital image from 4 x 5 to 8 x 10 will increase the number of pixels by how much?

7. What is the halftoning factor?

8. What is the bit depth of a typical grayscale image?

9. What is a byte in computer storage?

10. What is the approximate file size of a grayscale image that has a resolution of 150 ppi, a bit depth of 1 byte per pixel, and a size of 4 x 5 inches?

TEN

digital color photography

Promising the Past, 2, by Martina Lopez, 1995

digital color photography

***Promising the Past, 2,* by Martina Lopez, 1995**

(Schneider Gallery, Chicago, Illinois © Martina Lopez. Published with permission)

In the late 1980s, Martina Lopez began to use the computer to create images that documented her own family history. "I then started to incorporate family images from beyond my personal album as a way to create a collective history, one that would allow people to bring their own memories to my work," she told *Aperture* magazine in 1994.

For Lopez, an associate professor of photography at the University of Notre Dame, the horizon in her photographs "suggests endless time, the trees demarcate space, and the fragments of snapshots verify an actual lived experience." She says the reassembled figures help create a story that often reflects her own "personal dreams and contemplations."

olor in digital photography is produced in much the same way that it is in conventional photography. The additive and subtractive systems discussed in Chapter 9 in connection with conventional color photography are the basis for most color representation in digital photography as well. Digital image processors like Photoshop also give us other ways to view and interact with color images. Because color images are more complex than black-and-white images, they require more space to store them and more time to process or transmit them. As a result, ways of compacting and storing color images are important issues in digital color. While there are dozens of file formats that can be used to store color images, you can get by with only a few, each one offering special advantages.

DIGITAL COLOR REPRESENTATION

RGB color

The additive system creates a variety of colors by adding together various amounts of the three primary colors, red, green, and blue. In the world of computers and digital photography, this system is named for the primary colors themselves: **RGB color**. It is probably easiest to think of a digital RGB image as having three layers, one for each additive primary (Figure 11.1). In a typical RGB image, each primary color is represented by one byte, so the complete color information for each pixel is stored in three bytes. Because the bit depth for an RGB image is 24 bits (3 bytes x 8 bits per byte), it is often called 24-bit color. This three-byte representation allows for 256 x 256 x 256 distinct colors, or 16,777,216 colors in all.

Your computer is well matched to RGB color because that is the way the monitor displays color. If you use a magnifier to look closely at a white area on your monitor screen, you will see red, green, and blue dots or stripes (Figure 11.2).

Figure 11.1. RGB color. The additive primaries—red, green, and blue—are implemented as RGB color in digital imaging and are also the basis for the way computer monitors produce color. You can think of an RGB image as being made up of three layers, one for each of the primaries. An RGB image thus requires three bytes to store color information for each pixel.

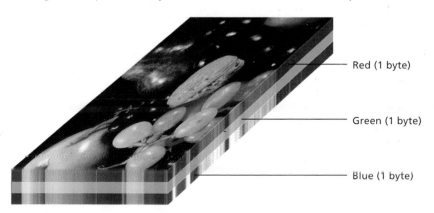

Red (1 byte)

Green (1 byte)

Blue (1 byte)

Figure 11.2. Close-up of monitor screen. The image on a computer monitor is composed of a pattern of red, green, and blue dots. By varying the intensity of the colored dots, many colors can be displayed.

Your monitor screen contains red, green, and blue phosphors which, when excited by the electron stream that creates the screen image, glow and emit red, green, and blue light. When all three primaries are mixed at full intensity, the monitor appears to be white. By making the three phosphors glow in differing intensities and different mixtures, the monitor can display a variety of colors. Most computer display adapters can be set to different modes, producing a smaller or greater range of colors on the monitor. If the display adapter can show all 16,777,216 values of 24-bit RGB color, it is said to be using millions of colors. Some computers can display only 16-bit color (thousands of colors) or 8-bit color (256 colors) on the screen. In those limited display modes the computer monitor may not appear to be truly photographic, although the computer will still be working with the full 24-bit complement of colors internally while processing the image itself.

The increased bit depth of an RGB image compared to a grayscale image will obviously have a significant impact on file size. An RGB image will require three times the storage of an equivalent grayscale image (one with the same resolution and of identical size) because each pixel requires three bytes rather than one. For example, a 4 x 5 RGB image at a resolution of 150 ppi will require this much storage:

File size = (4 inches)(5 inches)(150 x 150 pixels per square inch)(3 bytes per pixel)
= 1,350,000 bytes = 1.3 Mb

An equivalent grayscale file would require only 439 K of storage, a third as much. The added complexity of color doesn't just affect storage, however. Because they have greater bit depth than grayscale images, color images take longer to scan, to process, and to print as well.

The subtractive color system used in digital photography is called **CMYK color**. It is so named for the subtractive primaries, cyan, magenta, and yellow, with an added "K" layer, which contains the black and neutral gray values for the image. This is the same version of the subtractive system used in graphic arts for printing full-color (or **process color**) images in magazines, newspapers, and other printed publications. In graphic arts, the image is first separated into cyan, magenta, yellow, and neutral components. Those four separations are then overprinted one at a time onto a single sheet of paper using cyan, magenta, yellow, and black inks to yield the final full color image (Figure 9.23). The same system is used in digital imaging for the simple reason that most computer color printers use essentially the same methodology—cyan, magenta, yellow, and black inks or toners are separately applied to the paper to build up a full range of colors.

Most CMYK images store four bytes per pixel—one byte for each of the three subtractive primaries and one byte for the neutral "K" component. You can think of each byte as representing one layer in the full-color image (Figure 11.3). Because CMYK images require four bytes per pixel rather than the three used for an RGB image, CMYK files are a third again as large as equivalent RGB files. For example, a 4 x 5 CMYK image at a resolution of 150 ppi will require this much storage:

> *File size = (4 inches)(5 inches)(150 x 150 pixels per square inch)(4 bytes per pixel)*
> *= 1,800,000 bytes = 1.76 Mb*

This compares with 1.32 Mb for an RGB file and 439 K for a grayscale file.

Figure 11.3. CMYK color. The subtractive primaries—cyan, magenta, and yellow—form the basis of CMYK color, used widely in color printers. Besides the cyan, magenta, and yellow components, a neutral "K" component keeps track of grays and blacks in the image. You can think of a CMYK image as having four layers, one each for cyan, magenta, and yellow and one for the neutral gray values.

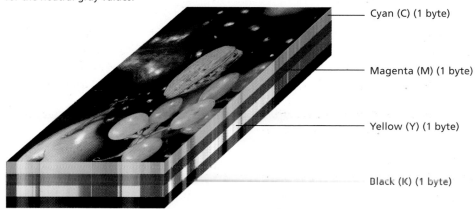

Cyan (C) (1 byte)

Magenta (M) (1 byte)

Yellow (Y) (1 byte)

Black (K) (1 byte)

Figure 11.4. Color balance dialog box. You can change the relative balance of each of the additive and subtractive primaries in an image, much as you would with a color enlarger.

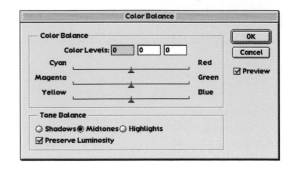

Color manipulation of RGB and CMYK images

Because the additive primaries are the color complements of the subtractive primaries, you can control the amount of red, green, and blue by manipulating cyan, magenta, and yellow—and vice versa. If you need to correct the overall color balance of an image, you can usually do so by manipulating the additive and subtractive primaries. Photoshop, for example, uses the Color Balance dialog box, which has sliders for each of the three complementary pairs (Figure 11.4). This is essentially the same approach that color photographers have been using to make conventional color prints for years; color heads on enlargers allow direct control of the amount of yellow, cyan, and magenta in the enlarging light. For example, you can use these controls to color correct an image taken under tungsten light using daylight film, or an image taken in the shade that has a bluish cast

Figure 11.5. Variations dialog box. This allows you to change the relative balance of each of the primary colors like the color balance dialog box, but adds a preview to make it easier to compare possible results. You can also make changes in lightness/darkness and in color saturation.

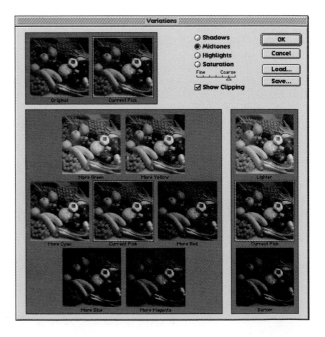

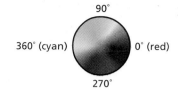

Figure 11.6. Color wheel. Hue is the color itself—blue as opposed to green or red. In the Hue, Saturation, and Brightness color model, hue is measured along a spectrum which runs around a color wheel.

from skylight. These types of corrections are even easier if you use something like Photoshop's Variations dialog box, which produces the equivalent of an instant color ring-around, previewing what your image would look like with added amounts of each of the three additive and three subtractive primaries (Figure 11.5). For simple color correction, the Variations dialog box is usually quick and easy, but many people still have to adjust the way they look at color to work with color shifts in terms of the six primaries. The RGB and CMYK color models are not very intuitive and many people have trouble adapting their color judgment to them. Many find it easier to work with the HSB color model.

HSB color

The **HSB color** model allows you to control hue, saturation, and brightness independently. **Hue** is the color itself—red, or green, or orange for instance. **Saturation** is the purity of the color—whether it tends to be grayish neutral at one extreme or pure color a the other. **Brightness** is the lightness or darkness of the color, and ranges from black to white. Many people find this model more intuitive than working with the color primaries because it mimics the way most of us think about color. The HSB color approach is really not a different color model, as RGB and CMYK are, but instead a different way to manipulate whatever color model you are using to store your image.

The range of hues is usually thought of as a spectrum running around a color wheel (Figure 11.6). Color complements are opposite one another on the color

ELEVEN

Figure 11.7. HSB color sliders. Separate controls allow you to manipulate hue (the color itself), saturation (the purity of the color), and brightness (the lightness or darkness of the color).

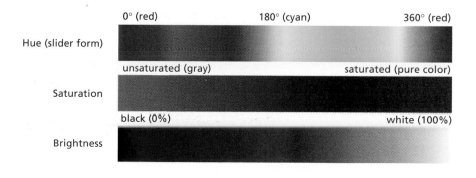

wheel. Red is located at 0° (or 360°). Cyan, the complement of red, is located at 180°. In image processing software, the range of hues is often displayed as a bar with a slider that you can use to adjust the selection of hue (Figure 11.7 top).

The saturation of a color can run from completely saturated to completely unsaturated. A completely saturated color is pure color—a single hue with no other hues mixed in. A completely unsaturated color will be utterly gray, with no "color" at all, nothing to differentiate it from other grays. If you were working with paint, you could most easily reduce the saturation of a color by mixing it with its complementary color. Most image processing software allows you to continuously vary color saturation from a neutral gray to pure color using a slider (Figure 11.7 middle).

The brightness (or luminance) of a color is its lightness or darkness. You can change the brightness of a color by adding or subtracting white light. At one end of the brightness scale there is no white light at all and the color appears as a dense black. At the other end, there is so much white light that it overwhelms the color and it appears as brilliant white. In between are colors with perceptible hue ranging from dingy looking colors at the dark end to washed-out, pastel colors at the bright end. Most image processing software allows continuous variation of brightness from black to white (Figure 11.7 bottom).

Color calibration

You may digitize a color image, slave over it on your computer, and create something that looks outstanding on your monitor, only to be disappointed when it's printed out because the people are green, the entire image is too dark, and it looks nothing like what you saw on the screen. In order to produce predictable results from screen to printer with an image processing system, you must calibrate the entire system so the individual components work in harmony. Essentially, this means adjusting the computer display so it accurately predicts what will happen when you print the image. Monitor calibration is equally important for grayscale images because it will make image density and contrast predictable in the final print. The problem in both color and grayscale is one of synchronizing the monitor and printer so they handle color and gray values the same way.

▸▸ **Step 1—Monitor calibration:** Although computer monitors all use the RGB color system, the precise colors displayed often vary from one monitor to another. Monitors may differ in the type of phosphors used to create the colors and employ different electronics to create and control the electron stream that forms the on-screen image. These differences result in a wide variation from one monitor to another. As a result you will need to calibrate your monitor. Monitor calibration involves setting the gamma, which controls midtone contrast, and removing color casts from the display. (Most computer monitors have a slightly blue tint.) Begin by warming up your monitor for at least 30 minutes to stabilize the display. Set

Figure 11.8. Gamma utility. This Photoshop utility allows you to calibrate your color monitor. It will help you set contrast and brightness, gamma, color balance, and white point to compensate for differences between one monitor and another.

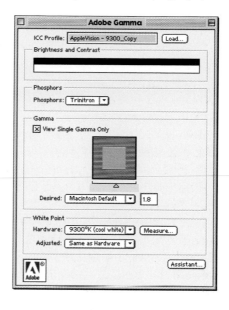

room lighting at normal working levels. Adjust the brightness and contrast of the monitor and tape down the controls. Then use a software utility like the Adobe Gamma utility (Figure 11.8) that comes with Photoshop to adjust screen gamma and remove color casts. When you are done, the white displayed on the monitor should match the white of a sheet of printer paper, and there should be no color casts in neutral areas (black and grays) on the screen. If you are using an RGB printer, like an inexpensive color ink-jet printer, that's all the calibration that you need to do.

▸▸ **Step 2—Printing ink colors:** If your printer requires CMYK color files, your image processing software will also need to adjust for the kind of inks your printer uses and its dot gain—the change in the halftone dot size when inks are absorbed into the paper during printing and bleed slightly. In Photoshop, these values are entered in the CMYK Setup dialog box. This information is used to convert RGB images to CMYK images for printing. If you're not sure about the values for ink colors and dot gain, ask your instructor or service bureau. The ink color and dot gain settings have a profound impact on the quality of the printed image. The ink colors themselves are usually consistent from one printer to another of the same type, for instance, from one Tektronix Phaser II printer to another, but dot gain can vary widely. As a result, you may need to adjust the value for the dot gain again after making a color proof.

▸▸ **Step 3—Color proof:** Print a CMYK image on the printer you are calibrating. This image must have been created in CMYK mode. It cannot have been converted from an RGB image because it is that conversion process that you are calibrating.

If you are using Photoshop, just use the CMYK test file that comes with it: *Olé No Moiré* (Macintosh) or *Testpict.jpg* (Windows). Simply open the image in Photoshop and send it to the printer.

▸▸ **Step 4—Calibrate screen image to the color proof:** Compare the printed CMYK color proof with the screen display of the image. You may find the screen is lighter or darker than the proof. Adjust for this difference by changing the setting for the printer's dot gain—in Photoshop, by using the CMYK Setup dialog box. If your screen display is too light, increase the dot gain; if the display is too dark, decrease the dot gain. When you close the dialog box, the display will change based on your new dot gain setting. If necessary, adjust the dot gain again until your proof matches the monitor. You should be able to adjust the dot gain until the monitor and proof density match exactly. Color casts are more difficult to correct, but are also fairly rare. If the color renditions in the proof and monitor do not match, check to see that you have the correct printing inks specified in the CMYK dialog box. You may need to check with your printer manufacturer for the correct calibration file.

Scanner calibration: Strictly speaking, your scanner must also be calibrated to make working with color images accurate and efficient. In general, however, you will not need to worry about it because nearly all desktop scanners—both film scanners and flatbed scanners—are self-calibrating. In the case of a film scanner, just make sure there is nothing in it when you turn it on and it will run through a calibration routine by itself. Then when you scan a negative or transparency, be sure to set the film type in the scanning software correctly so the scanner knows what kind of color dyes were used in the film and whether to compensate for the orange printing mask built into color negative films.

Color gamut and Lab color

Because a CMYK image requires more storage space than an RGB image, you might logically conclude that it contains more image information and that it encompasses a greater range of colors. It's actually the other way around. CMYK image information mimics the way process printing inks act and they do not produce as wide a range of colors as an RGB monitor because of the limitations of inks and paper. The range of colors produced by any color system is known as its **color gamut** (or color space). The color gamut for a CMYK image is less than for an RGB image, and both RGB and CMYK have a smaller color gamut than does the natural color spectrum (Figure 11.9). For example, the RGB system can produce a bright blue, but CMYK cannot. And neither RGB nor CMYK can produce a fluorescent orange, although the natural color spectrum obviously can (or you couldn't see the color). If you work in Photoshop, it can warn you if an RGB color cannot be reproduced in CMYK (Figure 11.10).

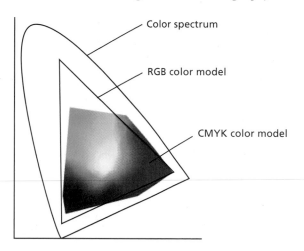

Figure 11.9. Color gamut. The range of colors produced by a particular color system is known as its color gamut, or color space. Different color systems produce different ranges of colors. The color gamut for the RGB system is larger than for CMYK color, for example.

Color spectrum

RGB color model

CMYK color model

If the RGB color model and the CMYK color model each contain a slightly different range of colors, how does a program like Photoshop manage to work with both color models and convert images back and forth between them? The answer is that Photoshop uses yet a third color model, called **L*a*b color**, or simply **Lab color**. This is a very nonintuitive, but mathematically precise, model for color representation. Like the RGB and CMYK models, Lab color breaks each color into three components—*L*, *a*, and *b*. The *L* component measures the brightness or luminance of the color. The *a* component measures the hue along a red-green axis. The *b* component measures the hue along a yellow-blue axis. Although Lab color is difficult to visualize, it has two significant advantages for an image processor like Photoshop. First, its color gamut encompasses all of the colors of both the RGB and CMYK color models, making it possible to convert

ELEVEN

Figure 11.10. CMYK out-of-gamut warning in Photoshop color picker

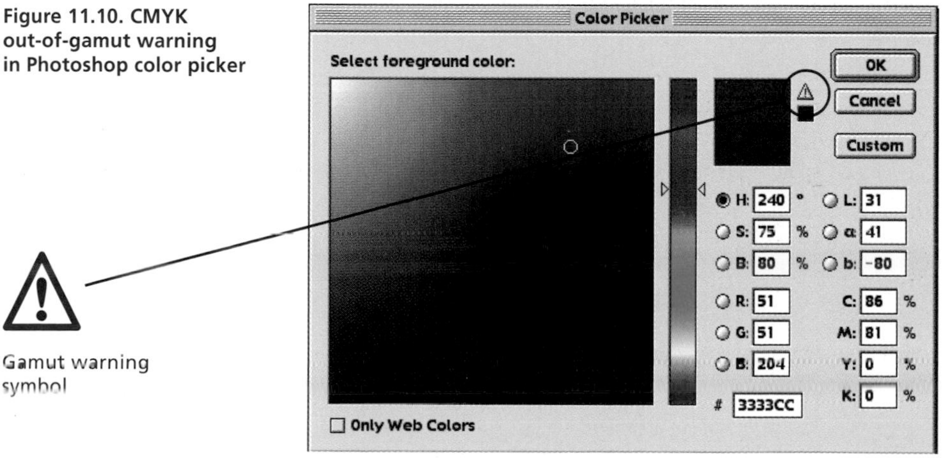

Gamut warning symbol

back and forth without losing color information. In fact, when you are working on an RGB image, Photoshop really stores the image in Lab mode and converts color information to RGB on-the-fly for the monitor display. The second advantage is that Lab color is device independent, that is, the color does not depend on the phosphors or settings on a computer monitor, nor does it depend on the type of printing inks used. Most digital photographers never use Lab color directly, but it's still there behind the scenes, keeping your images safe from restricted color gamuts and hardware limitations.

Indexed color

Because color image files are large, they require large storage devices and lots of computer memory to handle them. Their size is even more significant when you transmit image files from computer to computer over a modem. Not too many years ago, respectable modems transmitted information at 300 baud, or about 30 bytes per second. A 1.3 Mb color file would take about 12 hours to transmit at those speeds. As a result, early on-line services like CompuServe became interested in ways to store color images more economically so they could be transmitted more quickly. One solution was indexed color.

Indexed color is essentially a computerized version of paint by numbers. An indexed color image is similar to a grayscale image, but instead of having 256 gray values, an indexed color image has 256 distinct colors. That means an indexed color image takes about the same storage space as a grayscale image. If you use a program like Photoshop to convert an RGB image to indexed color, for example, it will first analyze the image to see what colors are actually used, then build a color table to represent those colors as closely as possible (Figure 11.11). Once the color table is built, the program assigns a color value to each pixel. In practice, the program may adjust color assignments so adjacent pixels mix colors from the color table and produce slight variations in color. As a result, the palette of available colors seems to be larger than 256 and the color fidelity of the indexed color image can be quite close to the original RGB image. The file that stores the image must contain the color table and the color values for each pixel, but an indexed color image is still about one-third the size of an equivalent RGB image. Despite vast increases in the speed of modems, indexed color images are still often used for transmission. For example, many of the images you see on the World Wide Web are in an indexed color format.

COMMON FILE FORMATS

Storing image information in computer files creates a number of challenges. Large image files tax storage space and take considerable time to transmit. The variety of color modes calls for flexible file formats that can store both RGB images and CMYK images in various bit depths. Image processing programs like

Figure 11.11. Indexed color image and color table. While an RGB image can have millions of different colors, an indexed color image cannot have more than 256. This saves storage space, but at the loss of some image quality, as seen in the details at right.

Original color image

Indexed color table

RGB image detail

Indexed color image detail

Photoshop require file formats that support advanced features by storing layers, selections, or device-independent color. In the process of addressing these challenges, image file formats have proliferated. Some file formats work on some platforms, such as Macintosh computers, but not others, like PCs. Some formats use special technology to compress files into a smaller storage area, which means that any program that uses the file must know how to uncompress the file. Some formats are specific to a certain application, like Photoshop, and other image processing programs are not likely to be able to use those files. Some formats can store color images, while others cannot. It is safe to say that there are scores of image file formats in use. At times, the digital photographer is likely to think he or she is in the Tower of Babel, where everyone speaks a different language and no one understands the other.

Fortunately a few of the file formats have become accepted so widely that they are likely to be all you need. In addition, high-end image processors like Photoshop can translate a number of these formats and even convert one format into another.

Figure 11.12. Bitmapped and object-oriented graphics. Bitmapped images are made of millions of pixels while object-oriented graphics are composed of lines and geometric shapes. Bitmapped images are especially useful for photographic images while object-oriented graphics are well suited to letter shapes and line drawings.

Bitmapped   Object-oriented

Bitmapped and object-oriented graphics

Computers deal with graphic information in two basic ways. One is to treat a picture as a pattern of pixels, as it does a digital photograph. This general approach is called a bitmapped or raster image because it consists of a series of pixels arranged in a grid. The second basic approach is to treat the picture as a collection of geometric figures. This approach is called an object-oriented or vector image because the complete drawing is a collection of individual geometric objects—lines, curves, circles, and so on. The bitmapped approach works well for photographs, while the object-oriented approach works well for things like line drawings, outline maps, type fonts, and the like (Figure 11.12). Many object-oriented file formats can actually contain bitmaps, which they treat as just another type of object. In order to work with photographs, any file format must be able to work with bitmapped images.

Figure 11.13. File compression. By condensing repetition, the storage required for image information is more than cut in half in this simple example.

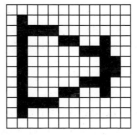

Without compression: 144 characters
WWWWWWWWWWWWWWWBWWWWWWWW
WWWBBBBWWWWWWWWWBWWWWBBWWWBW
WWWBWWWWWWBBBWWWBWWWWWWWWBBW
WBWWWWWWWBBWWWBWWWWWBBBWWW
BWWWBBWWBWWWWBBBBWWWWWWWWWBW
WWWWWWWWWWWWWWWWWWWWWWWW

With compression: 67 characters
13WB11W4B8WB3WBBWWB3WB5W3B3WB7WBB
WWB7WBBWWWB5W3B3WB3WBBWWWB3W4B8WB
22W

File compression

As the term suggests, file compression involves making files more compact, usually by eliminating redundant or unessential information. A simple example of a compression strategy is illustrated in Figure 11.13. Here we have a bitmap image of something that might be taken for a camera. Each pixel is either black or white. We can represent this image in a file with a string of *W*s and *B*s, a *W* for each white pixel and a *B* for each black pixel. When written out with no compression, the file would require 144 characters, equal to the number of pixels in the image. Note, however, that there is a great deal of repetition in the file—long strings of *W*s or *B*s repeating many times. We can shorten the file by using a kind of shorthand. We can put a number in front of a W or a B to signify that that value is repeated a certain number of times. So "13W" would mean that W is repeated 13 times, and we could store in those three characters the same information that required 13 characters in an uncompressed format. By applying this logic to the entire image, we shorten the file from 144 characters to 67 characters—a reduction of more than half. The amount of reduction given by a compression scheme is known as the **compression ratio**. The higher the compression ratio, the smaller the resulting file size.

The compression schemes used for photographic images are much more sophisticated than this simple example. They have to be, because pixel information in a photograph is not as simply repetitive as a black-and-white bitmap.

Two basic approaches to file compression are used for photographs. One is **lossless compression**, in which there is no loss of image information. Once the file is uncompressed, it is identical to the original file. Another approach is **lossy compression**, where subtle detail is sacrificed to make the file smaller. Lossy compression schemes involve a trade-off between compression ratio and image degradation: the greater the reduction in file size, the greater the loss in image quality. In most cases, you can select how much loss you are willing to accept

TIFF files

The Tagged-Image File Format (TIFF) may be the closest thing there is to a universal bitmapped image file format. It can be written or read by almost all computer applications that use images. So if you want to store an image from Photoshop and open it in your word processor to include in a newsletter, a TIFF file will almost always work. In addition, you can move TIFF files from one platform to another, so an image created on a Macintosh can be used on a PC. TIFF files support LZW compression, a type of lossless compression.

Photoshop files

While you are working on an image in Photoshop, this is the image file format to use. This format supports features of Photoshop that cannot be saved otherwise. It saves your image in any of the image modes that can be used by Photoshop

Figure 11.14. JPEG compression ratios. The more you compress a JPEG image, the greater the loss in image information and image quality, although JPEG files can be compressed a great deal with very little apparent loss in quality. You can usually select what you consider an acceptable trade-off when you save a JPEG file.

Original: no compression

JPEG: 1:10 compression

JPEG: 1:20 compression

and also saves selections (channels), paths, and layers. Saving this type of added information makes the file size larger but allows you to save your editing work in process. The Photoshop format cannot be understood by most other programs so this format is best used while working on an image. Once the image is finished, you can save it in another format to save space and make it more portable.

GIF files

The Graphics Interchange Format (GIF) was originally developed by CompuServe to facilitate transmission of bitmapped image files. GIF reduces the size of color files in two ways. First, it supports only indexed color, so the file is reduced to a third or a fourth of an RGB or CMYK file as a result of the mode change. Second, the file size is further reduced by LZW compression, a type of lossless compression. The color fidelity of a GIF image is limited by the fact that it uses indexed color, and thus the GIF format is not used for printing or publishing purposes. However, GIF files are still very common on the Internet. At one time, the only images that could be displayed alongside text on the World Wide Web were GIF files.

JPEG files

The most dramatic file size reduction for RGB and CMYK color files is achieved using the Joint Photographic Experts Group (JPEG) compression standard. Compression ratios of 1:10 (where the compressed file is one-tenth the size of the original file) are common, and the compression ratio can be much higher. JPEG compression is lossy—so when the compressed file is decompressed, it is not identical to the original. Some image information is lost. The JPEG standard uses a very sophisticated compression approach that minimizes the loss of contrast and brightness information, to which the human eye is very sensitive, but discards subtleties in color information, which human vision does not discern as readily. The result is some degradation in image quality, but usually not very noticeable. The loss in quality is greater with larger compression ratios (Figure 11.14). In most programs, including Photoshop, when you save an image in JPEG format, you can select the trade-off between image quality and compression ratio. Ordinarily, you should not save files in JPEG format while you are still working on them, for example, in Photoshop. When used repeatedly, the lossy compression can create artifacts in the image and further degrade quality. Keep the file in Photoshop or TIFF format until you are done working on it, then save it in JPEG format.

PNG files

The Portable Network Graphics file format was developed as an alternative to the GIF standard. It allows full RGB color but includes some characteristics common in GIF files that are often used in images intended for the World Wide Web: transparency, which allows your Web page background to show through portions of your image, and progressive loading, which displays your image in increasing detail as it is loaded onto your page.

PICT files

PICT files are a standard object-oriented format on Macintosh computers. Although they are object-oriented, a PICT file can contain a bitmap as one of its objects, or the only object. PICT files are not an ideal format for bitmapped image storage, but they can be useful as a way to transfer digital images from one Macintosh application to another.

BMP files

BMP files are the standard file format for Windows platform computers. They support RGB, indexed-color, and grayscale images. They can be compressed.

EPS files

Encapsulated Post Script (EPS) format is frequently used in digital photography for exporting images to desktop publishing programs like PageMaker, Quark Express, Freehand, or Illustrator. EPS is also often used to transmit CMYK image

ELEVEN

files to color printers. From one perspective, an EPS file contains two parts: a preview of the image and the image information itself. The preview is usually stored as a TIFF image (for PC) or a PICT image (for Macintosh). The full image information, on the other hand, is stored in a special page description language called PostScript, widely used in desktop publishing, that contains full instructions about how to print the image. A page layout program like Quark can use the preview to position the image without bothering with the full EPS file contents. When it comes time to print, Quark just sends the EPS file to the printer and the printer creates the image.

EPS format is extremely versatile. It can contain both bitmapped images like photographs and graphic objects like an outline map. It can contain both RGB and CMYK color, as well as black-and-white images. In the context of digital photography, however, EPS is almost always used to store CMYK color images. If you want to print a color image from Photoshop, for instance, you would first convert the image to CMYK mode. This conversion would use the printing inks and dot gain settings to adjust the CMYK files for the printer you use. Then you would use the Save As option to save the image in EPS format under a new name, possibly appending ".EPS" to the name to make it clear that it is stored in EPS format. This approach has two primary advantages. First it uses Photoshop to make the conversion from RGB to CMYK color, and Photoshop almost always does a better job of this than conversion routines built into printers. Second, it puts the image file into the PostScript language, which is the graphics language understood by almost all high-end color printers. Table 11.1 shows common image file formats.

Table 11.1. Common image file formats

TIFF	Tagged-Image File Format: Very versatile and very portable.
Photoshop	Native file format used by the Photoshop image processing program. Not portable, but able to work with Photoshop's many modes and features.
GIF	Graphics Interchange Format: An indexed color image format that is also compressed. Widely used for Internet images.
PNG	Portable Network Graphics: Emerging as a new standard format for Internet images.
JPEG	Joint Photographic Experts Group: An image file usually dramatically reduced in size using lossy compression. Also widely used for Internet images.
PICT	Standard image format for Macintosh computers, but not ideal for bitmapped images.
BMP	Standard image format for Windows platform computers.
EPS	Encapsulated PostScript: Frequently used for printing full-color images.

REVIEW **questions**

1. What is RGB color?

2. What is CMYK color?

3. What is the bit depth of a typical RGB color image?

4. What is the HSB color model?

5. How do you go about calibrating a color image processing system?

6. What is color gamut?

7. What is the Lab color model and what are its advantages and disadvantages?

8. What is indexed color and what is it used for?

9. What is the difference between a bitmapped (raster) image file and an object-oriented (vector) image file?

10. In general, how does file compression work?

ELEVEN

CHAPTER 12

The digital darkroom

Melting Beds, by Dan Burkholder

The digital darkroom

Melting Beds, by Dan Burkholder
(Published with permission, Dan Burkholder)

Dan Burkholder combines new technology and historic processes in his work. He uses digital photography to scan in images, combine them, and modify them. He then uses the computer to produce a large negative which is contact printed using platinum/palladium techniques, processes made popular by the Pictorialist photographers at the turn of the last century, but not in general use for decades. The digital negative offers several advantages. He can work from smaller negatives to begin with (most platinum/palladium printers must use view cameras that are 8 x 10 or larger).

He can create new visions by combining and modifying his images. By contact printing, he can take advantage of the long scale and delicate tones of the platinum/palladium print.

Melting Beds began with a 35 mm photograph (see inset) that Burkholder took in the Hot Springs National Park in Hot Springs, Arkansas. The room was part of a spa where gangsters and others relaxed early in the 20th century. Notice that Burkholder used Photoshop to correct most of the optical distortion introduced when the lens was tilted upward. He stretched the middle bed up at its back to strengthen the symmetry of the composition. He also used a melting effect on the edges of the beds to add to the slightly surreal quality of the image.

nce your photograph has been converted to electronic form, it can be fed into a computer, manipulated in a variety of ways, and then printed out in a number of formats—or published electronically. Within the computer, the millions of numbers that represent your digitized image can be altered and changed in ways that would be difficult or impossible in a conventional darkroom. Then when you're done working with the image, you can use various kinds of printers to transform those millions of numbers into a visual representation that can rival a conventional photographic print in sharpness and tonality. Or you can use the resources of the Internet to publish the image electronically.

PROCESSING DIGITAL IMAGES

In practice, you are usually not even aware of the millions of numbers that comprise your image when you work in an electronic darkroom. The computer displays the photograph on a monitor screen in full color or as shades of gray. Using a computer mouse, you can manipulate on-screen tools to change overall exposure and contrast, for instance. As you make adjustments, you see the effect immediately on the screen. You don't have to wait several minutes for the image to develop. You don't have to change contrast filters. And you don't get your hands wet. The computer is capable of quickly making the same sorts of image adjustments that you might make in a conventional darkroom. You can electronically burn and dodge selected areas of the image. You can even adjust the contrast in specific areas. You can magnify the image and fill in dust spots or repair scratches (Figure 12.1).

Figure 12.1. Digital retouching. The computer makes it easy to perform simple touch-ups for dust spots and scratches. Photoshop even includes a filter that will take care of minor problems automatically.

Before   After

TWELVE

A. Original image

B. Composite with new background

C. Mixed negative and positive image

D. Spatial displacement as a cube

Figure 12.2. Image manipulation. Photoshop and similar image processing programs offer a wide variety of manipulation possibilities. Some of these involve combining an image with a new background. Others involve manipulating pixel values to change brightness, contrast, and color levels. Others involve moving pixels to new locations, resulting in spatial distortions. Still others use sophisticated filters to create a variety of special effects.

E. Woodcut filter

But the electronic darkroom can also do things you only dream about in a conventional darkroom. You can cut and paste parts of your image, so you could take a picture of someone, cut him or her out, and paste him or her into an entirely new context (Figure 12.2B). This ability to seemingly alter reality is one of the most controversial aspects of the digital darkroom. It seems to call into question the very credibility of the photograph. Chapter 13 contains a fuller exploration of the ethical questions surrounding digital manipulation of photographs.

The digital darkroom allows you to produce numerous special effects. For example, you can selectively change some parts of an image to a negative and retain other parts as a positive (Figure 12.2C). Or you can tint a black-and-white image to produce a hand-colored effect. You can create false color by manipulating the relationship between pixel values and color representations.

You can spatially distort a picture to create a surrealistic effect (Figure 12.2D). Distortions are produced by displacing the location of the pixels that make up the image. In the example shown, pixels have been redistributed onto two surfaces of a cube-like structure. As a result, it appears that the subjects of the image are on two faces of a block. This is only one of many types of distortions that can be accomplished in the digital darkroom. You can also pinch, twirl, ripple, or shear an image. You can create wave effects. You can make the image look as if it were taken through a fish-eye lens.

You can apply effects filters that make the image look like a print from a woodcut rather than a photograph (Figure 12.2E). Various filters and screening patterns can create a new visualization of your image. You can create a watercolor effect or an oil painting effect. You can fracture the image into a mosaic or create a pointillistic effect reminiscent of a French surrealist painter.

One of the most powerful capabilities of the digital darkroom is its ability to composite and blend images to create entirely new realities (See Chapter 11 opener). The photographer can paint with pixels much as a painter uses oils or watercolors. The resulting images can be that much more evocative because they combine the realism of the photograph with the unfettered imagination of the painter's canvas.

Once you have adjusted and manipulated your image, you will probably want to produce a printed version so others can see it.

THE HALFTONE PROCESS

Any computer imaging device must translate the tone and color values for those millions of pixels that make up your digital image into visible form. Most computer printers display digitized images using the halftone process.

Halftones have been around since the late 1800s, when newspapers and magazines wanted to avoid having to hand-engrave printing plates in order to publish photographs. Printed publications needed a way to convert photographs directly into printable form. Such a process would not only be cheaper, it would

TWELVE

be more faithful to the original photograph. (Hand engravers were notorious for taking liberties with photographs to "improve" them.) The basic problem was one of representing the photograph, with all its variations of gray, using only black ink and white paper. The solution was to break the photograph into a pattern of dots (called halftone dots), with the dots varying in size to represent various shades of gray. Dark areas in the photograph were represented by large black dots; light areas, by tiny black dots (Figure 12.3). From normal viewing distance, the halftone dot pattern is nearly invisible and the viewer sees only the illusion of shades of gray.

Digital output devices like laser printers produce printed text by creating a pattern of tiny black dots on white paper. The letter *A*, for example, might be a pattern of dozens of tiny laser dots (Figure 12.4). The printer's resolution is determined by how small the dots are. Early laser printers produced 300 dots per inch. Most printers today can produce at least 600 dpi. But the printer's laser dots should not be confused with halftone dots. The printer's laser dots do not vary in size, as halftone dots do. The laser dots by themselves cannot create the illusion of a continuous grayscale.

To produce a grayscale, laser printers use the laser dots as building blocks to create halftone dots. For example, a halftone dot might occupy an area that is three laser dots wide by three laser dots high. Within this three-by-three halftone cell, the size of the halftone dot depends on how many of the laser dots are printed and how many are left unprinted (Figure 12.5). If most of the dots are printed, you get a large halftone dot. If only a few are printed, you get a small halftone dot. If all the laser dots are printed, you get black. If none of the laser dots are printed, you get white.

The size of the halftone cell—the number of laser dots that make it up—determines both the resolution of the halftone image and the number of gray values it can represent (Figure 12.6). The fewer the number of laser dots that are used to make the halftone dot, the higher the resolution of the halftone image. For example, if the halftone dot is constructed within a cell that is ten by ten laser dots and you were using a 300 dpi laser printer, the halftone dot would be ten laser dots wide, or 1/30 inch. Following terminology that printers have used for decades, this is called a 30 line per inch (lpi) halftone. If the halftone dot were made up of a pattern of laser dots four wide by four high, the resolution would be 300 divided by four, or a 75 lpi halftone. The smaller halftone dot would give higher resolution and finer detail in the printed halftone. It might appear that the secret to achieving high resolution, and thus higher quality, halftones is simply to use smaller halftone dots by using fewer laser dots to create each halftone dot. That would work except that the number of laser dots used to create each halftone dot also determines the number of gray levels that can be produced by the digital halftoning method.

Figure 12.3. Halftone dot pattern. The enlarged portion at left shows the dot pattern used in a halftone to simulate different values in the gray scale. Different sizes of dots create different proportions of black ink and white paper which in turn creates the illusion of different gray values.

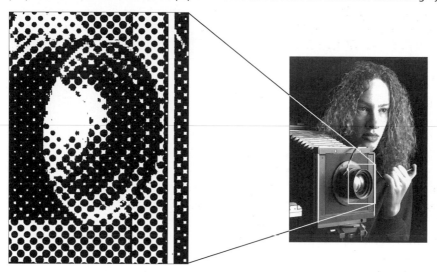

The fewer the number of laser dots used to build a halftone dot, the fewer the gray levels. A four-by-four halftone dot can produce 17 gray levels, but a two-by-two halftone dot can only produce five gray levels. The number of distinct gray levels is equal to the number of laser dots in the halftone cell plus one for the white level that is produced if none of the laser dots is printed. You can easily calculate the number of possible gray levels for a halftone cell using the following formula:

$$gray\ levels = (cell\ size)^2 + 1$$

Figure 12.4. Laser dots. Laser printers work by producing a pattern of tiny dots, in this case to build a letterform in the shape of a capital "A." In most laser printers, there are 600 dots per inch.

Figure 12.5. Halftone dots. Small dots in a laser printer combine to form various sizes of halftone dots. This 3 x 3 arrangement of laser dots allows for ten different sizes of halftone dots, ranging from solid white to solid black.

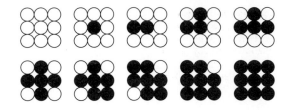

where *cell size* is the width of the halftone dot in laser dots. If the cell size were ten laser dots wide, the number of gray levels would be

$$\textit{gray levels} = 10^2 + 1 = 100 + 1 = 101$$

If the cell size were 16 laser dots wide, the number of gray levels would be

$$\textit{gray levels} = 16^2 + 1 = 256 + 1 = 257$$

Thus it would take a halftone dot that is 16 laser dots wide to produce a 256-level grayscale. To achieve that many gray levels using a 300 dpi laser printer, you would be forced to employ an 18 lpi halftone screen, which would yield extremely coarse resolution.

Obviously you must make some compromises between resolution and gray levels when you produce halftones on a laser printer. If the resolution is too high, you will posterize the image or produce banding effects. If you try to produce too many gray levels, the resolution will become unacceptably coarse. Commonly recommended compromise settings that produce acceptable results are shown in Table 12.1. These settings, or something close to them, are probably already in effect as the defaults for your printer and you can use them without change.

Table 12.1. Commonly Used Halftone Resolutions for Various Printer Resolutions

Printer resolution (dpi)	Halftone resolution (lpi)	Number of gray levels
300	60	26
600	75	65
1200	100	145
2400	150	257

FIGURE 12.6. Trade-off between halftone resolution and gray values. The smaller the halftone dot cell, the greater the resolution, but the smaller the range of gray values.

A. 2 x 2 cell: 5 gray values, resolution of 150 lpi on 300 dpi printer

B. 4 x 4 cell: 17 gray values, resolution of 75 lpi on 300 dpi printer

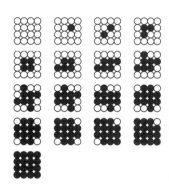

C. 10 x 10 cell: 101 gray values, resolution of 30 lpi on 300 dpi printer

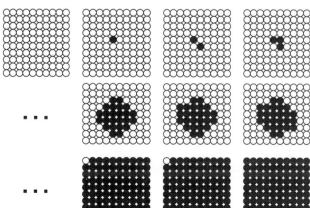

DISPLAY DEVICES

Laser printers

A laser printer is like a copy machine in that it uses an electrically charged surface to create the image. Instead of using light reflected off a paper original, however, the laser printer uses a computer-controlled laser beam to form the image.

A metal plate, usually in the shape of a drum, is first given an overall positive charge (Figure 12.7). The laser beam scans across the metal surface, rapidly turning on and off under the control of a computer built into the printer. In spots where laser light hits the charged surface, the electrical charge is neutralized. In spots that are not hit by laser light the positive charge remains and will eventually become the laser dots that create the image. Once the laser beam has scanned the surface, negatively charged black powder is dusted over the drum. Where the surface has retained its positive charge, the negative powder adheres to the drum; where the surface has been neutralized, no toner powder adheres. Next, a sheet of paper is given a positive charge and passed over the drum. The negatively charged powder transfers to the paper and is heated to fuse it in place, creating the final image.

The first laser printers produced 300 laser dots per inch (300 dpi). Most laser printers now produce 600 dpi and some can produce 1,200 dpi or even more. Higher resolution printers give better results with halftone images because they can produce small halftone dots, and thus higher resolution, at the same time they produce an acceptable number of gray values. Photographs printed on most laser printers will never be mistaken for a conventional photograph, but those printers can still be useful for proofing digital images or for small quantities of publications.

Color laser printers can produce full-color photographs using a CMYK imaging approach. Four toners are used, one each for cyan, magenta, yellow, and black. High-end color laser printers can produce continuous tone color, making the halftone pattern almost imperceptible and achieving near-photographic quality. These printers are usually found only at service bureaus.

Imagesetters

Imagesetters are the modern version of the typesetting machines used by newspapers and print shops for the past three decades. As the name suggests, an imagesetter can produce images as well as type. It creates an image the same way a laser printer does, by building a pattern of tiny dots. An imagesetter generates the dot pattern on a cathode ray tube and then exposes conventional photographic paper to the image on the tube. After development, the type, photographs, and line drawings all appear on the paper. The imagesetter dot pattern is much finer than a laser printer's—usually at least 1,200 or 2,400 dpi—and the sharpness

Figure 12.7. Laser printer. This schematic diagram shows how a laser printer uses electrical charge and laser light to create a printed image.

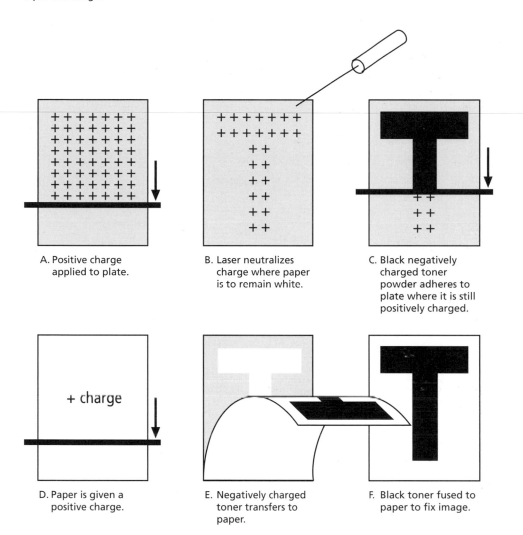

A. Positive charge applied to plate.

B. Laser neutralizes charge where paper is to remain white.

C. Black negatively charged toner powder adheres to plate where it is still positively charged.

D. Paper is given a positive charge.

E. Negatively charged toner transfers to paper.

F. Black toner fused to paper to fix image.

TWELVE

and detail of the resulting image is correspondingly greater. Even working at 1,200 dpi, an imagesetter can produce a 100 lpi halftone dot with 145 gray values. Many experts believe that the human eye does not readily perceive more than about 150 shades of gray anyway, so even at these settings an imagesetter produces essentially a full range of tones.

The imagesetter can produce a printing master that contains both photographs and text side-by-side, positioned just the way they are to appear on the finished page. For photographs that are to appear in newspapers and other printed publications, this is the ideal method. In fact, in many newspapers today, this will be the first printed version of the photograph. Frequently, the image is scanned directly from film into the computer, where it is cropped and positioned on the page, then printed out for the first time with the rest of the master page.

Ink jet printers

Many ink jet printers are similar to laser printers in that they create an image by creating a pattern of tiny dots on the paper. The difference, as the name suggests, is that the ink jet printer forms the dots by squirting ink on the paper through a small nozzle. The ink jet print head moves back and forth across the paper and where a dot should appear, ink inside a reservoir is heated almost instantly until pressure forces the ink out through a tiny nozzle onto the paper. In effect, the print head spray paints the image onto the paper.

Ink jet technology is employed in very inexpensive desktop printers as well as high-end color printers used to preview color separations prior to publishing them on a printing press. Compared to laser printers, ink jet printers are somewhat slower. On the other hand, ink jet technology has made color printing much more affordable and many moderately priced models produce results nearly indistinguishable from a conventional photograph. Color ink jet printers produce full color by spraying cyan, magenta, yellow, and black inks simultaneously (and some models add two more colors to achieve greater color fidelity). Maximum quality requires the use of special papers, which tend to be expensive. Thus, although the equipment is relatively inexpensive, the costs of ink and paper can be quite high. Still, the ink jet printer is probably the best option for high-quality output without having to go to a service bureau.

Thermal printers

Thermal printers (also called thermal dye-transfer or dye-sublimation printers) use heat to transfer dyes from a color ribbon to a receiver sheet to produce a full-color image of photographic quality. A thermal printing head containing a long row of tiny heating elements heats the color ribbon and deposits color dye on the receiver sheet (Figure 12.8). The temperature of each heating element is computer controlled and regulates the amount of dye transferred to the paper, so no halftone dot pattern is required to create variations in gray values or colors. The color ribbon contains separate sections for each of the subtractive primaries—yellow, magenta, and cyan. Three separate passes, one for each primary color, are made across the receiver sheet to build up a full-color image, in much the same way a full-color image is produced by a printing press. Thermal printers can print on a glossy receiver sheet, which produces an image like a conventional glossy print, or on a transparent sheet, which produces an image like a color transparency. Black-and-white thermal printers are also available. Thermal printers are relatively expensive but can be found at most service bureaus.

Film recorders

Film recorders can produce a full-color image on conventional color film. The film is exposed through color filters to a very high resolution TV screen that is controlled by the computer. More sophisticated film recorders can produce results that are indistinguishable from conventional photographic methods. Once the image is on film, it can be used to make conventional photographic prints or displayed as a slide.

The list of possible printing technologies for digital photography does not end here. Scores of other processes—based on lasers, dry-transfer dyes, fiber-optics, and light valves, to name a few—are under development and being tested. It

Figure 12.8. Thermal printer. This schematic diagram shows how a thermal printer uses tiny heated wires to melt colored dyes and transfer color to a paper surface. The amount of color transferred can be controlled by the heat of the wire so this type of printer does not need to use a halftone dot pattern. The result is a print almost indistinguishable from a conventional photographic print.

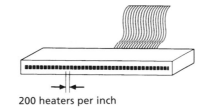

200 heaters per inch

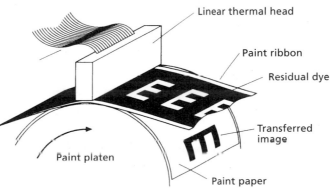

Linear thermal head

Paint ribbon

Residual dye

Transferred image

Paint platen

Paint paper

TWELVE

seems likely that no one technology will vanquish the others because of trade-offs in cost, quality, speed, and appearance. Digital photographers will probably continue to have a variety of approaches to getting printed copy from their electronic darkrooms.

NEWSPAPER USE OF DIGITAL PHOTOGRAPHY

Newspapers have been among the pioneers of digital photographic technology, especially the digital camera. The sharpness of the digital camera is adequate for much newspaper photography. In addition, digital cameras have distinct advantages for the newspaper photographer. Its speed is a great help on deadline. And the ability to transmit digital images quickly over telephone wires is a boon to news syndicates and photographers covering events at great distances from their home newspapers. For instance, a newspaper photographer might travel several hundred miles to cover a football game involving a local team. At one time, it was necessary to take the film back to the newspaper to be used. Newspapers even used portable darkrooms so the photographer could process film in the car or on an airplane to cut precious minutes off the deadline squeeze. With a digital camera, however, the photographer can simply dial up the newspaper's computer from the press box and transmit the images over the telephone. Even when using conventional film, a photographer can use a film scanner to transmit the images once they have been processed. One of the early practitioners of digital deadline photography was Associated Press photographer Ron Edmonds, who used a still video camera to cover the 1989 swearing-in of

Figure 12.9. Digital cameras in photojournalism. Photojournalists can check images in the preview window of a digital camera at the news scene, a habit called "chimping" among news photographers. The digital camera is valuable primarily because it eliminates darkroom processing and allows images to be transmitted quickly.

President George Bush. His photograph was on its way to more than 1,000 newspapers nationwide within 40 seconds of the time it was taken.

Nearly all daily newspapers in the United States are now involved in digital photography to one extent or another. All Associated Press newspapers now use an electronic darkroom to receive and edit wire photos (Figure 12.9). A few newspapers already use digital cameras, especially for tight deadline assignments. Most newspapers that continue to use conventional film and cameras now employ film scanners to move images into their electronic systems. Many newspapers bring text and digitized images together in electronic layouts on the computer before producing the printing plate.

DIGITAL PUBLISHING

Increasingly, you don't need paper or film at all for others to see the results of your efforts in the digital darkroom. More and more, the digital image itself is the final product as digital publishing and Internet communication prove more widespread. You can look at photographs in books published on CD-ROM directly on your computer screen. You can visit virtual art galleries on the Internet. You can create your own home page on the World Wide Web and put your own photographs on exhibit for others to see.

One of the first photography books published on CD-ROM was Rick Smolan's *From Alice to Ocean*, the story of Robyn Davidson's 1,700-mile solo journey across the Australian outback. The book is interactive. You can click on a map and look at a photograph of the place where you clicked. As you look at the photograph, you can click on a button and hear the photographer explain how the photograph was made or hear comments by the subject. Smolan has since published a second interactive book on CD-ROM, *Journey to Vietnam*. The list of similar interactive photography books grows daily.

Quickly growing as sophisticated as CD-ROM multimedia presentations are sites on the World Wide Web. To use the World Wide Web, you need a browser and a connection to the Internet. The browser displays document files stored on other computers using a coding system known as hypertext markup language, or HTML. More powerful sites add Java scripts and Flash presentations. Web documents can contain digitized images in GIF or JPEG format and the browser will display the photographs as part of the Web page. Any Web page can contain links that the user clicks to display yet another Web page, which could be stored on another computer halfway around the world. Because the links weave together millions of computer documents from country to country around the globe, it is indeed a world wide web. If you have an account on a Web server, you can probably set up your own home page.

TWELVE

REVIEW **questions** ?

1. What types of special effects and manipulations can be produced using image processing software?

2. What is the halftone process and how is it used to produce a digital image?

3. How does a laser printer produce halftone dots from laser dots?

4. How does a color laser printer produce color images?

5. What is the trade-off between halftone resolution and number of gray values in a digital halftone?

6. How many gray levels can be produced on a 600-dpi laser printer using a halftone resolution of 60 lines per inch?

7. Compare the following digital printing technologies: laser printer, ink jet printer, imagesetter, thermal printer, and film recorder?

8. What are the advantages of digital photography to a newspaper photographer?

9. What is digital publishing?

10. What is the World Wide Web?

professional issues in photography

"I'm not interested in taking pretty pictures. I'm anxious to tell a story.
You never know when things are going to
happen. They may happen just as the light
goes. I'd rather have a strong image that
is technically bad than vice versa."

Robert Capa

photography,
ethics,
and the # law

Princess Diana with Photographers, New York, 1997, by Emile Wamsteker

photography, ethics, and the law

***Princess Diana with Photographers*, New York, 1997, by Emile Wamsteker**
(Published with permission, AP/Wide World Photos)

Nothing stretched the boundaries of photographic ethics and laws governing invasion of privacy in the late 1990s more than the relentless pursuit of Princess Diana of Britain by the *paparazzi*, a group of British and European photographers. As exemplified in this shot taken in New York as she left a charity auction, photographers chronicled her every move. They often used any means possible to snap photos of the famous princess, once Princess of Wales and wife of the heir to the British throne. At times, this pursuit bordered on the unreasonable, with photographers intruding on her personal life as well as recording her official duties with their high-powered lenses and often boorish behavior. Her death in 1997 was at first blamed on the *paparazzi* chasing her car. This led to attempts to enact laws restricting the taking of photographs of celebrities. Although most of these attempts failed, the uproar served as a warning to all photographers to consider their behavior in pursuing their subjects.

Mastering the technical skills of photography and acquiring the ability to recognize a good photo isn't all there is to being a successful photographer. In the real world, there are rules beyond the rule of thirds and laws beyond the law of reciprocity. People will expect you to abide by the rules of ethical behavior and the laws of the legal system.

ETHICS

Many times, who or what you photograph, how and when you take the picture, and what you ultimately do with it is simply a matter of ethics. In many ways, journalistic **ethics** are like good taste: you acquire them slowly over time. Hopefully, you will eventually reach the point where you know something is unethical the minute you encounter it.

Unfortunately, there are no rigid rules to guide you. Photography is not governed by a binding and formal code of ethics. Unlike licensed professions like medicine and law, where people who are unethical can be prevented from working, journalism is more flexible and compliance is voluntary. It isn't that journalists or photographers are less ethical than doctors or lawyers. There is just no formal mechanism to police and discipline them.

Professional photo organizations like the National Press Photographers Association have codes of ethics. They exert moral pressure on photographers to be ethical as they do their jobs. "It is the individual responsibility of every photojournalist at all times to strive for pictures that report truthfully, honestly, and objectively," reads one principle. "As journalists, we believe that credibility is our greatest asset. In documentary photojournalism, it is wrong to alter the content of a photograph in any way (electronically or in the darkroom) that deceives the public. We believe the guidelines for fair and accurate reporting should be the criteria for judging what may be done electronically to a photograph." The code goes on to urge photographers to have "in them a note of sympathy for our common humanity and shall always require us to take into consideration our highest duties as members of society."

Photographers who don't live up to such high ideals will eventually earn reputations for being unethical and might have trouble getting jobs or free-lance photo assignments. That most photographers and other journalists do follow such high standards—based on their training, experience, and individual consciences—is one of the wonders of modern journalism. Few other professions exercise such self-restraint.

THIRTEEN

KNOWING THE LAW

If photo ethics are intangible, legal questions are not. Various laws have developed to protect both the subjects of photographs and the photographers taking the photographs. When you work as a photographer, you must observe some basic rules. First of all, you can't create a public nuisance. For example, you cannot impede traffic or create a fire hazard by blocking a door as you take pictures. You cannot intrude on a person's home without permission, nor unduly disturb even a well-known celebrity. You usually are not allowed to take a photo of a theatrical presentation, a professional sporting event, or a painting in a museum without permission. Most courtrooms are off limits to you, as are military installations.

And, in perhaps what will seem the most surprising prohibition of all, you are restricted in photographing money and postage stamps. This law used to bar all photos of these items to discourage counterfeiting. The law has been modified in recent years to allow such photographs for philatelic, numismatic, historical, educational, or newsworthy purposes, but never for advertisements except in stamp and coin publications. All photos of money must be in black and white, although colored pictures of postage stamps are allowed.

Privacy questions

Basically, the law has defined the photographer's right to take pictures of people or things in "public" places. But there are some qualifications that primarily stem from the ultimate use of the photographs.

For example, amateur photographers who take photos for their own interest or pleasure are free to photograph, say, the performers or spectators at a public parade without danger of violating anyone's rights. Similarly, professional news photographers can take the same type of photo, provided the event is considered newsworthy and the photos are used in a news story. On the other hand, a professional photographer who photographs a majorette in the parade and then sells it for advertising purposes is violating her right to privacy unless the photographer has her explicit permission to use it in that way.

The law attempts to protect individuals' rights to privacy and, in many cases, must balance these rights against the public's right to information or news. There are four basic types of **invasion of privacy:** appropriation, intrusion, publication of private matters, and false light.

▸▸ **Appropriation** occurs when you use someone's name or likeness, such as a photograph, for trade or advertising purposes without his or her permission. To do so is an invasion of this person's privacy. Most of the time, this issue arises with well-known people who are photographed in public places and the photos are used to sell products without their consent. The people may not want to be associated with the products—or perhaps they want to be paid for endorsing them.

But the privacy of anyone you photograph in a public place—not just well-known personalities—can be invaded if you use his or her photo without permission for advertising or trade purposes. You can even invade the privacy of someone who consents to your taking his or her picture in a private place—for example, a model who agrees to a photo session in your own studio. If you have a chance later to sell the photos to an ad agency, you need the model's permission to use the photos for that purpose.

FIGURE 13.1. A model release form

MODEL RELEASE

Date: _____

Photographer: _____

Address: _____

_____

For valuable consideration, I hereby irrevocably consent to and authorize the use and reproduction by you, or anyone authorized by you, of any and all photographs which you have this day taken of me, negative or positive, for any purpose whatsoever, without further compensation to me. All negatives and positives, together with the prints shall constitute your property, solely and completely.

I am over 21 years of age.   Yes _____   No _____

Model: _____
       (signature of model)

Address: _____

Witnessed by: _____
              (signature of witness)

(If the person signing is under 21, consent must be given by the parent or guardian.)

I hereby certify that I am the parent or guardian of _____
the model named above, and for the value received, I do give my consent without reservations to the foregoing on behalf of him or her or them.

Signed: _____   Date: _____
        (signature of parent or guardian)

Witnessed by: _____
              (signature of witness)

While most people who are not famous celebrities may actually be flattered and may not make an issue if you use their photos without permission, your own sense of ethics should lead you to avoid invading their privacy by appropriation. One way to do so is to get everyone you photograph in anything but a straight news situation to sign a model release. A **model release** is a standardized form in which the person signing gives his or her consent both to take the photograph and to use it. There are many variations of model releases. Figure 13.1 shows a standard form that you can adapt to your needs.

For example, you can substitute a specific amount of money for the phrase, "for valuable consideration." The standard form gives you permission to use the photos in any way you wish, but if the subject is reluctant, the form can be revised to mention one specific use, such as to illustrate one particular story or to use in a textbook. It might also prohibit a specific use, such as in an advertisement.

Once signed, the model release form goes into your file or the file of your employer for reference. In most cases, the form will never be looked at again. In rare instances when a subject objects to a photograph—usually after its sale and/

or publication—it is very comforting to be able to protect yourself and answer the objection by producing the signed release.

▸▸ **Intrusion**, as defined by law, is an invasion of privacy akin to trespassing. It occurs when a photographer goes to unreasonable lengths to take photographs of people, almost always without their consent or knowledge, in places where they have a reasonable expectation of privacy. Accordingly, it is not only unethical, but in violation of a person's rights if you use a telephoto lens, for example, to photograph your neighbor sunbathing in the privacy of her own backyard. The issue here is not so much the ultimate use of the photo, but how you took it.

When it comes to celebrities, intrusion applies not only to how you attempt to photograph them in private places, but also to how you treat them when you attempt to photograph them in public places. Celebrities are deemed newsworthy and are thus fair game for photographers whenever they appear in public. Nevertheless, you must be cautious of unreasonable harassment or interference in their activities when attempting to photograph them in public.

The courts have placed a lot of emphasis on reasonableness, as photographer Ron Gallella found out in 1972 and again in 1981. For years, Gallella, a New York free-lance photographer, had made his living taking photographs of Jacqueline Kennedy Onassis. She was able to convince a New York court that he had invaded her privacy by harassing her and her children indoors and outdoors at all times. He concocted ruses and wore disguises to take her picture. He was first required to stay a specified number of feet away from their residences and from her and her children when in public. After he failed to do so, he was then barred from photographing her altogether. Compounding his situation was the fact that Gallella had sent Christmas cards to editors with her photo on one side and his own on the other, which the court judged to constitute an advertisement and thus a further invasion of her privacy by appropriation.

Intrusion became a big issue again in 1997 at the time of the death of Princess Diana of Britain in a car crash in Paris. After her marriage in 1981 to Prince Charles, the heir to the British throne, Diana was constantly pursued by photographers. In time, a number of staff photographers and free-lancers made their living from taking and selling photos of the princess and her two sons. Their interest was only heightened after she and the prince separated. At times, their pursuit bordered on the unreasonable as the photographers went beyond depicting her official duties and intruded into her private life with their high-powered lenses and brash manner. For her part, the princess seemed to welcome the coverage at times when she was promoting a cause, then suddenly to try to stop it by becoming angry and defensive and fleeing like a hunted animal. Most of the time, the *paparazzi*—named for the fictional photojournalist Paparazzo in Frederico Fellini's 1960 film "La Dolce Vita" who would stop at nothing to get his shot—paid no attention to her demands for privacy. When her death was at first blamed on the group of European photographers chasing her car, there were immediate calls for restrictions on the *paparazzi*. Indeed, seven of them were detained for questioning after the accident but were eventually released. Even though bills were introduced in the U.S. Congress and several states, no new restrictions on taking photos of celebrities were ever enacted except in California where Hollywood personalities brought significant pressure to bear. The furor died down, but the incident should serve as a cautionary tale to photographers and those wanting to become photographers. There are limits to zeal when it comes to pursuing people to photograph, even public figures.

▸▸ **Publication of private matters** involves the "common sense" notion of invasion of privacy—that is, revealing private information about a person that most of us would consider personal, private, and no one else's business. For the most part, this type of invasion of privacy applies in issues involving public

Figure 13.2. Lindbergh trial. In this photograph taken by an Associated Press photographer in 1934, Charles Lindbergh testifies at the Hauptmann trial. Hauptmann was accused of kidnapping and killing Lindbergh's baby. Photographers were part of a circus-like atmosphere that led to a ban on cameras in courtrooms that lasted for decades. Cameras are still not allowed in federal courtrooms, but most states allow them at some level.

(Reprinted with permission. AP/Wide World Photos)

THIRTEEN

figures and the concept of newsworthiness. Given that public figures are newsworthy and that the public has the right to information, the question becomes one of what the public really needs to know.

For example, you might take sexually explicit photographs of friends at a fraternity party at which everyone agrees that the pictures are to be taken for their own interest and amusement. If one of the participants later becomes a candidate for the United States Senate, it would not be difficult to find a publication willing to buy the photos from you. The ethics involved, not only on your part but on the part of the publisher as well, are obvious. As a legal matter, the issue would be whether the public really needed to know about the candidate's behavior among friends.

⇥ **False light** is the use of a person's name or likeness in a way that gives a false impression. In an actual case, a news photographer took a photograph of a young girl immediately after she had been hit by a hit-and-run driver. The photograph ran the next day in the local newspaper along with information about the accident. There was no problem with that use of the photograph. But several months later, a national magazine ran the same photograph in connection with an article on pedestrian carelessness entitled "They Ask to be Killed." This context completely misrepresented the circumstances of the incident; it cast the girl in a false light. The girl's parents sued and won.

Courtroom rules

Long before the O.J. Simpson trial raised questions about the advisability of allowing cameras in the courtroom, there was the Hauptmann trial. Bruno Richard Hauptmann went on trial in 1934 for the kidnapping and murder of the baby of Colonel Charles A. Lindbergh, the famous aviator.

The presiding judge, Thomas W. Trenchard, had forbidden the taking of photographs while court was in session. The many photographers assigned to the story took them anyway, concealing their cameras in mufflers, both to deaden the sound of the clicking shutters and to hide their equipment from the eyes of the judge. Despite his prohibition, photographers managed to record key moments in the trial, such as Lindbergh himself on the stand testifying that he had heard Hauptmann's voice giving directions about picking up the ransom money (Figure 13.2).

The actions of reporters, photographers, and the crowd outside the courthouse created a circus-like atmosphere that made a fair trial impossible, or at least that was the popular characterization at the time. Historians have since disputed this account, but when a committee of the American Bar Association made a recommendation a few years later to ban cameras in the courtroom, they used the Hauptmann trial as evidence of the need for greater courtroom decorum. In 1937 the American Bar Association adopted Canon 35 of the Canons of Judicial Ethics, which read in part: "The taking of photographs in the courtroom, during sessions of the court or recesses between sessions. . .are calculated to detract from the essential dignity of the proceedings, degrade the court, and create misconceptions with respect thereto in the mind of the public and should not be permitted."

After many years of confusion, the question of cameras in the courtroom was finally clarified by the 1981 decision of the U.S. Supreme Court in *Chandler v. Florida*. The Court ruled that state courts have the authority to allow broadcast and still photographic coverage of criminal trials, even if defendants object. The Court, however, left the actual decision to state court systems.

The Supreme Court's ruling removed uncertainty in the 27 states then permitting trial coverage. By 2001, all states except Mississippi and South Dakota allow cameras in some courtrooms, if only experimentally. Despite its decisions, the U.S. Supreme Court still does not permit cameras in its own chambers. It did allow sketch artists to work during deliberations that decided the presidential election of 2001.

The states that do allow cameras in the courtroom are still experimenting with arrangements that will allow photographic coverage without interfering with the business or decorum of the court. Local courts or chapters of the Society of Professional Journalists, should be able to provide information on the current courtroom rules within a particular state.

Libel and photography

The dictionary defines **libel** as "defamation by written or printed words, pictures, or in any form other than by spoken words or gestures." A news photographer has less to worry about in the area of libel than a reporter. The grounds for a libel suit rest more with the words of the text and captions accompanying a photograph than the photograph itself.

Photographs can make the persons in them subject to the same ridicule, contempt, or hatred that written words can, however. So you need to be careful to consider how the subjects in your photos will appear to others. Printed publication of libelous photographs is your major concern here, but you can also libel someone by displaying an unflattering or ridiculous pose of him or her in the window of your studio.

One of the classic defenses in a libel suit is truth. If a libelous statement is true, it can be safely published as long as it is published without malice. In general, it is exceedingly difficult—but not impossible—to take a photograph that is untrue. Nonetheless, the photographer should be on guard against photographs that somehow distort the subjects in such a way that they do not fairly represent them. Ethics and common sense should govern your use of the

THIRTEEN

photographs you take. Before using a photograph, ask yourself this question: If this were a photo of me, would I be offended by its use?

New digital dilemmas

The advent of digital photography has caused new and vexing ethical and legal problems. These problems revolve around one key question: Just because new digital tools allow you to do something technically, is it acceptable to do it?

As early as 1860, photographers created images that were photographic fictions. While they appeared to be authentic portrayals of reality, they were not. But such manipulated photographic images were rare. It took a great deal of skill and care for photographers to create them using purely photographic means. The electronic darkroom has changed all of that. Now, it is possible for anyone with patience and a few hours on a desktop computer to alter the content of photos. This trend has been especially prominent in advertising photographs, which are often manipulated, sometimes drastically.

Altered advertising imagery is usually considered acceptable. So are altered images in art photographs where the new techniques of image processing have given art photographers a flexibility that in the past belonged only to painters and sculptors. Photographers used to be constrained to produce only faithful reproductions of the reality that lay in front of their cameras. This limited the ability of the artist to interact with the medium. A painter could return to the canvas and revise, remove, restore. The photographer was usually limited to slight modifications in the darkroom.

Today's image processors have made the photographic image as malleable as the painter's canvas. Computer operations can darken, lighten, sharpen, or blur the image—or completely transform it by creating what seems to be entirely new. The computer can combine images easily. That capability opens new doors for the artist because "anything goes" in the postmodern art world. The same does not hold true for documentary photographers and photojournalists, however, who lose a lot of credibility by even making slight modifications to an image. Magazines, which have used image processing technology for more than a decade, occasionally have manipulated images to improve their composition—often with controversial results.

In one well-known case, *National Geographic* electronically picked up one of the five-million-ton Egyptian pyramids and moved it to one side to improve a color photograph. In another, a photographer superimposed the head of TV personality Oprah Winfrey on the body of actress Ann-Margret for a cover shot on *TV Guide*.

Although seemingly harmless, both of these cases raise a fundamental question: How much manipulation can be tolerated without damaging the credibility of a documentary or news photograph?

As earlier noted, the National Press Photographers Association, which represents most of the newspaper photographers in the United States, has tackled the issue head-on. Its basic position is that any manipulation beyond what could be achieved easily in a darkroom should not be tolerated. Burning, dodging, adjustments in contrast and exposure, or repair of dust marks and scratches are all acceptable. But anything that changes the content of the photograph—removing or relocating objects within the image, for instance—are beyond acceptable bounds because they damage the credibility of the newspaper photograph.

What seems clear is that the future believability of the news photograph will be based not on the nature of the technology but on the credibility and honesty of those taking and editing the images. As a photographer, you need to ask yourself the question posed at the start of this section: Just because I can do this electronically, should I do it?

UNDERSTANDING COPYRIGHT LAWS

Copyright is the exclusive right to reproduce, publish, and sell the matter and form of literary or artistic work. The U.S. Copyright Law that went into effect in 1978 provides protection for photographs as well as written material. Under the law, all unpublished work is automatically protected by copyright if it is original. To protect published work, it is only necessary to require proper **copyright notice** of your ownership whenever one of your photographs is published. The notice ("Copyright 1984 by Jane Doe") must appear in a location in the publication where it can be easily found.

Exclusive rights

Under copyright law, owners of literary or artistic work have five basic rights, called **exclusive rights.** The first exclusive right is the right to reproduce the work. The second is the right to prepare derivative works (second editions or translations, for example). The third is the right to distribute the work to the public. The fourth is the right of public performance. And the fifth is the right of public display of the work. While all these rights are intended to protect the owners of creative work, the first, third, and fifth exclusive rights are the important ones for photographers.

Many photographers and authors routinely register their work with the Copyright Office, Library of Congress, Washington, D.C., 20559, as a way of indisputably establishing ownership. However, whether you register your work or not, copyright protection for your own photographs extends for the duration of your life, plus 50 years. For works made for hire, and for anonymous and pseudonymous works (unless the author's or photographer's identity is revealed in Copyright Office records), the protection term for the

THIRTEEN

owner or publisher is 75 years from publication or 100 years from creation, whichever is shorter. If you become involved in a legal dispute about copyright ownership, you must file the proper form with the Copyright Office. The growth of millions of Web sites in recent years has created new problems for both photographers and the owners of the sites. In most cases, the difficulties stem from the use of a photographer's work on a site without permission and compensation to the photographer.

The Copyright Act does cover new technological advances. An illustration or photograph must be licensed for use on the Internet. The unauthorized reproduction of an illustration or photograph from a Web site without permission is viewed as if it was taken from a magazine. That protects Web site owners from having their content appropriated by others. But these owners have used a provision of copyright law to avoid paying photographers for using their work: fair use. Fair use includes the use of copyrighted work for educational purposes, criticism, comment, research, and news reporting. Several factors qualify a work as coming under this doctrine: purpose and character of the use, nature of the work, amount of work used in relation to the whole, and the effect the use has on the market value of the work. With no final, all encompassing legal ruling yet made, individual cases provide some guidance. For example, a photo of a food vendor in Fenway Park in Boston was published with permission on the Web site of The Discovery Channel. Although the Web site warned that all photos were copyrighted and could not be reproduced without permission, The Boston *Herald* used the photo to illustrate a story about the vendor being fired. The photographer filed a copyright infringement lawsuit against the paper. In its defense, *The Herald* said it had noted The Discovery Channel Web site address in its story and also that the usage qualified as news. In the end, the newspaper lost because it had cropped the image, making it appear that it had been taken by one of its own photographers.

Defining ownership of photographs

If a local retail store hires you to take fashion photographs for them to use in their newspaper advertising, who owns the rights to the photographs—you or the store? The answer depends on whether you are working as a free-lance photographer or under a **work-made-for-hire agreement.**

Work-for-hire agreement

Under current copyright law, works made for hire belong to the person who commissioned and paid for them. For instance, the photographs taken by a newspaper photographer while working on the job are considered works made for hire. They are the property of the newspaper, not the photographer, because the photographer is an employee and taking pictures is part of the photographer's job. On the other hand, if you are hired by someone to produce advertising photographs on your own, you are considered a free-lance photographer and the photographs will belong to you. You can sell them to whoever hired you and can also use them in whatever other way you see fit.

In general then, photographs made by employees are works made for hire and belong to the employer, while photographs made by independent photographers are free-lanced works and belong to the photographer. When it is not clear whether photographers are acting as free-lancers, the courts have tended to treat them as free-lancers anyway, to give the benefit of the doubt to whoever created the photograph. The exception occurs when a photographer who is not actually an employee is heavily supervised while producing the photographs; if the photographer is not really working independently, a court is more likely to consider the photographs produced to be works made for hire. Obviously, in cases where there may be any uncertainty about the ownership of the photographs, it is best to have a written understanding between photographer and client. That will prevent misunderstandings and possibly costly litigation.

When you take photographs as a free-lancer, you have a number of options. You can, for example, sell both the photograph itself and your rights to it as well. In this case, you transfer ownership of your work and can no longer claim any rights to it.

Licensing agreement

A more desirable alternative in the eyes of most photographers is to "lend" or "rent" the right to reproduce a photograph to a customer for a specific fee under a **licensing agreement.** In this case, you can also limit the use of the photograph, say, to a particular edition of a publication. You can restrict where the publication may be distributed and sold. For example, it is common to sell North American serial rights, which means a publication can use the image once in a magazine or newspaper to be distributed in Canada, Mexico, and the United States. You can also specify the credit line you want and stipulate the date by which the print or slide must be returned to you, as well as the fee for failure to return the print or slide.

Just as when you make an agreement to take pictures for a customer, you should spell out the terms in writing when you agree to sell a photograph that you own. Most established magazines have their own forms that spell out the understanding they have with photographers who shoot assignments for them. Figure 13.3 shows a standard licensing agreement that you can adapt to your own needs when you use it.

THIRTEEN

FIGURE 13.3. A licensing agreement

LICENSING AGREEMENT

Client: _____

_____

_____

Material for use: _____ Delivery date: _____

Rights granted: _____

Model release: _____

Reproduction fee: _____ Service fee for prints: _____

Credit line to read: _____

Color transparencies and negatives and black-and-white negatives remain the property of the photographer and are to be returned by the client within 10 days of delivery. Client agrees to pay a holding fee of $20.00 per week per transparency or negative held beyond 10 days.

Client agrees to assume all responsibility for the safe and undamaged return of transparencies or negatives to the photographer. In the event that the client's use of the material results in loss or damage, the client agrees to pay monetary damages to the photographer. The client further agrees that the minimum reasonable value of a lost or damaged color transparency is no less than $1,000, and the minimum reasonable value of a lost or damaged black-and-white negative is no less than $250.

The photographer will not be liable for any legal action or claim arising from publication of the material by the client in uses other than those specified by model release.

Any objection to these provisions must be made in writing prior to any use of delivered materials.

Accepted by: _____ Date: _____
(signature of user)

_____ Date: _____
(signature of photographer)

Defining ownership of digital images

As with the copyright law, the Internet has created many questions relating to who owns a photograph. One source of controversy occurs when publishers "re-purpose" photographs. Say a publisher pays for and prints an image in its magazine. So far so good. The problem arises when the publisher decides to use that same image on its Web site. As a result of the original payment, the owner says it already owns the work and does not have to pay to use it on its Web site. The photographer thinks otherwise and wants additional payment.

One case illustrates the problem clearly. In 1997, *National Geographic* was clearing rights for an anniversary CD-ROM and sent letters to 2,500 photographers and writers saying they wouldn't be paid for the use of their work. The magazine reasoned in its letter that because "the CD-ROM archive consists of an exact image of the page as it was originally published, this reissuance (or reprint) is not a 'further editorial use' of material such as requires additional payment to the photographers whose contract commit the Society to payment under these circumstances." The *Geographic's* argument was that the CD-ROM did not constitute a new use of the material, but was more like selling additional copies of the original magazine.

Other problems stem from the interpretation of first rights, that is, one-time publication in a magazine or newspaper, with all other rights belonging to the writer. One case highlights this dilemma. In 1997, Jonathan Tasini, president of the National Writers Union, and five other writers, sued the *New York Times* and several other publications and database corporations over use of their work without permission and additional payment. The writers argued they still owned their own work and thought publishers were illegally getting paid for making the work available through database owners. In their response, the publishers said the writers had already been paid for their free-lance work. They consider the archive a revision of the original publication, just like microfilm.

A federal district court judge ruled in favor of the defendant saying the use of contents of a print publication on a database qualifies as a permitted "revision" of the original publication. Two years later an appeals court reversed the original decision and sent the case back to the lower court to determine damages. In its decision, the appeals court asserted two basic principles: 1) on-line and database uses of articles that originally appeared in print may not be considered part of the first rights but are instead additional uses; 2) additional uses of an article are not permitted without a contract signed by both parties that specifically grant the additional uses.

In March 2001, the United States Supreme Court heard argument on this case. This marked the first time the murky issue of ownership of digital material was considered at that high level. Although the Tasini case dealt with printed material, it also applies to photographs.

The matter of copyright and the Internet and the ownership of photos reused on a Web site is far from settled. What is clear is that photographers would be wise to spell out in writing the terms and conditions of sale: where the image may be used, whether it can be used more than once, whether it can be used for other purposes, etc. Most established publications, not wanting the distraction of legal suits, will already have contracts and licensing agreements drawn up and ready to sign.

THIRTEEN

REVIEW **questions**

1. What basic rules does a photographer need to observe?

2. When does privacy become a concern for a photographer?

3. What are the four types of invasion of privacy?

4. What is appropriation?

5. What is intrusion?

6. What is a model release form and when should it be used?

7. What rules apply to taking photographs in the courtroom?

8. What role does libel play in photography?

9. What ethical dilemmas have been created by digital photography techniques?

10. How can such problems be avoided?

11. Why should a photographer obey copyright laws?

12. Who owns a photograph?

13. How has the Internet created new problems in copyright and ownership of photographs?

CHAPTER 14

careers in photography

Ronald Fischer, beekeeper, Davis, California, May 9, 1981, by Richard Avedon

FOURTEEN

331

careers in photography

Ronald Fischer, beekeeper, Davis, California, May 9, 1981, **by Richard Avedon**
(© 1981 by Richard Avedon)

The power of Avedon's image of the beekeeper is generated by the vulnerability of naked flesh covered by hundreds of stinging bees. The head and body are completely hairless, seemingly the more exposed to attack, yet the figure of the beekeeper is composed and dignified.

The image of the beekeeper is in Avedon's signature portrait style, shot against a white background that forces the viewer to confront the subject with no extraneous visual details. The image seems to distill the essence of the subject.

Richard Avedon is probably best known for revolutionizing fashion photography following World War II by moving it from the staid confines of the studio out into the streets, giving his images new life and energy. His fashion career has spanned decades and he has always been among its most innovative practitioners.

But what is probably most remarkable about Avedon's career is its breadth. Although extremely successful in his commercial work, Avedon has been at least as successful in his other work—his portraits and his personal documentaries. He has photographed the famous and the infamous. His personal essays have taken him to Vietnam during the war. He photographed the last days of his father as he was dying of cancer. He made a series of images about mental hospitals. For Avedon, the camera does not seem to be an option. It is a way of confronting and understanding life.

Why study photography? There are many reasons. Beginners want to learn how to operate a camera, take pictures, develop their film, and make enlarged prints. Experienced amateur photographers want to improve their techniques, yet remain nonprofessional; others strive to make photography a career, as professional art photographers, industrial photographers, commercial photographers, free-lance photographers, or photojournalists. The list is endless, but the point is simple. People study photography because it is a fascinating and rewarding way to spend time, whether it be purely for pleasure or because it is a job.

CAREERS IN PHOTOGRAPHY

There are many kinds of careers in photography. Pursuing any of them on a full-time basis, however, requires ability and persistence.

▸▸ **Photojournalism** has become a highly prized segment of the profession. More young photographers want to become photojournalists than any other kind of photographer. But the field is crowded. There are only a few positions for photographers on large daily newspapers and weekly news magazines that place an emphasis on photography. Magazines like *National Geographic* that are oriented toward photographers are even harder to crack, again because only a limited number of positions are available. A small number of free-lance photojournalists make a living by working for a number of publications at the same time, usually with the help of an agent or photo agency like Black Star or Magnum.

The best way to enter photojournalism is on the level of a small or medium-sized daily or weekly newspaper. Such positions are usually gotten by photojournalists who have had experience on their college newspapers or yearbooks. Although the assignments on small or medium-sized dailies or weeklies are rarely national fast-breaking news stories, a photographer can get excellent training there. Sometimes, however, even a relatively inexperienced photographer can get lucky. In 1980, Roger Werth of the Longview, Washington *Daily News*, was probably the first photographer to get up in an aircraft to record the eruption of Mount St. Helens on film. His spectacular shots (Figure 14.1) were widely used and one was even published on the cover of *Time*.

Often photographers on daily and weekly newspapers are called upon to write captions or copy blocks or to design and lay out photo pages. Writing skills and design experience are a definite advantage on smaller publications that cannot afford to have a full complement of specialists.

As with other jobs in photography, photojournalists need to be familiar with digital equipment and processes, as explained in Chapters 10, 11, and 12. They

FOURTEEN

**FIGURE 14.1.
Photojournalism:
Mount St. Helens,
by Roger Werth.**
Most photojournalists
work for newspapers
covering everyday
events like community
activities, local sports,
and the occasional fire
or traffic accident.
Once in a while a
volcano will go off in
your backyard. When
Mount St. Helens blew
in 1980, Roger Werth
was one of the first
photographers to get
up in the air and
begin photographing.
His photographs were
published nationally.

*(Published with
permission)*

develop film and scan it into the halftones that will eventually become the images on the final printed page. For reasons of cost and time, making prints in the conventional way has become old-fashioned and unnecessary. In this kind of system, there is no darkroom.

▶▶ **Art photographers** probably have the most difficult time of all in making a living from their work. Although many people collect photographs the same way they collect paintings—and many museums feature art photographs in their exhibitions—only a few art photographers succeed at their craft without other means of support. Many supplement their photo sales by teaching art photography.

FIGURE 14.2. Commercial photography. Commercial photographers record the key moments of everyday life: weddings, graduations, school classes, job promotions, honors, along with portraits of individuals, families, and even pets. These photos are often very conventional, but imaginative photographers will find their work in demand.

(Photo by Ball Studio. Published with permission)

People who study photography with the goal of becoming art photographers will find that it is very different from other segments of the profession. The work can be demanding, especially in the darkroom, because print quality must be flawless. The demand for art photographers is not as great as that for photojournalists, largely because of the unique nature of the photographs. Like photojournalists, art photographers often find it helpful to work digitally. Digital photography has opened up new avenues of creativity for art photographers.

▸▸ **Commercial photographers** operate their own studios from which they take photographs of weddings, families, individual portraits, school class members, and pets. Most photos are not candid, but well-planned and taken under carefully controlled lighting conditions (Figure 14.2). While a photojournalist deals with the unexpected, the commercial photographer knows precisely what to expect in the work to be done. Commercial photographers charge a set rate for taking the pictures and also make money on the prints sold to the people in the photos—for example, all the members of a class or a wedding party. Although they are often called upon to record the boring and mundane, commercial photographers can excel by coming up with ideas that are new, fresh, and eye-catching. There is no reason that their everyday subjects need look dull and predictable in the final photograph.

FOURTEEN

FIGURE 14.3. Fashion photography. Photos of the latest in clothing and accessories appear in fashion magazines, advertisements, portfolios, and catalogs. The image of the fashion photographer is that of a glamorous artist surrounded by glamorous models in glamorous locations. But in a business where photographic styles come and go along with the fashions they document, most fashion photographers have to work very hard and keep incorporating fresh ideas into their work.

⏵ **Fashion photographers** specialize in illustrating new clothing and accessories (Figure 14.3). They are much in demand in big cities to take photographs of models that will appear in advertisements and on the editorial pages of newspapers and magazines. Some fashion photography is done in studios; some, on location in real settings. Fashion photographers must know how to work with models to achieve the proper "look." They must also be able to satisfy their often demanding customers who want to be sure that the clothes are displayed properly. On location, the work of a fashion photographer often resembles that of a movie director in that all the disparate elements must be brought together to produce a successful photograph. Fashion photographers usually work free-lance, though a few big department stores and publications employ their own.

⏵ **Advertising photographers** take photographs of products that appear in newspaper and magazine advertisements (Figures 14.4 and 14.5). Whether the product is a jet airplane or a can of peas, the advertising photographer must show it in a way that will enhance it and make people want to buy it. Most ad photos are taken in a studio under carefully controlled lighting conditions. The more realistic orientation of advertisements in recent years, however, has required that some shots be done on location. An advertising photographer must coordinate his or her work with the art director, ad designer, and copywriter to make sure it

**FIGURE 14.4.
Advertising
photography.**
The advertising
photographer is part
of a team including
art directors, copy
writers, and clients,
which translates ideas
into images, words,
and designs intended
to appeal to buyers.

*(Published with permission
of Hewlett Packard
Company)*

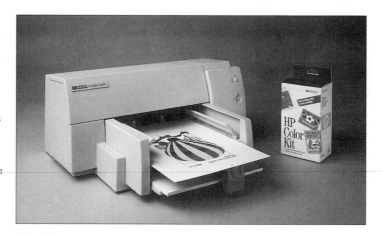

**FIGURE 14.5.
An advertisement
using photographs.**
The advertising
photographer must
usually plan for the
fact that his or her
images will be inte-
grated into work
that includes text
and other images.

*(Published with permission
of Hewlett Packard
Company)*

FOURTEEN

FIGURE 14.6. Architectural photography. Photographs of buildings, both during construction and as a completed project, are used by contractors, developers, and architects. This work is often done with a large format camera, which allows the photographer to render the building from a correct perspective.

(Photo by Randy Wood. Published with permission)

conveys the desired message. Most ad photographers work on a free-lance basis, although a few big advertising agencies employ their own.

A lucrative segment of advertising photography is catalog photography. Photographers who work in the area specialize in product illustrations for direct-mail advertising.

▸▸ **Architectural photographers** take pictures of buildings (Figure 14.6) in the way fashion photographers take pictures of models wearing new clothes. They take specialized photos of buildings—not people—for architects and contractors. Contractors want to show the progress of a building from empty lot through the various stages of completion, while architects want to show the completed structure in flattering views that please customers and can help get more business.

Architectural photographers' clients also include large management companies that own buildings and use images to lease or rent the buildings. Commercial real estate—where photographers take photos of houses for sale—is another potential area for work.

▸▸ **Industrial photographers** provide a variety of photographic services to business and industry. They may provide advertising photographs of products (Figure 14.7) and processes, portraits of company personnel, visual aids for training programs, or photographs for company brochures and reports. Among those who did much of their early work in industrial photography are Ansel Adams and Margaret Bourke-White. It was Bourke-White's simple, graphic photographs of industrial subjects that brought her to the attention of Henry Luce. He hired her as the first staff photographer for *Fortune* and eventually for *Life* when it was created a few years later.

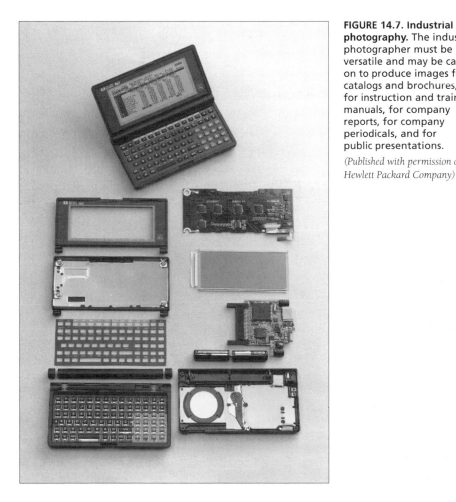

FIGURE 14.7. Industrial photography. The industrial photographer must be versatile and may be called on to produce images for catalogs and brochures, for instruction and training manuals, for company reports, for company periodicals, and for public presentations.

(Published with permission of Hewlett Packard Company)

FOURTEEN

**FIGURE 14.8.
Law enforcement
photography.**
Crime scenes,
homicide victims,
and criminal suspects
are all subjects for
the law enforcement
photographer.
Because their photos
may be used as
evidence in court,
their work must be
accurate and detailed.

*(Photo by Corvallis Police
Department. Published
with permission)*

▸▸ **Law enforcement photographers** work for police and sheriffs' departments to take photos of crime scenes (Figure 14.8), homicide victims, and criminal suspects. The photographs are used to help solve crimes and as evidence in court, so they must be very accurate with proper documentation so they will hold up in court. Police photographers do their work soon after a crime has been committed and have to be careful not to disturb evidence. Most law enforcement photographers are employees of the police or sheriffs' departments for which they do their work.

▸▸ **Free-lance photographers** work for themselves and hire their photographic services out to others. Some free-lancers provide a variety of photographic services to a variety of clients—from industrial and advertising photography to portraiture and feature photography. Others may specialize, for example, in advertising or photojournalism, but they are not employees of any particular advertising agency or publication. Many employed photographers envy the apparent freedom of the free-lancer. But the job is usually accompanied by irregular hours and irregular pay. And the free-lance photographer must work hard to establish a reputation and maintain it. The free-lancer must also be prepared to spend time selling his or her work to prospective clients.

After her graduation from Oregon State University, Cheryl Hatch paid her own way to Cairo, Egypt, where she established herself as a free-lancer shooting photos in the Middle East and Africa (Figure 14.9) and selling them to a number of publications.

▸▸ **Photo editors** are the hidden player in the complicated process that carries a photo from the click of the camera to its final appearance in print, broadcast, or

FIGURE 14.9. Free-lance photography: Eritrea, by Cheryl Hatch. Cheryl Hatch has spent years in Africa photographing the lives of women caught up in the many conflicts there. Here, in a culture where it is taboo to talk about sex, women soldiers attend an AIDS awareness lecture at a military base near Keren, Eritrea. Free-lancing gives the freedom to photograph what you think is significant, but also means you are often on your own, financially and personally.

(Published with permission)

on the Internet. Editors play a role in determining how a story will be illustrated. They assign a photographer to cover the subject. When the photos are turned in, the editor sees that they are combined with the text in the final layout, hopefully giving the best play possible to the photos. Photographers sometimes become photo editors later in their careers and it is considered a step up into management, unless you will miss the rough and tumble of work in the field. The job requires the ability to visualize how photos can enhance a story.

▶▶ **Photo archivists** organize and maintain the millions of photographs owned by the ever-growing number of photo archives. These archives include those operated by universities, private companies, art museums, news organizations, private collections of one or more individual photographers, and government organizations like the Library of Congress. Photo archivists' customers range from publications and television stations to book authors and educational institutions. Archivists must have a love of photography and be knowledgeable about photo history and the collections they oversee. When customers call, it is

FOURTEEN

the archivist who locates the photo, grants the permission to reproduce it (usually after a fee is paid), and sends out the photo, making sure later that it is returned to the collection. Most photo archives make money because of the high fees many of them charge for the use of the photos in their collections.

Corbis is one of the newest—and largest—photo archives in the world. It is organized in a way that is typical of how many old photos or those by specific photographers are now handled. It owns 65 million images, more than 2.1 million of them online. It includes the Bettmann Collection, with its 17 million historical and news photo images, and Sygma, with 40 million images, the largest news photography agency in the world. Corbis, owned by Microsoft founder Bill Gates, also holds 3,000 images from such creative sources as Ansel Adams, the National Gallery-London and the State Hermitage Museum-St. Petersburg. Corbis also offers Digital Stock, a source of royalty-free stock photos on a wide range of subjects.

For people who study photography with the intention of becoming professionals, the choices are many and depend on individual interests. Beyond the specialized photography already noted, there are a number of other areas that offer jobs: photo laboratory processing, camera repair, audiovisual photography, medical photography, and public relations photography.

ASSEMBLING A PORTFOLIO

If you plan a career in photography, you need to prepare a portfolio to sell yourself and your work. A portfolio is a set of mounted photos or slides that you carry around with you to show prospective customers your worth as a photographer. Portfolios are very personal statements, so they vary greatly between individuals.

It is a good idea to have your portfolio ready at all times, updating it with new work from time to time. When you put your portfolio together, you'll want to keep certain basic points in mind.

Select only the best photographs for your portfolio. You shouldn't try to show how you have improved over the years. Don't feel the portfolio has to be large. Ten superb prints are better than a collection of 20 prints that includes one mediocre example of your work. It is only human nature that the photograph most likely to be remembered by a prospective employer will be the mediocre one.

Make good prints and mount them carefully. You can then place them in a large leather or cardboard folder that closes or ties for showing your photos one by one when you meet prospective clients. It is a good idea to identify the photos on the back.

Consider preparing several portfolios. If you take various kinds of photographs, it's a good idea to have more than one portfolio—for example, one for architecture and one for advertising.

Gather printed examples of how your photos were used. If you've had photographs published in annual reports, brochures, magazine articles, or the like, you can take tear sheets from the publications along in another folder when you meet prospective clients.

Prepare a portfolio on slides. You can easily send such a portfolio to potential clients out of town. This concise record of your work is less bulky and easier to ship than the portfolio you carry around with you. If possible, you should also prepare several "credit" slides that introduce your work ("The photographs of Jane Doe") along with your name, address, and telephone number.

Keep your portfolio updated and ready to show. Customers usually want a photographer on the day they call you and can't wait to make a decision while you spend a day in the darkroom making prints of your last three assignments.

SELLING YOUR PHOTOGRAPHS

The selling of photographs can consume a book longer than this one. The business side of photography is complicated and less rewarding than the enjoyable hours spent behind the camera or in the darkroom. If you want to become more than a "weekend photographer," however, you will need to know how to sell your photos.

You must first decide how serious you are about becoming a professional photographer or, at least, a good amateur who sells photos regularly. This decision will lead you in one of two directions.

The task of the amateur is relatively easy. Make contact with your local newspaper editor to find out that publication's photo needs. If the newspaper has no regular photographer, you might be able to take photos to illustrate travel articles or feature stories. If you want to go beyond that kind of occasional work to augment your income, you might want to take out an advertisement offering to do wedding shots, baby photos, or pictures for local clubs and organizations or school districts. This kind of photography is sometimes repetitious and, for the wedding, school, and baby portraits, requires that you buy special lighting equipment. It can be lucrative, however, especially in the repeat business that comes from school and wedding shots.

For the professional photographer wanting to branch out beyond the kind of local business noted above for the amateur, the way is more complicated. The best approach requires that you take yourself seriously as a photographer and set yourself up in business, just like you were opening a small store or going into business as a plumber. There are a number of things you can do to make the process a little easier.

Organize an office. Whether in your home or in a commercial office building, you should have an office complete with desk, files, and, most important of all, letterhead stationery, envelopes, business cards, and statements for billing

FOURTEEN

customers. You will want to select a name and have a logo designed for your business. You can use that logo and name—set attractively in readable type—on the letterhead, envelopes, cards, and statements. Since you will be operating a small business, you may want to consult an accountant about bookkeeping and tax matters. You will need to keep records for income taxes and may have to collect sales taxes, as well as obtain a local resale license from your city and state tax boards.

Your potential customers needn't know that your office is at home in a room that is used to hold dust mops. The important thing is for you to look professional upon your first meeting. The quality of your photographs is more important, of course, but you may not get the chance to display your ability if your business operation looks sloppy and amateurish to an outsider.

Decide what kind of photographer you are and study the market for such photos carefully. All of these segments include customers with special needs. You should study books like *Photographer's Market,* which tells what many magazines and newspapers around the country want in the way of photographs from free-lancers. Other free-lance assignment categories are detailed in such books as well. If you are aiming at a more local market—for example, advertising agencies, architects, or industrial firms—you can start calling on potential customers personally to make contacts and show your work. You can also consider feeding photographs to stock picture agencies as a supplement to your income. Such agencies, which are listed in *Photographer's Market,* collect photos on many subjects and sell them for various uses.

Prepare a brochure. It helps to have a brochure that details your capabilities and shows examples of your work. You can then mail the brochure to prospective clients or have it ready to leave behind after one of your personal visits.

Start taking the kind of pictures that fit the market you are trying to reach. Don't snap the camera shutter until you have put yourself in the shoes of a prospective client, whether that person be an advertising account executive, an architect, or a magazine photography director.

Try to sell the same photograph to several, non-competing markets. You can thus make your ideas pay off with only an initial investment of time and money.

File your negatives, contact sheets, and prints carefully. You will know where everything is quickly if you develop a good filing system. Selling your own photos from your stock is lucrative as is the selling of additional prints to a customer who hired you to take them initially. Your photos won't do you any good if you can't find the negatives when a call comes in.

Be prepared to move quickly to sell photos to national publications. When a major news event happens in your area, you must be able to assess the importance of the event instantly and to be there to take the pictures no one else can get. It helps to have contacted photo editors at national publications in a routine way beforehand. Luck plays a big part in this, of course, but you can let a good opportunity slip by if you don't know how to handle it. The photographer who took some of the first (and only) shots of the eruption of Mount St. Helens in 1980 (Figure 14.1) was a 23-year-old staffer on a nearby small daily newspaper who happened to be in the right place at the right time. His photos of the event have appeared in *Time, Life,* and several books.

Enter contests and brag about your awards. You can boast about your awards in your brochure and on your personal visits to clients. You can also set up displays of your work at local galleries, public buildings, or even shopping malls and department stores. All of this attracts attention to you and your work.

Set your prices carefully. You will want to make sure you do not give your work away, but you do not want to lose business either by charging too much. Photo organizations like the National Press Photographers Association can give you the standard rates in your area for certain kinds of photo work. Professionals usually charge a day rate plus expenses for assignment work and so much per print for sales of their own photos.

Never let your quality slip. When you get an assignment, you must take the time to shoot the job well, making sure you know in advance what the customer wants and then giving exactly what has been asked for. You must also take pains in the darkroom with printing and be sure to meet deadlines scrupulously.

Improve your photography. It is important to work constantly at improving your skills as a photographer. You can do this in a number of ways: by attending workshops and taking classes, by joining a local camera club, by visiting photo exhibits. Good professional photographers are always striving to learn new and different techniques. The workshops have the additional advantage of allowing you to meet people, both noted professionals and others at your same skill level.

FIGURE 14.10. Support photography. A photograph of an emu illustrates an agricultural technical report. Photography can similarly be used to support communication in business, construction, science, or any other field where it helps to show as well as tell.

(Courtesy of Agricultural Communications, Oregon State University. Published with permission)

FOURTEEN

PHOTOGRAPHY AND OTHER CAREERS

Students of photography who do not intend to become professional photographers can enhance other careers by knowing how to take and use photos well. Many projects require the taking of photos from time to time. For example, a real estate agent must usually take exterior and interior views of all houses listed for sale. If the photos are good, the chances for a sale of the property are greatly enhanced. Similarly, an insurance adjuster has to take photos of items being turned in as claims against an insurance policy. Good, clear photos speed the process immeasurably.

In such fields as science, forestry, agriculture, construction, and general business, taking photographs is not required, but you can make an impression if you illustrate a technical report (Figure 14.10) or oral presentation with photographs. Let's say you are a building contractor. You may want to keep a photographic record of the various stages of construction for your information and to show that construction followed specifications—for instance, that reinforcing steel and other hidden structural supports were properly installed. Similarly, a forester wanting to show the success of new tree species or an agricultural researcher illustrating the way a new fertilizer aids plant growth will tell the story better with pictures.

In all such instances, the photographs must look professional. Badly composed, out-of-focus photos are worse than none at all. It helps to know the possibilities and limitations of photography. You must have a rudimentary knowledge of camera, composition, film, developing, and print enlarging to succeed, whether you take the photographs yourself or hire a professional photographer.

PERSONAL PHOTOGRAPHY

Beyond the dreams of having a full-time career in photography or enhancing another job by taking pictures from time to time, there remains another vast reason for studying photography: because you enjoy taking pictures. From children to retirees, thousands and thousands of people have turned to photography as an avocation. They constantly take pictures of family and friends, animals, houses, special events, and travel. They spend millions of dollars every year on cameras, lenses, accessories, supplies, processing, and books like this one.

Why do people take photographs? There are probably as many reasons as there are people offering them. It is a relaxing, enjoyable way to spend your time. Concentrating on photographing a subject can make you forget your cares. The hours you spend in the darkroom make you equally oblivious to everyday pressures. Photography is an endeavor that requires a single-minded devotion not needed in most other avocations.

FIGURE 14.11. Personal photography. Photography can be a very satisfying avocation. It offers end-less opportunities for expression and enough challenges to hold your interest indefinitely. Histori-cally, some of the finest and most influential photographers started their careers as amateurs.

(Photo by Randy Wood. Published with permission.)

In short, photography is a creative and rewarding way to spend your free time. Like any other craft or art form, photography can offer a sense of accomplishment and fulfillment. If you pursue it with creative interest and hard work, you will have photographs you are proud to claim responsibility for taking (Figure 14.11). And as an amateur photographer, you will have an advantage over professionals: You will have the freedom to shoot whatever subject matter interests you, and your photos will have to please no one but yourself.

The same principles apply to achieving good photos, whether they be of family members or a high-fashion model. This book has introduced you to the fundamentals. Your own experience, further reading, and conversation with other photographers will take you beyond.

FOURTEEN

REVIEW questions

1. Why do people study photography?

2. What is art photography?

3. What is photojournalism?

4. What is the best way to become a photojournalist?

5. What kinds of photos do commercial photographers take?

6. What is the most important factor in becoming a successful fashion photographer?

7. How should advertising photographers depict the products in their photos?

8. What does an architectural photographer do?

9. What is the difference between an industrial photographer and an advertising photographer?

10. What is the most important task of a law enforcement photographer?

11. What does a photo editor do?

12. What is a photo archive?

13. What is a portfolio?

14. What are the main considerations in assembling a portfolio of work?

15. Why is it important to study various photo markets?

photo history

"I can only think in terms of my own field, how a photographer tries to help—how all the best photographers I know have tried to help by building up the pictorial files of history for the world to see. Just one inch in the long mile."

Margaret Bourke-White

CHAPTER 15

A short history of photography

Migrant Mother, Nipomo, California, 1936, by Dorothea Lange

A short history of photography

Migrant Mother, Nipomo, California, 1936, by Dorothea Lange
(Courtesy Library of Congress)

Dorothea Lange joined the photography staff of the Farm Security Administration in 1935 to document the human face of the Depression. As with many of her photos, the "Migrant Mother" series came about largely by happenstance and luck because she never planned her field trips in advance. Instead, she preferred to start out in one direction and drive until she saw something worth photographing. At the end of a trip in March 1936, Lange had already passed the entrance of a pea picker's camp near Nipomo, California, when she decided to turn back and drive in. When she got there, she immediately saw a women sitting in a tattered tent with two of her seven children. The woman told Lange the family was living on wild birds. There was no work because the pea crop had frozen on the ground. She hadn't moved on, however, because she had sold the tires off her car to pay for food. Although Lange spent only 10 minutes taking six exposures, what emerged was what Roy Stryker, head of the FSA project, called *the* picture from possibly the most ambitious documentary project ever undertaken.

Lange, trained as a portrait photographer in the Pictorialist tradition, helped put a human face on one of the most disruptive social events in U.S. history. She continued to work as a documentary photographer after leaving the FSA project in 1940 and photographed the detention centers where Japanese-Americans were interned as a result of the hysteria following Pearl Harbor at the beginning of World War II.

Photography has a history as exciting and varied as the subjects its millions of cameras have captured on film. From primitive beginnings over 170 years ago, photography has emerged into its present position as one of the dominant creative forces of our time.

The men and women who made photography what it is today built their contributions, one upon another, in a solid progression of accomplishments. The results of their efforts are enjoyed today even by those who pick up and use the most simple camera.

CAPTURING THE IMAGE

Early developments

The forerunner of the modern camera was the **camera obscura,** a room with a single small opening to the outside in one wall. An inverted image of the outdoor scene was projected on the opposite wall. Although well known for centuries, the camera obscura was not put to general use until it was described by Giovanni Battista della Porta in his book *Natural Magic* in 1544 (Figure 15.1).

Artists began to use the device to achieve the correct perspective demanded of Renaissance paintings. By this time, a lens had been placed in the hole to improve the image and the camera obscura was made smaller and more portable—first to the size of a small hut, then to a sedan chair, next to a small tent, and eventually to a portable box. These later versions enabled amateur artists to trace inexpensive portraits conveyed directly from the outside world to the wall of the camera obscura.

Inventors were working on other developments that led eventually to the photographic process. In 1727, Johann Heinrich Schulze discovered that light darkened a solution of silver nitrate. By 1802, Sir Humphry Davy and Thomas Wedgwood had soaked paper and leather in silver nitrate, laid objects on the sensitized surface, and exposed the arrangement to sunlight. This method gave them silhouettes that were later called **photograms.**

FIGURE 15.1. The Camera Obscura, 1544. The camera was known for centuries before the invention of photography. The camera, first with a pin-hole lens and later with an optical lens, created a precise image, all the more tantalizing because there was no way to record it.

(Courtesy Gernsheim Collection, Harry Ransom Humanities Research Center, The University of Texas at Austin)

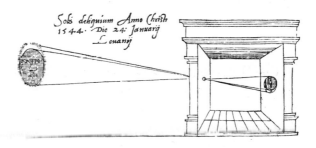

The first "photographs"

The next important development came in 1816 when French physicist Joseph Niépce made a negative image, in which dark and light were reversed, by placing a piece of paper sensitized with silver chloride in a camera. Niépce was unhappy that the image was a negative and that it was not permanent. By 1822, Niépce found a way to produce a positive copy of an engraving by exposing a glass plate coated with an asphalt-like substance. He called the process **heliography.**

Niépce continued work to perfect the technique so it could be used to make positive pictures in a camera. He finally succeeded in 1826 when he recorded the view from his second floor window (Figure 15.2). By today's standards, the image is extremely primitive, showing only the outlines of trees and buildings with very little detail. But it is still considered the world's first photograph—the first permanent image made with a camera. His "film" was a piece of pewter coated with the same asphalt-like substance used in his earlier experiments. The exposure time was at least eight hours; his effective ISO rating was thus on the order of 0.00001, about one-ten millionth the sensitivity of modern films.

FIGURE 15.2. The first photograph. In 1826, Joseph Niépce took a photograph from a second floor window of his house, requiring an exposure time of at least eight hours. He called his process heliography.

(Courtesy of the Gernsheim Collection, Harry Ransom Humanities Research Center, The University of Texas at Austin)

FIGURE 15.3. Daguerreotype. Daguerre took this plate of a Parisian boulevard from his apartment window in about 1838. The exposure time was so long that all the pedestrians and boulevard traffic are blurred out with the exception of the figure having his boots polished in the foreground.

(© Copyright by the Bayerisches Nationalmuseum, Munich)

In 1829, Niépce and Parisian painter Louis Daguerre formed a partnership to work together on the improvement of heliography. Daguerre began experimenting tirelessly with silver, despite Niépce's misgivings about its potential for producing a positive image.

Daguerre finally discovered by accident that he could produce a permanent positive image by sensitizing a silver-plated metal sheet with iodine fumes, exposing it to light, developing it over mercury fumes, and then fixing the image in a concentrated salt solution. Niépce died in 1833, and when Daguerre perfected his process in 1839, he considered it different enough from his earlier work with Niépce to call the resulting images **daguerreotypes** (Figure 15.3).

Meanwhile, English inventor William Henry Fox Talbot had been working with paper soaked with silver chloride. He produced his first paper negative in a camera in 1835 and then went on to produce a positive image from it by waxing the paper negative to make it translucent, sandwiching it with another light-sensitized paper, and then exposing the sandwich to light. In 1839, Talbot announced his process, which he called **calotype,** that allowed him to make

FIGURE 15.4. *The Open Door,* **by William Henry Fox Talbot, 1843.** A salted paper print from a calotype negative, this is one of the plates Talbot produced for *The Pencil of Nature.*

(Courtesy Gernsheim Collection, Harry Ransom Humanities Research Center, The University of Texas at Austin)

multiple copies of a positive image from a single "negative." Talbot's calotype images did not match daguerreotypes in sharpness or popularity. Nonetheless, it is Talbot who worked out the outlines of photography as we know it today: a negative-positive process based on the light-sensitive properties of silver salts. Talbot foresaw many of the future applications of photography and published demonstrations of them in a book, *The Pencil of Nature,* illustrated with original photographic prints (Figure 15.4).

At the same time, English astronomer Sir John Herschel was experimenting with photography. He discovered the use of hyposulfite of soda as an effective chemical for fixing, or making permanent, a silver image. Herschel also discovered the cyanotype (blueprint) process and is credited for coining the term *snapshot.*

The rise of portraiture

After Daguerre demonstrated in public how he produced his very detailed positive miniature images, there was immediate interest in them. People clamored to learn the new process and buy the pictures.

Because of the long exposure time required, Daguerre's process was first used for landscapes, architecture, and other inanimate subjects. However, American scientist John Draper was able to make a daguerreotype portrait in 1839, using an exposure time of a half hour. Draper and inventor Samuel F.B. Morse promoted daguerreotype portraits in the United States, and daguerreotype studios sprang up in nearly every sizable town and city throughout the country.

Portrait photography quickly became extremely popular in both the United States and Europe even though very early portraiture bordered on cruel and unusual punishment. It required you to sit still, staring unblinking into the direct sun. To keep you from moving, your head was held tightly in a special clamp. All of this probably accounts for the rather austere expressions found in early portraits of the day.

Within a few years, however, inventors developed more sensitive coatings and better lenses. The quality of the images improved, and exposures were reduced to only a few minutes, then to less than a minute, thereby making portraiture more humane.

Improving the process

The introduction of the **wet collodion** process in 1851 all but replaced the previous processes. It was as sharp as the daguerreotype but also reproducible in the same way as the calotype in that it was a negative-positive process. It was more sensitive to light than the previous techniques, enabling photographers to use exposures as short as five seconds.

Perfection of the wet collodion process followed a long search by inventors for a substance that would bind a light-sensitive emulsion to a glass plate. Glass, they thought, would be better than paper or metal as a support for light-sensitive emulsion since it was textureless, uniformly transparent, chemically inert, and less expensive than metal.

English sculptor Frederick Scott Archer tried collodion, a mixture of gun cotton dissolved in alcohol, which is sticky when wet and dries into a tough, transparent skin, that had been used for several years to dress wounds for surgery. Archer had been making calotypes of his sculpture subjects and discovered that collodion was good for binding emulsion to glass. The glass plate had to be exposed and processed, however, while the collodion was still wet and transparent. As a result, photographers always had to have a darkroom nearby.

For portraits, this was not a great problem and photographers like Julia Margaret Cameron and Nadar produced studies that went beyond the assembly line images typical of the commercial portrait studios (Figure 15.5). The wet plate process was far more a problem for photographers who ventured into the field. But that did not stop French photographer Francis Frith from barging wet plate apparatus up the Nile and dealing with collodion plates that sizzled in the desert heat to bring home images of the wonders of Egypt. In the United States, William Henry Jackson and Timothy O'Sullivan travelled west with geologic survey expeditions to chart the

FIGURE 15.5. Sarah Bernhardt, by Nadar, 1859. Nadar (Gaspard Félix Tournachon) ran a very successful studio, where he photographed many of the prominent political and artistic figures of Paris. He was also an active experimenter. He was among the first to photograph using electric light and he was one of the first aerial photographers, shooting pictures of Paris from a lighter-than-air balloon in 1858.

(Courtesy George Eastman House)

territories acquired in the Louisiana Purchase (Figure 15.6). Pack mules did much of the work, but the photographers still had to carry large cameras and heavy plates up hillsides and across rocky terrain to get the vantage points they needed.

Over the decade following the discovery of the wet collodion process, inventors attempted to free wet-plate photographers from the necessity of carrying their darkrooms with them. Dry collodion emulsions were introduced in 1865, but were no more sensitive than wet plates. By 1871, collodion was replaced by a **gelatin emulsion** in **dry plates.** Ways were found to make the gelatin emulsion much more sensitive, allowing exposure times of a fraction of a second. Early plates were sensitive only to blue light. Plates were gradually made sensitive to more of the visible spectrum by the addition of dyes, or color sensitizers.

But the major contribution of the dry plate was to cut the umbilical cord that tied photographers to their darkrooms. The new technique allowed photographers to concentrate on new subjects. Aerial photography from hot air balloons was possible. Photographs could be made under water. Despite the great improvements, plates were still made of glass; they were bulky and fragile.

In 1888, another inventor would change everything. In that year, George Eastman introduced **roll film** having a gelatin and chemical coating on a paper backing. Shortly afterward, he substituted celluloid for paper. This type of film allowed many exposures to be taken on one roll of film and made photography more portable.

Eastman aimed directly at the amateur market, offering a simple camera loaded with a 100-exposure roll of film for $25. When the roll was completely exposed, the photographer returned the camera. Eastman's company developed the roll and returned prints together with the camera loaded with a new roll of film. The slogan used in ads of the time told it all: "You press the button, we do the rest."

PHOTOGRAPHY AND ART: STRANGE BEDFELLOWS

When photography first appeared on the scene, it was viewed with deep suspicion by established artists. Because they judged it an essentially mechanical process, artists felt photography did not allow for the expressive qualities that exemplified True Art.

As a result, photographers with artistic aspirations found themselves imitating the painterly arts. One of the most ambitious was Oscar Gustave Rejlander. He

FIGURE 15.6. *Hot Springs on the Gardiner River, Upper Basin (Thomas Moran Standing),* by William Henry Jackson, 1871. Jackson was one of several photographers who joined survey expeditions to explore the uncharted Western territories of the United States. He had to pack heavy glass plates, all his processing chemicals, and a portable darkroom in order to use his wet plate camera. Like many scenics of the time, Jackson's work was widely published in the form of stereograms. By placing the card in a simple viewer, the image appeared as a three-dimensional scene and was a common parlor diversion before the days of radio and television.

(Courtesy George Eastman House)

FIFTEEN

Figure 15.7. *Two Ways of Life,* by Oscar Gustave Rejlander, 1857. Photography was at first thought too mechanical to qualify as art. A composite print of some 30 separate negatives, this large print was an attempt to accomplish with photographic processes what the great painters did with oils and canvas.

(Courtesy George Eastman House)

was a trained artist and a photographer who attempted to translate the aesthetic of his academy training into photographic images. His *Two Ways of Life* (Figure 15.7) is a history painting in the style of the painter Raphael, but executed with a camera rather than a paintbrush. The finished contact print is 31 by 16 inches, a composite of some 30 individual negatives. By taking pictures of two or three figures at a time, Rejlander gradually pieced together the image in much the same way that a painter might build an image on canvas.

Pictorialism

But it wasn't long before photographers were arguing that theirs was a medium with its own unique visual characteristics that did not need to imitate anything else to be a legitimate means of artistic expression. One of the most persuasive voices in this debate was that of Alfred Stieglitz, an American who studied in Europe and brought new ideas of photography with him back to New York near the turn of the 19th Century (Figure 15.8). Stieglitz organized exhibitions, opened a gallery, and published *Camera Work*, the most influential photography publication in the country at the time. He became the father of the Pictorialist movement in the United States. He was the center of a group of photographers who changed the rules of art photography, among them Edward Steichen and Clarence White. The Pictorialists eschewed the manipulations of combination printing and favored everyday subject matter, but they also used processes that allowed for considerable manipulation during printing. These "ennobling

Figure 15.8. *Paula,* **by Alfred Stieglitz, 1889.** Stieglitz was one of the most influential voices arguing that photography did not need embellishment to be an art form. He constantly tested the limits of the medium, making pictures in inclement weather and available interior light.

(Chloride Print 22.7 x 16.9 cm, Alfred Stieglitz Collection 1949.698. Photograph © 2000, The Art Institute of Chicago. All Rights Reserved.)

Figure 15.9. *Ring Toss,* **by Clarence H. White, 1899.** Like other Pictorialists, White usually photographed everyday scenes. He brought to his images a fondness for natural light and a compositional style influenced by the Japanese print.

(Courtesy Library of Congress)

FIFTEEN

processes" were thought to elevate an otherwise mechanically made print into a hand-made art object. They insisted that these prints hang alongside other works of art at exhibitions.

Clarence White was in many ways the quintessential Pictorialist photographer. He was fond of domestic scenes and strong compositions. *Ring Toss*, among his best images (Figure 15.9), shows a sensitivity to light and a sensibility not unlike a painting by John Singer Sargent. White remained loyal to the Pictorialist aesthetic long after Stieglitz and Steichen had moved on to other approaches.

Modernism

At about the time of World War I, new voices began to champion the very precision that set photography apart from other artistic media. These photographers set aside the hand-work processes and soft focus lenses of the Pictorialists and embraced what came to be known as straight photography. Artistic truth, they seemed to say, lay in the unvarnished surface details of the subject.

Figure 15.10. *Blind Woman, New York, 1916* **by Paul Strand.** Strand wanted his street photographs to be as objective as possible and used a trick lens so people wouldn't know he was photographing them. The result is a very direct, almost brutal, image.

(© 1971 Aperture Foundation, Inc., Paul Strand Archive)

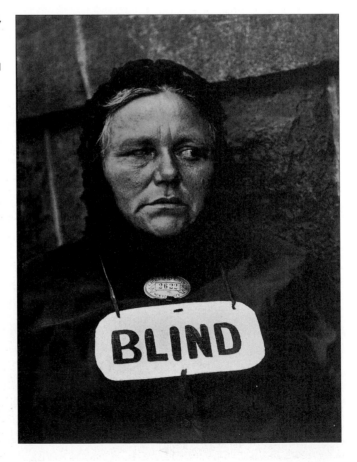

Paul Strand, one of Stieglitz's disciples, was one of the first to create these direct, almost confrontational images (Figure 15.10).

Other photographers of the era, involved in the Dadaist and surrealist movements in Europe, experimented with photographic processes that lent themselves to accident and surprise. Man Ray, an American who lived most of his life in Paris, was identified with his photograms (which he called Rayographs) and with his solarizations (images which are part negative and part positive due to exposure during development) (Figure 15.11).

On the West Coast of the United States, a small group of photographers banded together to create Group f/64. The group, named for a very small aperture which produces large depth of field with a view camera, also espoused the precision and sharpness that seemed to be unique to photography. The head of the group was Edward Weston, whose landscapes, figure studies, and still lifes seemed to define this aesthetic (see opening photograph for Chapter 7). He used an 8 x 10 view camera and insisted on contact printing his images for maximum sharpness. He

Figure 15.11. *Solarization,* **by Man Ray, 1929.** Man Ray, an American painter, moved to Paris and became a fixture in the Dadaist and surrealist movements following World War I. Although he took a number of very straightforward portraits of many of his fellow artists—Pablo Picasso, James Joyce, Gertrude Stein, among others—he was fascinated by processes which seemed to encourage experiment and discovery. This solarization is the result of briefly exposing the negative to light during development, producing an image that is part negative and part positive.

(© Man Ray Trust/Artists Rights Society (ARS), NY/ADAGP, Paris. Courtesy George Eastman House)

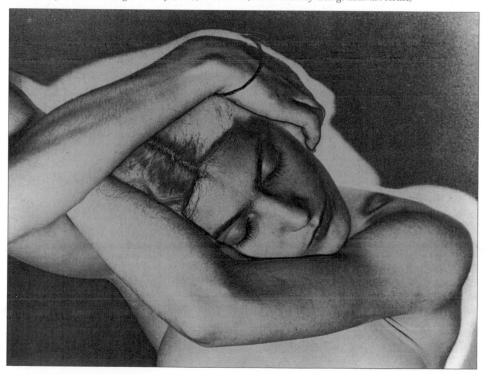

FIFTEEN

introduced the idea of previsualization, the notion that the photographer should be in such perfect control of his medium that he could see the final print in his mind's eye before the exposure, then execute his craft in such a way as to produce that print. Another member of the group, Ansel Adams, (see Chapter 8 opener) became an exponent of previsualization and developed the zone system, an approach to exposure and development that gives the photographer great control over the final result.

Personal vision

The approach of the modernists seemed to suggest that the truth of one's vision lay in precisely seeing the outward appearance of things. That was the power of the straight photograph. There were a number of photographers who grew up in this tradition who wanted to see more, to somehow see beneath the surface. They felt that a photograph should create an emotion in the viewer somehow equivalent to the form of the image. The idea of *equivalence* had been suggested by Stieglitz many years before and in his later years he took many abstract photographs of clouds that he called equivalents. Many other photographers also expanded the ideals of straight photography to include more personal and perhaps less objective views of the world.

Henri Cartier-Bresson, a French photographer, took pictures in a seemingly documentary style, but described himself as a surrealist. He photographed street scenes and everyday events, usually in places far away from France, and always with a strong sense of design (see opening photograph for Chapter 3). His work is a personal vision of a world carefully ordered, but always about to dissolve into disorder and change.

Figure 15.12. *Pacific, Devil's Slide, California, 1947,* **by Minor White.** White intended his images to be "equivalents," symbolic of inner emotional and spiritual states that the viewer brings to the picture. He was very influential as a teacher, as one of the founders of *Aperture,* and as a proponent of the Zone System.

(Reproduction courtesy Minor White Archive, Princeton University. Copyright © 1982 by the Trustees of Princeton University. All rights reserved)

Minor White was directly inspired by Stieglitz's idea of equivalence. He followed a regime of Zen meditation and sought not just the emotional, but the spiritual, in his images (Figure 15.12). He wrote, "I photograph not that which is, but that which I AM." White was the cofounder of *Aperture* magazine, the reigning publication for art photography in the United States to this day, and was its editor for more than 20 years. He extended and helped popularize the zone system approach to photography, inculcating a mastery of materials and processes in his students, many of whom went on to become influential photographers in their own right.

Diane Arbus developed a uniquely personal vision in her short career. She photographed on the fringes of society, always seemingly examining the boundary between what we consider normal and what we exclude. Her photographs seem to embrace the outcasts of society while questioning those we think of as unquestionably normal. She photographed circus people, transvestites, and the mentally retarded with haunting compassion. But her photographs of "normal" families and children at play seem to question the surface normalcy (Figure 15.13).

Yet another photographer who developed a personal visual mythology through photography was Jerry Uelsmann. He advocates a post-visualization approach in which he gathers together images from his own contact sheets and looks for combinations of individual images that will create interesting combinations. He

Figure 15.13. *Child with a Toy Hand Grenade in Central Park, New York City, 1962, by Diane Arbus.* Arbus's photographs test the boundaries between what we consider normal and what, abnormal. She photographed social outcasts in a sympathetic way and photographed "normal" people, like the child playing in the park, in a way that questions their normalcy.

(Copyright © Estate of Diane Arbus 1970. Courtesy of the Robert Miller Gallery, New York)

FIFTEEN

then combination prints several negatives on one sheet of paper to make a completed image (see opening photograph for Chapter 6). No longer a slave to the moment the shutter is tripped, his approach allows for discovery and alteration as he is working on the final image, just as a painter or sculptor might try different ideas as he or she is working. He calls his images "obviously symbolic, but not symbolically obvious."

Postmodernism

While the period that followed modernism and a preoccupation with the straight image found photographers seeking personal truths, the postmodern period finds photographers questioning whether there is any such thing as truth, at least in any absolute sense. Postmodern photographers are very concerned with what gives photographs meaning and with examining a world in which truth seems largely conditioned by our media environment. The concern becomes less about discovering truth or documenting truth, since if there is such a thing, we probably generated it ourselves anyway. Instead, the preoccupation is with examining how we create meaning. Because they have often been marginalized by the media environment in the past, women and minorities are among the most interesting of the postmodernist photographers.

Figure 15.14. *Untitled Film Still,* 1979, by **Cindy Sherman.** Taking on the appearance of a single frame from a "B" movie, Sherman's self-portraits are not really about her personally, but about how media depictions of women—and by extension everyone—shape our self-concepts and our understandings of others.

(Courtesy of Cindy Sherman and Metro Pictures)

Cindy Sherman photographs what might be taken for self-portraits, although her images are not so much introspective as they are examinations of how women are portrayed in the media and how female and male identities are defined. Her series of *Untitled Film Stills* shows women (actually herself) in what might be single frames excerpted from a "B" movie (Figure 15.14). Because it is a known fiction, the image in essence asks us to consider how much of our own reality is unconsciously formed from similar media messages.

Barbara Kruger worked as a graphic designer in the magazine industry before she entered photography. Her work is deliberately conceived as a series of media messages, usually in the form of simple advertisements (Figure 15.15). She takes simple imagery and adds wording which seems to expose the nearly invisible messages carried by mainstream media: am I attractive enough? am I complete? do I need to look like this to be accepted? Her images invite us to examine whose standards and assumptions we use to measure ourselves.

Figure 15.15. *Untitled,* **1989, by Barbara Kruger.** Kruger's images usually consist of a simple image with a verbal label. Her works resemble advertisements, but really call into question the unspoken messages we all receive from advertisements and other media. In this example, we are reminded not only of the controversy over abortion rights, but also over contradictory images of the role of women in the family and in society.

(Courtesy of Mary Boone Gallery, New York)

FIFTEEN

DOCUMENTARY PHOTOGRAPHY

The wet-plate era

Among the first photographers to use the camera for documentation were the early war photographers, Roger Fenton and Mathew Brady. Fenton photographed the Crimean war in 1855. Brady, the very successful owner of daguerreotype studios in New York and Washington, D.C., set out with a group of photographers to document the battlefields of the Civil War in the United States in 1861. Because they used the wet plate process, these photographers had to carry their darkrooms with them, often in horse-drawn wagons (Figure 15.16). Because their plates were not very sensitive to light, they were forced to use long exposures and they brought back images of the dead strewn on the battlefield rather than the action of the battles themselves (Figure 15.17).

Aside from the cumbersome equipment and slow materials, another challenge faced early documentary photographers: lack of a way to translate the photographic image directly into printing plates. Because it was necessary to hand engrave printing plates and because the engravers were known to take liberties in the process, the printed photograph lacked the impact and verisimilitude of the photograph itself. However, this problem was solved by the turn of the century and photographs, printed from mechanically produced plates, became a staple of newspaper and magazines everywhere.

Social documentation

One of the first photographers to turn his camera on social problems was Jacob Riis, who photographed the plight of immigrants flooding into New York near the turn of the 19th century who were forced to live in overcrowded tenement slums. Riis published books, mostly illustrated with hand engravings from his photographs, but also gave many lectures illustrated with lantern slides made from his pictures.

Figure 15.16. Roger Fenton's *Photographic Van with Aide Sparling.* Because he used the wet plate process, Fenton had to carry all his photographic supplies with him, coat the glass plate, then expose and develop it before it dried.

(Courtesy Gernsheim Collection, Harry Ransom Humanities Research Center, The University of Texas, Austin)

Another photographer interested in the problems of immigrants was Lewis Hine. He photographed at Ellis Island, where many of the new arrivals first set foot on United States soil. Soon, his attention turned to the problems of child labor. Children of poor families were often expected to work ten and twelve hours a day, depriving them of a childhood and an education. Hine travelled all over the eastern United States photographing children working in mills, factories, and mines (Figure 15.18). His photographs became part of the evidence considered by Congress in establishing the U.S. Children's Bureau in 1912 and a later ban on child labor in 1938.

Figure 15.17.
Confederate Dead by a Fence on Hagerstown Road **by Alexander Gardner, 1863.** Gardner was one of "Brady's men" who carried their large wet plate cameras to the battlefields of the Civil War. Because the photographic plates were relatively slow and exposure times long, their images are primarily of the dead.

(Courtesy Library of Congress)

Figure 15.18.
A Raveler and a Looper at Work, London Hosiery Mill, Tennessee, **by Lewis Hine, 1910.** Hine was interested in using his camera to fight what he saw as social injustice, in particular the exploitation of children who were often expected to work ten or twelve hours a day under dirty and often unsafe conditions.

(Courtesy Library of Congress)

FIFTEEN

The FSA project

By the Depression of the 1930s, the U.S. government had begun to see the value of photography as a documentor of social conditions.

The Farm Security Administration hired photographers—including Dorothea Lange, Walker Evans, Arthur Rothstein, and John Vachon to document on film the devastating social conditions in rural America caused by the drought and economic depression. Although the thousands of photographs taken for the FSA often depicted hard times (see opening photograph for this chapter and Figure 15.19), they also captured on film scenes of everyday life in an America that was changing. The photos were part of an evolution into a form of journalism that was something new to its practitioners and its audiences: using photographs rather than words to tell a news story.

Life magazine and photojournalism

Camera design would influence photojournalism in the 1920s. Early cameras had been simple boxes, not all that different from the original camera obscura except for the smaller size. Just before World War I, however, the Leitz Company, manufacturer of motion picture cameras, designed a small camera for testing motion picture film. The camera was intended as an exposure meter of sorts; it made trial exposures on a strip of film to test quality. The images on the test film were so good, however, that they could be enlarged into very presentable prints.

World War I interrupted this work, but by 1924, the first Leica camera was introduced. It used film the same size as motion picture film: 35 mm. The high

Figure 15.19. *Dust Storm, Cimarron County,* **1937, by Arthur Rothstein.** Rothstein's image, part of the Farm Security Administration documentary project, became emblematic of the dust bowl era and the plight of the farmers devastated by drought and the depression.

(*Courtesy Library of Congress*)

quality of the photos produced by this lightweight, easy-to-use camera made it immediately popular with photojournalists. To a certain extent, the Leica led to a fascination with "candid photography" and the rise of the weekly picture magazine, first in Europe and then in the United States.

Nowhere was this newly emerging segment of the profession—magazine photojournalism—practiced with more distinction than in the pages of *Life*, which began weekly publication on November 23, 1936. The magazine was an immediate success, quickly selling out its entire press run of 466,000 copies.

The emphasis on photographs in *Life* relegated writers to second place for the first time in journalism. In the hands of *Life* photographers like W. Eugene Smith, the photo essay became a powerful form (Figure 15.20). Before the arrival of television news, the public waited eagerly each week to see how *Life* would cover a story. The imaginative photo compositions, cropping, layout, and design set a standard never seen before. When it died in its weekly version in 1972—a victim of increasing postal rates and television's ability to deliver national audiences to advertisers—a part of journalistic history died with it. (The magazine continued as a monthly until 2000, but it was never the innovative and lively publication it had once been.)

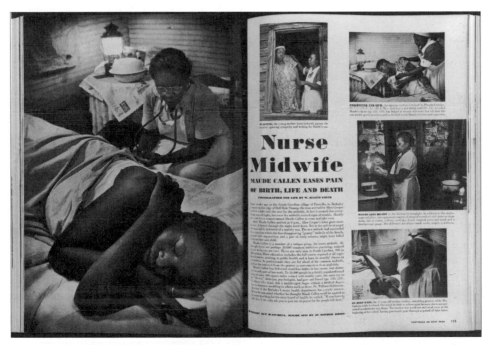

FIFTEEN

Figure 15.20. *Nurse Midwife,* **by W. Eugene Smith, 1951.** Smith's essay appeared in *Life* magazine on December 3, 1951. It focused on the tireless work of Maude Callen, who looked after the health needs of hundreds of rural residents.

(Estate of W. Eugene Smith/Black Star. Courtesy George Eastman House)

Recent documentary photography

The influence of the original *Life* has continued in other forms. The only national magazine that continues to engage in serious documentary work is *National Geographic*. The *Geographic* is financially able to allow photographers enough time to develop depth in their coverage and, while the magazine tends to focus primarily on noncontroversial topics, it does occasionally tackle social issues, following in the footsteps of Hine and Smith.

But most social documentary work today is developed by committed individuals who want to address a problem and feel they can best do that with their camera. Among them are Eugene Richards, who has photographed the problems of drug addiction and the drama of the emergency room at a metropolitan hospital. Mary Ellen Mark immerses herself in her subject, often living among her subjects and shooting for weeks or months at a time. She has produced books about life in a women's mental ward, young prostitutes in Bombay, and runaways on the streets of Seattle (Figure 15.21). Sebastião Salgado is a trained economist who has produced haunting images of the exploitation of manual workers throughout the world (Figure 15.22).

Figure 15.21. *Lillie, Seattle*, by Mary Ellen Mark, 1983. This is an image from Mark's documentary series on runaway children living on the streets of Seattle, published in a book titled *Streetwise*. In this image, the photograph derives power from the seeming contradiction of a person so young she finds comfort in a doll, yet mature enough to be smoking.

(Courtesy Mary Ellen Mark and George Eastman House)

Figure 15.22. *Gold-miners in the Serra Pelada Mine, Brazil,* by **Sabastião Salgado, 1986.** This image is part of a project that Salgado photographed over a number of years focused on the exploitation of manual workers around the world. This image shows the mine as something out of Dante's Inferno, a kind of living hell.

(© Sabastião Salgado/Contact Press Images)

HISTORY OF PHOTOGRAPHY
Timeline

1800	1850	1900

Processes

Heliography

Daguerreotype

Calotype

Wet Collodion

Dry Plate

Roll Film

Photographers

Niépce

Daguerre

Herschel

Morse

Talbot

Brady

Riis

Stieglitz

Steichen

Weston

Man Ray

Applications

Portraiture

Landscape

Motion Studies

War Photography

Social Documentary

Photojournalism

HISTORY OF PHOTOGRAPHY
Timeline

1900	1950	2005

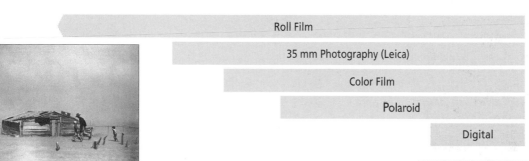

Roll Film

35 mm Photography (Leica)

Color Film

Polaroid

Digital

Riis

Stieglitz

Steichen

Weston

Man Ray

Adams

Evans

Bourke-White

Smith

Portraiture

Landscape

Motion Studies

War Photography

Social Documentary

Photojournalism

FIFTEEN

REVIEW **questions ?**

1. What was a camera obscura and why is it important to modern photography?

2. What is reported to be the first photograph?

3. What was the daguerreotype and how did it affect photo history?

4. How did the wet collodion process and the dry plate affect photography?

5. Who was Mathew Brady and why is he an important figure in photo history?

6. What did Alfred Stieglitz contribute to the recognition of photography as a legitimate art form?

7. When did photojournalism become an important profession?

8. Who was George Eastman and what role did he play in photo history?

9. What is postmodernism and what issues does it confront?

10. What was the Farm Security Administration photographic project?

glossary

accent light: often a spotlight that is placed high above and to the rear of the subject.

activator: an ingredient in the developer that makes it alkaline. A strong alkali produces a rapid-acting developer and high contrast; a weak alkali gives a relatively slow-acting developer and less contrast.

additive primary: one of the three colors (red, green, or blue) that create white light when added together.

advertising photographer: a photographer who takes photographs of products or people that appear in advertisements.

agitation: turning the developing tank upside down and back so the developer flows freely and evenly over the entire surface of the film; rocking the developing tray gently back and forth so the developer flows evenly over a print.

ambient light: light that surrounds a subject to be photographed, usually continuous light as distinguished from light added by flash.

angle of view: the angle, or width of the scene in front of the camera, which is "seen" by the lens.

anti-halation layer: the layer of film that keeps light rays from being reflected back up through the film and exposing it a second time.

aperture: the adjustable opening of a lens through which light passes, used to adjust the intensity (brightness or dimness) of the light.

aperture priority: an automatic exposure mode that permits you to set the aperture and select the depth of field. The camera will automatically set the shutter speed to give the correct exposure.

appropriation: a violation of a person's privacy rights by using the person's name or likeness for trade or advertising purposes without his or her permission.

architectural photographer: a photographer who makes a living taking photographs of buildings and building interiors.

artificial light: light added to a scene by the photographer—for example, floodlights or flash.

art photographer: a photographer whose photographs of people and objects are works of art like those created by a painter or a sculptor.

ASA (American Standards Association): the numerical rating indicating the light sensitivity of a particular type of film. It was replaced by ISO index in recent years.

autofocus lens: a lens that can be electronically focused by circuitry built into the camera body.

automatic exposure: the feature on some cameras that automatically sets the aperture or shutter speed or both.

autowinder: a camera attachment that automatically advances the film and cocks the shutter after each exposure is made at a rate of about two frames per second. It is slower and less expensive than a motor drive.

average gray: 18% reflectance of the incident light, the same amount of light reflected by an average scene; the tone used to calibrate reflected light meters.

averaging meter: a through-the-lens metering system that measures and averages varying intensities of light and shadow areas electronically.

background light: light that shines solely on the background.

banding: abrupt transition from one gray level to another in a digital photograph.

bit: a binary digit. Can contain a value of 0 or 1.

bit depth: in a digital photograph, the amount of computer storage allotted to each pixel.

bleaching: lightening or removing areas of a print by applying chemical bleach and then fixing the print again.

bleed mount: a means of mounting a print that allows the photo to extend to all four edges of the board, with no border.

body: the housing for all the parts of the camera. It is designed to keep out light.

bounce light: light, usually from a flash that is indirectly bounced or reflected off a surface toward the subject. The light is thereby softened or made more diffuse.

bracketing: taking photos at several exposure settings to offer insurance against incorrect exposure and to experiment with exposure effects on the final negative or transparency.

brightness: the lightness or darkness of a color.

built-in light meter: a metering apparatus incorporated into the camera body; many use a light-sensitive cell located behind the lens.

burning: manipulating a print in the darkroom to give one part of it additional exposure to darken it.

byte: a group of eight binary digits, or bits. Can contain values between 0 and 255.

C-41: a chromogenic processing system used to produce color negatives.

cable release: a long, flexible wire with a plunger at one end and a socket at the other that attaches to the shutter release of the camera.

calotype: a photographic process developed by inventor William Henry Fox Talbot in 1835 that allowed him to make multiple copies of a positive image from a single "negative."

camera: a box-like device with a shutter that, when opened, admits light to enable an object to be focused by a lens on a photo-sensitive film or plate thereby producing a photographic image.

camera bags: made of canvas, leather, plastic, or aluminum, a camera bag both protects and makes transportable all photographic equipment and supplies.

camera cases: protects the camera, especially the lens, from damage, dust, and moisture.

camera obscura: the forerunner of the modern camera, a room with a single small opening to the outside in one wall. An inverted image of the outdoor scene was projected on the opposite wall.

can opener: a device used to open chemical containers and to pry open film cassettes.

cassette chamber: the part of the camera that holds the film cassette.

CCD: see charge-coupled device.

center of interest: the focal point within a photograph, usually the subject.

center-weighted meter: a metering system that calculates exposure settings by operating through the lens. It bases the exposure more on light reaching the center of the viewfinder area than light at the frame edges.

charge-coupled device (CCD): a sensor that can convert light into an electronic signal. It captures the image in a still video camera in the way film does in a conventional camera.

chromogenic: a system for creating a color image by forming dyes in each emulsion layer of color film. Black-and-white chromogenic films use color processing chemicals to form a monochromatic dye image.

clamp tripod: an alternative to a full-size tripod. The clamp tripod is screwed into the tripod socket of the camera, then clamped to a firm surface.

CMYK color: color formation using the three subtractive primary colors (cyan, magenta, and yellow) plus a fourth neutral ("K") layer.

cold mount tissue: a thin paper used for mounting a print. Simple pressure, without heat, is enough to bond the print to its backing.

color balance: a match between the color sensitivity of color film and the color of the light source.

color complements: colors opposite one another on the color wheel.

color gamut: the range of colors produced by a color system.

color temperature: the general coloration of a light source.

color wheel: a diagram showing the relationship between the additive and subtractive primaries.

commercial photographer: a photographer who operates a studio and/or laboratory and takes pictures to sell to the public.

compression ratio: the amount of reduction in file size produced by a compression approach.

contact sheet: a proof print of every frame on a roll of film, so named because the negative and photographic paper are in direct contact when made.

continuous light: a steady source of light, such as light bulbs or floodlights; as distinct from flash or strobe light.

contrast: the range of tones in a negative or print; the difference in extremes between highlights (light areas) and shadows (dark areas).

contrast filter: in taking pictures, a colored filter used to control the tonal rendition of colored objects on black-and-white film, often used to darken the sky so clouds stand out; in enlarging, a plastic filter used to control the contrast of blacks and whites in the finished print.

contrast grade: the contrast characteristics of a particular batch of enlarging paper. For example, a number 2 grade paper is considered normal contrast.

contrasty print: a print with exaggerated differences between light and dark tones.

copyright: the exclusive right to reproduce, publish, and sell the matter and form of a literary or artistic work.

copyright notice: a legal phrase displayed on material giving notice that the material is protected by copyright law.

copyright registration: a procedure for establishing and maintaining copyright claims, made through the Copyright Office of the Library of Congress in Washington, D.C.

correction filter: used to compensate for differences between the color sensitivity of a certain type of film and the type (color) of light used to expose it.

crop marks: marks made to indicate the part of the frame to be used.

cropping: selecting the portion of a frame of film to be printed in an enlargement.

daguerreotypes: In 1839, painter Louis Daguerre discovered by accident that he could produce a positive image by sensitizing a silver-plated metal sheet with iodine fumes, exposing it to light, developing it over mercury fumes, and then fixing the image in a salt solution. He called the resulting images daguerreotypes.

darkroom: a room in which illumination can be controlled or eliminated so that photographic material can be processed.

daylight film: used with daylight, whether outdoors or coming indoors through a window or skylight.

density: the opacity ("blackness") of an area in a film or print image.

depth of field: the zone in front of, and behind, the subject that is acceptably sharp.

developer: a chemical solution that makes the latent image on film or photographic paper visible by converting exposed silver halide crystals to metallic silver.

developing agent: an ingredient in film or paper developer that converts exposed silver halide crystals to the metallic silver that forms the image.

developing tank: a processing tank made of plastic or metal in which film is placed for developing.

diffusion: to scatter light so it is less directional and casts less distinct shadows.

direction: the angle at which light strikes a subject, a factor that affects the way texture and shape are depicted in the photograph.

dodging: manipulating a print in the darkroom to give one part of it less exposure and thus lighten it.

dryer: a machine for drying film or prints after they have been processed.

dry mounting: a means of attaching prints to a cardboard backing for more permanence and easy display through use of a heated press, an iron, and special adhesive tissue.

dry mount tissue: a thin paper coated with adhesive that gets sticky when heated. The tissue holds the photographic print to the mounting board.

dry plate: early photographic process involving an emulsion coated onto a glass plate.

dusting equipment: soft brushes used to remove dust and pieces of lint from negatives and from the enlarger lens.

DX-coated film: film cassettes that are printed with a pattern of black and silver squares which represent the film's ISO index.

dye-destruction system: a system for creating a color image by beginning with a full set of dyes and then removing those that are not needed in the image.

dye-incorporated system: a system in which potential dyes are included in color film during manufacture and are converted to visible dyes during processing.

dye-injection system: a system in which dyes are introduced into each emulsion layer of color film during development. The layers are developed and dyed one at a time.

E-6: a chromogenic processing system for producing color positive transparencies.

easel: a fixed or adjustable frame placed on the baseboard of an enlarger to hold the paper flat for exposure.

electronic darkroom: a computer used to make photographs electronically without the need to develop negatives and print them conventionally.

emulsion: the photographically active layer of film or paper containing silver halide crystals suspended in gelatin.

enlarger: a piece of equipment used to project an image from a negative to a sheet of photographic paper to make prints of a size larger than the original negative.

enlarging: the process of making an enlarged photographic positive image from a negative.

exclusive rights: under copyright law, the owners of literary or artistic work have five basic rights: 1) right to reproduce the work, 2) right to prepare derivative works (second editions or translations), 3) right to distribute the work to the public, 4) right of public performance, and 5) right of public display of the work. Only these owners have such rights exclusively.

existing light: light already existing at the scene to be photographed; usually distinguished from natural or artificial light.

exposure value: the value that can be used by photographers to refer to the group of all the shutter speed-aperture combinations that give correct exposure with a certain brightness level.

f/16 rule: an exposure guide which says to use an aperture of f/16 at a shutter speed equivalent to 1/ISO (for example f/16 at 1/125 for an ISO 125 film) when photographing in direct sun on a sunny day.

false light: a violation of a person's privacy rights by using the person's name or likeness in a fictionalized or semifictionalized account so as to give a false impression.

fashion photographer: a photographer who takes pictures of models wearing different kinds of clothes for use in fashion magazines and advertising.

fast: a type of film or paper that is very sensitive to light; a lens with a large maximum aperture for its focal length (e.g., a f/2.8 200 mm lens).

fiber-base paper: "conventional" photographic paper; an emulsion coated onto paper that is durable when wet.

file: a computer stores each image as a separate collection of numbers, called a file. File sizes are commonly given in kilobytes or megabytes.

fill flash: artificial light directed at subjects to fill or lighten shadow areas usually created by strong sunlight.

fill light: the light that is used to fill in and soften the shadows created by the main light when using artificial light.

film-advancing mechanism: moves the film from left to right in order to expose as many pictures as are on the strip of film.

film base: the acetate or polyester layer of film on which the other layers rest.

film clips. devices that hold film for drying.

film development time: the amount of time film is exposed to developer.

film-holding mechanism: the part of the camera that holds film at the focal plane.

film recorder: can print a computer-processed image on conventional color film or paper.

filter: a tinted or colored piece of optical glass, plastic, or gelatin attached to the lens of a camera to modify light before it reaches the film.

filter factor: a multiplying number that serves to compensate for the absorption of radiant energy (light) by a filter.

fish-eye lens: an extreme wide-angle lens, usually with a focal length of 8 mm or less and characterized by a circular image.

fixer: the chemical that renders a photographic image stable on film or print.

fixing: making a photographic image stable by removing unexposed silver halide crystals from the emulsion.

flash: a brief burst of high intensity light, synchronized with the shutter opening of the camera.

flat print: a print that lacks contrast—that is, it has no dark blacks or clear whites.

floodlight: a light source that spreads its illumination over a wide area.

focal length: the distance between the lens and the plane of focus when the lens is focused at infinity.

focal plane shutter: a shutter built into the camera body just in front of the film plane, or plane of focus, made of two overlapping curtains forming an adjustable window.

focusing mechanism: the part of the camera that moves the lens toward or away from the subject to be photographed, and toward or away from the film upon which the image will be recorded.

focusing screen: a piece of etched glass used to view and focus upon the scene in front of the camera.

frame: one of a succession of pictures on a strip of film.

framing: selecting a portion of the scene in front of the camera to be contained in the viewfinder frame; also, using a natural frame (window, arch, tree branch, etc.) as an element in composing a photograph.

free-lance photographer: a photographer who is self-employed, works independently, and is generally hired to do specific jobs, from portraiture to news photography.

fresnel lens: a focusing aid with concentric line patterns that is used to brighten the outer edges of the screen.

f-stop: a numerical indicator of the size of the aperture. The larger the f-number, the smaller the physical lens opening.

gelatin supercoating: a light-sensitive emulsion containing silver halide crystals, and a paper base that protects the emulsion from scratches.

grain magnifier: an optical device that helps focus the image from an enlarger.

gray card: a card that is gray in color (one having 18 percent reflectance) used to achieve the "average gray" standard needed for photography. It is made by Kodak and called the Kodak Neutral Test Card.

gray scale: in any photograph, conventional or digital, the patterns of gray tones that are produced by the direct action of light.

ground-glass system: a focusing system wherein light from the lens is projected onto a viewing screen.

guide number: used to calculate flash exposures. It is the product of the flash-to-subject distance and the aperture that gives correct exposure at that distance.

halftone: the process that breaks a continuous tone photograph into a pattern of black-and-white dots that can be printed on a printing press or computer printer.

halftoning factor: the oversampling factor used in making digital scans that will later be printed using halftone dots.

heliography: a process developed by French physicist Joseph Niépce in 1816 that produced a positive copy of an engraving by exposing a glass plate coated with an asphalt-like substance.

high contrast film: black-and-white film that combines very high contrast with extremely high resolution and virtually microscopic grain.

highlights: the light areas in the original scene that appear on the negative as the relatively dense or opaque areas.

HSB color: a color model that allows control of hue, saturation, and brightness independently.

hue: the color itself, for example, red or blue or green.

hypo clearing agent: a solution that speeds the removal of fixer during the wash, thus reducing wash times.

imagesetter: typesetting machines capable of printing computer-processed images with a relatively high resolution.

incident light meter: an exposure meter that measures the intensity of light striking the subject.

industrial photographer: a photographer who works for a large corporation to take pictures of its products and personnel.

infrared film: black-and-white and color film possessing sensitivity in the infrared portion of the spectrum as well as in the visible region. It is ideal for experimental photos.

ink jet printer: squirts colored inks onto paper to print a computer-processed image.

intensity: the brightness or dimness of light.

intrusion: a violation of the privacy rights of another person when he or she has a reasonable expectation of privacy, for example, by using an extremely long telephoto lens or a concealed recording device.

invasion of privacy: a violation of the right of someone to be left alone. See appropriation, false light, intrusion, and publication of private matters.

ISO index: a numerical rating indicating the light sensitivity, or speed, of a particular type of film. It replaced the ASA rating in name, although the rating values are interchangeable.

Lab (L*a*b) color: a mathematically precise model for color representation that breaks each color into three components—L, a, and b.

laser printer: can print computer-processed images, but with relatively low resolution.

latent image: an image recorded in a light-sensitive emulsion upon exposure, but invisible. It must be developed to become visible.

latitude: the tolerance of a film for exposure error.

law enforcement photographer: a photographer who works for police and sheriffs' departments to take photos of crime scenes and homicide victims.

law of reciprocity: the photographic principle that you can interchange shutter speeds and aperture settings without changing overall exposure. For example, f/5.6 at 1/60 is the exposure equivalent of f/8 at 1/30.

leaf shutter: a shutter built into the lens consisting of several small overlapping spring powered metal blades.

lens: the part of the camera that views the subject to be photographed and projects it onto the film as a completely reversed image; the part of the enlarger that projects a flat image (the negative) onto a flat plane (the enlarger baseboard).

lens hood: a detachable camera accessory that shields the lens from extraneous light.

libel: defamation, or holding someone up to ridicule, by written or printed words or pictures.

licensing agreement: a contract between a photographer and a second party to use a photograph for a specific purpose.

light-sensitive emulsion: in printmaking, light-sensitive emulsion is exposed to light and silver ions in the silver halide crystals are converted to metallic silver atoms to make a latent image.

line-conversion: a grayscale image is converted into an image that has no intermediate grays.

lossless compression: a method of making computer files smaller without losing any data.

lossy compression: a method of making computer files smaller where subtle information is sacrificed.

l-shaped croppers: cardboard guides that "frame" a contact sheet image before printing.

macro lens: a lens that enables a photographer to take pictures very close to the subject. A true macro lens permits shooting so close that the negative image is the same size as the original subject.

magnification: the size of the image on the film or final print relative to the original subject or negative.

main light: the major artificial light source used to illuminate a scene and used to create the primary shadowing on the subject; also called the key light.

manual exposure: the ability to vary camera aperture and shutter speed manually until the meter indicates correct exposure.

merger: a confusing association of subject with background.

microprism grid: a focusing spot that consists of many tiny prisms that break up, or exaggerate the blur of, an out-of-focus image. When focused, the image is clear and intact.

model release: a standardized form in which the person signing gives his or her consent to have the photograph taken and used by the photographer.

monopod: a one-legged stand for holding the camera.

motor drive: a camera attachment that automatically advances the film and cocks the shutter after each exposure. It operates at the rate of about five frames per second.

mounting: the process of attaching a print to a cardboard backing. See dry mount and wet mount.

"M" synchronization: the designation for "medium peak" flash bulbs; camera synchronization for use with regular wire-filled flash bulbs.

natural light: a term photographers use to refer to light found outdoors in nature. (Strictly speaking, of course, all light is natural; or at least none is unnatural.)

negative: the developed image in which the light and dark tones of a photograph are reversed.

negative carrier: a frame for holding the negative inside an enlarger for printing.

negative sleeves: cellophane or plastic holders that protect negatives from damage.

neutral density filter: a filter that cuts down on the brightness of a scene, but it is "neutral" in that it does not alter color rendition.

normal lens: a lens with a focal length of approximately the same length as the diagonal measurement of the film format used (50 mm for 35 mm film).

overexposure: the result when too much light reaches the film or paper. It causes a denser than normal negative or print.

panchromatic: film that is sensitive to the wavelengths from all colors of the visible spectrum.

panning: moving the camera with a moving subject. The background will blur, but the subject should be relatively sharp.

paper base: the support for the gelatin supercoating and light-sensitive emulsion in photographic paper.

paper developer: a chemical used to bring out the visible images on photographic paper.

paper grade: see contrast grade.

paper safe: a special box designed to keep photographic paper from being exposed to light.

paper weight: the thickness of photographic paper: single or double for fiber-based paper, medium weight for resin-coated paper.

parallax effect: the difference between what is seen through the viewfinder of the camera and what is recorded on film due to the distance between the viewfinder and the lens; also called parallax error.

photo archivist: someone who preserves and indexes large collections of photographs.

photo editor: the editor responsible for securing and selecting photographs for publication in magazines or newspapers.

photoflood: an incandescent light bulb of high efficiency but limited life that works well to light interior scenes and portrait subjects.

photogram: a photographic image made without a camera, generally by contact printing objects placed directly on the photographic paper.

photographic paper: a sensitized paper designed for use in making photographic prints.

photojournalism: a career in which a photographer uses a camera, in much the way a reporter uses a pencil, to record news events for newspapers and magazines.

pixel: picture element. A small cell, a component of a larger image, that may vary in tone from black through various shades of gray to white.

plane of focus: the hypothetical flat surface in image space that represents the focus of a distant flat object surface perpendicular to the lens.

polarizing filter: used to cut out polarized light primarily to eliminate reflections or to increase cloud contrast.

portfolio: a sheaf of mounted photos that a photographer uses to display his or her work for prospective customers.

portraits: photographs of people, usually of their faces.

posterization: an image that is composed of only a few distinct gray values.

preservative: an ingredient (usually sodium sulfite) in developer or fixer that prevents or retards spoiling and thus prolongs the life of these solutions.

pressure plate: a part of the film-holding mechanism of a camera that keeps the film flat against the shutter.

privacy: the legal right to be left alone.

process color: the subtractive system used in graphic arts for printing full-color.

programmed exposure: an automatic exposure mode that sets both shutter speed and aperture.

proper contrast: a print with proper contrast contains a solid black, a bright white, and a full range of tones between.

publication of private matters: violation of a person's privacy rights by revealing private, intimate details about a person that others have no right to know.

pushing film: the technique for compensating for known underexposure of film with special development, often by prolonging development or using a high-energy developer.

push processing: giving extra development to a film to make up for loss of contrast that comes from underexposure.

rangefinder system: a system that allows the photographer to focus by superimposing one image over another.

reel: a spool or frame upon which exposed film is wound for developing.

reflected light meter: a meter that measures the light reflected from, or produced by, a subject to be photographed.

reflectors: a surface that reflects light toward the subject, usually used to throw light into shadow areas and increase shadow detail.

resin-coated paper: photographic paper that has been coated with a water-resistant plastic to allow faster processing, washing, and drying.

resolution: the ability to resolve fine detail in a film, lens, or electronic imaging device.

restrainer: a chemical that holds back developer action, thus keeping fogging of film or paper at an acceptable level.

rewind knob: the foldable crank of the camera that rewinds film back into the cassette.

RGB color: color formation using the three additive primary colors, red, green, and blue.

roll film: photographic emulsion coated onto a flexible film base. This made smaller cameras and motion pictures possible.

rule of thirds: a rule of thumb for composition that entails dividing the frame into thirds horizontally and vertically to form four intersection points at which the subject can be effectively positioned.

safelight: a darkroom light with a built-in filter that screens out rays harmful to film or paper.

saturated colors: slight underexposure creates more intense, more saturated colors. Because many photographers want saturated colors, they routinely underexpose slide film by inflating the ISO speed rating by one-third stop.

saturation: the purity of a color—whether it tends to be grayish neutral or pure color.

scanner: a device for exposing an image on film by tracing light along a series of many closely spaced parallel lines. Both film scanners and print scanners capture visual images in electronic form.

scissors: used to cut the leader off the film before winding it on the developing reel.

scratch-resistant substance: a coating of hard gelatin applied to the film to help protect it from abrasion.

shadows: the dark areas in the original scene depicted in the negative as relatively thin or transparent areas.

shutter: the gate-like mechanism that controls access of light to the film.

shutter curtain: the part of a focal plane shutter that moves across the film plane to expose it.

shutter priority: an automatic exposure mode that permits you to set the shutter speed to capture the subject at either a high speed or to show movement of the subject at a slower speed. The camera will automatically set the aperture to give the correct exposure.

silver salt/silver halide crystals: light-sensitive compounds used in photographic emulsions to record the image.

single-lens reflex: a camera design that uses a mirror system to allow the photographer to view the scene through the lens.

skylight filter: a filter intended to warm the slightly bluish shadows often encountered with color film, but often used simply for lens protection.

slow: a type of film that has low sensitivity to light; a lens with a relatively small maximum aperture for its focal length (an f/3.5 50 mm, for instance).

specularity: the degree of diffusion in a light source. Specular light has sharp-edged shadows while diffuse light has shadows with softly defined edges.

speed: a particular setting for the camera shutter; the light sensitivity of photographic materials as measured by the ISO or ASA of film or the ANSI rating for paper; the relative size of the maximum aperture for a lens of given focal length. See fast and slow

split-image rangefinder prism assembly: the rangefinder focusing spot consists of two small prisms that cause an out-of-focus image to appear split in half in the viewfinder. Focusing brings the two halves together to form a whole image.

spotlight: a light that concentrates its output on a relatively small area of the subject.

spot meter: a meter that measures a small portion of the light reflected from a subject.

spotting: using dye to fill in and thus eliminate a dust spot or scratch on a print.

sprocket wheel: a device in the camera that engages the edge of the film and pulls it through the camera.

stop bath: a chemical solution that stops the action of the developer by neutralizing it for both film and paper.

straight print: an unmanipulated enlargement made at a single exposure time.

strobe: an electronic flash unit that puts out a powerful, extremely brief burst of light.

subtractive primary: one of the three colors (yellow, magenta, cyan) used in photography and graphic arts printing to produce full-color images.

synchronization: coordination between the peak of flash light and the opening of the camera shutter so the flash output is used most effectively to expose the film.

tacking iron: an iron used in dry mounting prints.

take-up reel: the part of the camera that winds up film after it has been exposed.

telephoto lens: a lens of longer-than-normal focal length that magnifies objects.

test print: a contact print or enlargement containing trial exposure times.

test strip: a contact print containing trial exposure times done on part of a piece of photo paper.

thermal printer: uses heat to transfer dyes from a color ribbon to a receiver sheet to produce a full-color image of photographic quality from a computer-processed image. Also called thermal-dye transfer or dye-sublimation printer.

toning: using chemicals called toners to alter the tint or color of the silver image of a black-and-white print.

tri-pack construction: color film with three emulsion layers, one for each subtractive primary, coated onto a single film base.

tripod: a free-standing three-legged support for a camera.

tungsten film: used with light bulbs or photoflood lamps.

twin-lens reflex: a camera with one lens to focus light on the film and another to focus light on the viewing screen via a mirror.

ultraviolet filter: a filter intended to remove ultraviolet light and eliminate a secondary "ghost" image, but often used simply for lens protection.

umbrella: a studio device used to diffuse light.

underexposure: the result when too little light reaches the film or paper. It causes a thinner-than-normal negative or a lighter-than-normal print.

value: the lightness or darkness of a color. It is comparable to brightness in the hue, saturation, and brightness (HSB) color system.

variable contrast paper: photographic paper that allows control of contrast on the same paper through use of filters.

view camera: a camera design, the oldest in existence, in which the lens is separated from the film plane by an adjustable bellows.

viewfinder: the part of the camera that allows a photographer to see the subject to be photographed; a type of camera in which the light from the object to be photographed travels through the viewfinder to the eye, and separately through the lens to the film.

visible image: an image that has been developed.

wet collodion: a negative material consisting of a glass plate coated with a mixture of cellulose nitrate and potassium iodide and sensitized with silver nitrate. Developed in 1851, it all but replaced the previous processes. It was as sharp as the daguerreotype but also reproducible in the same way as the calotype in that it was a negative-positive process.

wet mounting: the use of a paste-like substance to mount large size prints to a cardboard or wooden backing, normally done when a print is too large to be dry mounted. See dry mount.

wetting agent: a chemical that promotes even film drying when it is added to the final processing rinse.

wide-angle lens: a lens of shorter-than-normal focal length that offers a wide angle of view.

work-made-for-hire agreement: an agreement between a photographer and a customer which gives ownership of resultant photographs to that customer, not the photographer.

Wratten: a system for numbering black-and-white filters.

"X" synchronization: the camera setting to be used with electronic flash.

zoom lens: a lens of variable focal length.

index

GLO
AND